The ILFRACOMBE LINE

By John Nicholas

On Saturday 27th July 1963 ex-GWR 2-6-0 No.6346 heads the 8.50am Taunton to Ilfracombe four coach train past the Heddon Mill up distant signal climbing the 1 in 40 bank towards the summit at Mortehoe, banked by Ivatt 2-6-2T No.41298. Then there was no traffic to be seen on the adjacent main A 361 road. Many passengers on this train would have travelled overnight on long distance services from London, the Midlands and the North, and have almost reached the end of their holiday journey. Incidentally during this period through services between Taunton and Ilfracombe ran only on summer Saturdays; on other days a change of trains at Barnstaple Junction was required. *Peter W.Gray*

IRWELL PRESS

ACKNOWLEDGEMENTS

A book of this kind could not be written without the kind and generous help of many people over years of research, drafting, and checking. It is a matter of regret that over the years several of them have not lived to see the fruits of their labours but members of their families will recognise their contributions.

Numerous railwaymen have given generously of their time to provide a very full account of the operation of the line. These include Messrs. K.Almond, W.Darke, G.Facey, W.Hatchley, F.Kidwell, K.Ley, E.McLaughlan, D.Matale, W.Muskett, C.Nott and N.Wheeler. Staff at Shapland and Petter and RAF Chivenor have been most helpful. A considerable number of local people have also contributed, including L.Andrews, S.Taylor, and Mrs H. Chugg.

A particular feature of this book is the wide variety and high quality of photographs taken over a very long period of time, many of the early examples coming from the era of plate glass negatives. Some of the early photographers are not known but two were - Mr R.L.Knight, whose grandson continues to run the family photographic business in Barnstaple, and Mr F.E.Box who not only photographed the line over more than 30 years but also wrote several very detailed articles on it. Other photographers include H.C.Casserley, R.J.Sellick, A.E.West, R.E.Tustin, S.C.Nash, P.Swift and M.Squire. I am most grateful to the owners of all photographic collections for their permission to publish, and these include Ilfracombe Museum, National Railway Museum, Knights Photographers, Minerva Gallery, Mr D.Casserly, Mrs J.Sellick, Mr P.Gower and Mrs R.Tustin. All photographs are individually credited and I am most grateful for their use.

Considerable reference has been made to the standard works on the London and South Western Railway by R.A.Williams, on South Western and Southern locomotives by D.L.Bradley and on South Western carriages by G.R.Weddell, and a number of articles on the Barnstaple and Ilfracombe Railway by F.E.Box, particularly three published in *The Railway Magazine* in 1919 and 1920. Reference has also been made to *Southern Titled Trains* by D.W.Winkworth, *Track Layout Diagrams* of the Southern Railway Section 6 by G.A.Pryer, *Ilfracombe Postcard Views* by Tom Bartlett, and *Clinkers Register of Closed Passenger Stations and Goods Depots*.

A.Shelley kindly supplied details of the BR(SR) Locomotive and Carriage Workings, and M.King has identified much of the rolling stock seen in the photographs. R.Whitehouse has checked the later chapters and supplied additional material. For assistance with the signalling I am indebted to both C.Osment, and R.Palmer whose own research was published in the Signalling Record Society magazine, and both have very carefully checked the original manuscript. Mr D.Cullum and Mr N.Pomfret have kindly made available Southern Railway records from their collections. E.Youldon of Exeter has provided a great deal of information on train and locomotive workings, and has meticulously checked and commented upon the original manuscript, but of course the responsibility for any error rests with the author. The author acknowledges the assistance of the staff of Ilfracombe Museum, the Public Record Office at Kew, the British Museum Newspaper Library at Colindale, and D.Steggles of the Railway Studies Collection of the Devon Record Office.

Reference has been made to Acts of Parliament, Board of Trade Inspecting Officers and Accident Reports, Public and Working Timetables, South Western and Southern Signalling Instructions, other South Western, Southern and British Railways records, the *North Devon Journal*, the *North Devon Herald*, and the *Ilfracombe Gazette*. The 1963 traffic survey was published in the *North Devon Railway Report* by David St John Thomas. Other sources used include the files of several magazines and periodicals including the *South Western Railway Magazine*, *Southern Railway Magazine*, *Railway Observer*, *Railway Magazine*, *South Western Circular*, and the magazines of the Bideford and Instow Railway Group, Lynton and Barnstaple Railway Association, North Devon Line Railway Development Group, and Southern Railways Group.

A NOTE ON SPELLING

Over the last two centuries the spelling in current usage for several locations has varied. At Barnstaple Westacotts shipyard and crossing became Westcott's, Rolle Quay has sometimes been called Rolle's Quay or Rolles Quay, Vellator Crossing was sometimes Velator, Mortehoe and Woolacombe station was opened as Morthoe and later became Mortehoe. Further afield South Molton was known as Southmolton. For consistency the spelling in use in British Railways records has been used in much of the book, excepting the historical chapters.

First Published in the United Kingdom by
IRWELL PRESS 1998
59A, High Street, Clophill, Bedfordshire MK45 4BE
Printed in Huddersfield by The Amadeus Press

CONTENTS

In May 1964 Battle of Britain class 4-6-2 No.34081 92 SQUADRON emerges from the second Slade tunnel of 1891, coasting down the 1 in 36 bank into Ilfracombe with the 11am from Waterloo 'Atlantic Coast Express'. This well-known service had but a few months left to run, it being withdrawn a few months later. *G.F.Heiron*

INTRODUCTION

The picturesque but isolated North Devon resort of Ilfracombe became a favourite holiday destination in Victorian times. The *Ilfracombe Gazette* included in its weekly pages lists of guests residing at each of the town's hotels, in an age when rank, status and knowing the right people was a social imperative. Guests arrived by road, steamer and railway and there was great competition, particularly for the prestigious first class traffic. Both the South Western and Great Western Railways opened offices in the town years before their trains arrived and the Midland advertised services to and from its system via Bristol, Portishead and a connecting steamer service.

Serious consideration of a railway commenced with the opening of the North Devon Railway to Barnstaple in 1854, and took two decades to bring to fruition. Curiously the promoters of the first line authorised by parliament, the Ilfracombe Railway of 1864, neglected Barnstaple and due to the opposition of a prominent landowner also avoided Braunton. It was therefore fortuitous that the mixed gauge line, jointly financed by the standard gauge South Western and broad gauge Devon and Somerset Railways collapsed when the latter failed to pay its first call, which was hardly surprising for an impoverished company which struggled to complete its own line. The successful

Barnstaple and Ilfracombe Railway of 1870 had the backing of both the South Western and Barnstaple Corporation, on a line which served both it and Braunton well. Construction was slow with two major engineering works at Barnstaple, the long iron viaduct over the Taw and the swing bridge over the Yeo, and the long summit cutting through the rocks at Mortehoe. Lack of labour was blamed for the delays but it seems more likely that this was due to shortage of funds, part of the line being built with lightweight track. Another economy was the provision of a large number of level crossings, rather than the construction of road bridges. This made the line very expensive to operate, particularly in later years.

Initially a single track line with a couple of passing places, the train service was provided by the universal 'Ilfracombe Goods', a light class of 0-6-0 built to a standard Beyer Peacock design, so useful on light railways that when the South Western had finished with them Col. Stephens bought most of them for use on his lines. Traffic steadily increased, to the extent that the South Western uprated the track, doubled most of the line, and gradually extended the Ilfracombe terminus. To avoid the competition of a threatened Great Western rival line to the resort, a loop line was built to connect the systems at Barnstaple and through car-

riages from Taunton and Paddington were added to South Western trains at Barnstaple Junction. A new Barnstaple Town station was provided for the interchange of traffic with the narrow gauge line to Lynton which had a short life, although restoration of part of it has now begun.

For its first half-century the line was known as the Ilfracombe Branch, for the principal North Devon line ran from Exeter to Torrington, but the new Southern Railway changed this round, providing a large new turntable at Ilfracombe for the new N class moguls, and the Great Western engines which began to appear. The Torrington line then became the branch. The Southern Railway, which further extended the terminus, and later the Southern Region, encouraged the growth of holiday traffic to the extent that by the 1950s some ten thousand holidaymakers used the line each Saturday of the peak season. Decline set in 1964 but it was not until 1970 that the line closed and, following an abortive preservation attempt, was dismantled in 1975. The line had a number of distinctive features. In its short length there were more than a dozen level crossings, each one protected by signals controlled from crossing or signal boxes, often so close together that the home signal post for one crossing also had the distant for the next one. At Pottington

Drummond S11 class 4-4-0, still in LSWR livery in the early Southern Railway period, awaits the road at Barnstaple Junction with a freight for the Torrington line. The photograph shows the enlargement of the down platform to provide two down roads, which was brought into use in 1924. *R.C.Riley Collection.*

A Taunton line train of Western Region stock hauled by a 43XX class 2-6-0 curves over Barnstaple bridge on 8th August 1964. *P.Swift*

the swing bridge was opened manually by a team of gangers working a capstan every time seagoing vessels sailed in or out of the Yeo estuary on a high tide. To reach the resort the line had to go over the top of the hills behind, with gradients of 1 in 40 from Braunton and 1 in 36 from Ilfracombe up to the summit at Mortehoe; heavy holiday trains required two or sometimes even three locomotives to ascend the banks. For many years the line saw very heavy passenger traffic during the summer season.

For almost all of its life the Ilfracombe line enjoyed through services from Waterloo, two or three coaches at quiet times extended to full length dining car expresses on peak summer Saturdays. Ilfracombe was a principal destination for the Atlantic Coast Express, the 11am express from Waterloo with the up departure at 10.30am. An equally fa-mous, but short-lived express was the Devon Belle which ran for eight post-war summer seasons. On peak summer Saturdays there were not only some nine departures for Waterloo but also another eight for the Great Western routes to Paddington, Cardiff, Manchester, Wolverhampton and Taunton, together with some local services. In earlier years there were also through carriages from the Great Central and Brighton lines. During

On 18th April 1954 West Country class 4-6-2 No 34004 YEOVIL crosses the River Taw viaduct at Barnstaple with the Ilfracombe portion of the 11am 'Atlantic Coast Express' from Waterloo. *Peter W Gray*

The 1 in 40 bank near *Hunters Inn* about 1930 with an eleven coach train, the maximum allowed on the line. The train engine is an N 2-6-0, piloted by M7 No.322, and banked by another M7. Trains exceeding 280 tons, such as this one, had to have an assisting engine at the rear. Judging by the nameboards on some of the coaches this appears to be a Saturday Atlantic Coast Express, the 10.35am restaurant car train from Waterloo to Ilfracombe only. *A.Halls courtesy R.J.Sellick.*

the summer peaks of passenger traffic many extra railwaymen, locomotives and coaches were drafted on to the line to play their part.

Despite its heavy holiday traffic on summer Saturdays Dr Beeching saw no future for the Ilfracombe line; passenger and freight traffic over the rest of the year was light and the many level crossings made it expensive to operate. Diesels were introduced, all freight services withdrawn, and the line was singled so that by the late 1960s it was but a shadow of its former self. Summer Saturday expresses

to and from Paddington continued to run to support the tourism trade of the resorts until complete closure came in 1970; paradoxically they ran to the fastest schedules ever seen, due to much faster running on the main line. A preservation attempt was made, but failed when it transpired that all the funds raised had been spent; this proved to be a big setback for other railway preservation attempts in the area.

Now much of the dismantled line has been converted into a footpath, but the two major bridges at Barnstaple have

been removed. Some of the crossing keepers cottages along the line have been converted into private homes, the sites of the stations at Braunton and Ilfracombe have been re-developed, but the station buildings at Barnstaple Town, Wrafton and Mortehoe survive, all now in connection with the leisure industry which the line did so much to develop. This book provides the fullest account yet published of the Ilfracombe Line, including a wide variety of track plans, signalling diagrams and photographs, many of which have not previously been published.

Battle of Britain class 4-6-2 No.34079 141 SQUADRON coasts down the 1 in 36 bank into Ilfracombe in May 1964, the train here approaching bridge No.31. *G.F.Hieron.*

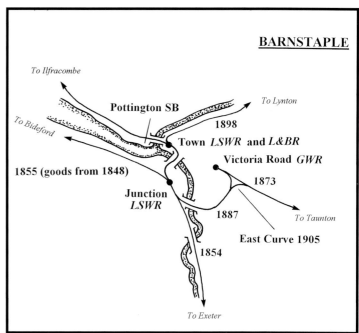

A standard Exmouth Junction concrete gradient post was about ¾ mile north of Mortehoe, marking the commencement of more than two miles of 1 in 36 to Ilfracombe. *J.Scrace*

Below. A local train from Barnstaple comprising West Country class 4-6-2 No.34002 SALISBURY and a three coach set descends the 1 in 36 bank past the Slade reservoirs towards the Ilfracombe terminus in May 1964. Note that the up track has been re-laid with flatbottom rail on concrete sleepers to cope with the pounding of heavy up trains. *G.F.Heiron*

CHAPTER ONE

THE LINE DESCRIBED

The Ilfracombe Line commenced at Barnstaple Junction West Signal Box, recorded here in October 1907. The lines to the left follow the original line to Fremington and Bideford, whilst the (then) Ilfracombe Branch curves sharply away to the right, under the Sticklepath Road bridge, No.1 on the Civil Engineer's list of structures on the branch. By 1924 the layout became more complex with the installation of the second down platform face, and the movement of the 1912 replacement of this tall signal box. *F.E.Box courtesy National Railway Museum*

BARNSTAPLE JUNCTION

The Ilfracombe line began immediately at the end of the down platform at Barnstaple Junction station. The platform opened with the branch in 1874, and in 1924 was enlarged to an island, to cater for increased traffic. The older main line to Bideford and Torrington carried straight on under Sticklepath Road bridge (No.97 on the Coleford Junction to Torrington line system of numbering employed by the South Western). Apart from the photographs in this volume the reader is referred to *The North Devon Line* (OPC 1992) for a full description of Barnstaple Junction station, and *Lines to Torrington* (OPC 1984) for the line on to Bideford.

The first half mile to Ilfracombe consisted of a long reverse S curve from the platform end of Barnstaple Junction to the far end of the bridge over the River Taw. At Barnstaple Junction West Signal Box the train driver collected the Tyers No.6 tablet for the single track section to Barnstaple Town. The original 1874 tall stone signal box towered over the western end of the station, and carried a notice 'Maximum Speed to Town Station 15mph'. The box was replaced by a shorter brick and concrete one in 1912; this was modified and moved in 1924, but the speed restriction dictated by the sharp curves remained. There was an accident in 1922, when a goods train bound for

Ilfracombe was turned into a siding through a signalman's error; full details are given in Chapter Four. The up and down tracks continued their sharp right hand curve past the signal box and under Sticklepath Road which was carried on a substantial and attractive stone-built bridge, No.1 on the branch. The up and down lines rapidly converged and past MP

211½ (from Waterloo) there was a down signal post with two arms. The upper arm was the Barnstaple Junction West down advanced starting signal, and the lower arm the Barnstaple Town down distant, which was fixed at caution. The line, almost level for about the first six miles, ran here on a low embankment and crossed over a minor bridge with an iron

The Southern Railway established the Southern National bus company to augment its train services. Here we see No.3101, registration DR 8804, in the Barnstaple Junction station approach on 18th April 1954, with the houses of Sticklepath Road behind. *Peter W Gray*

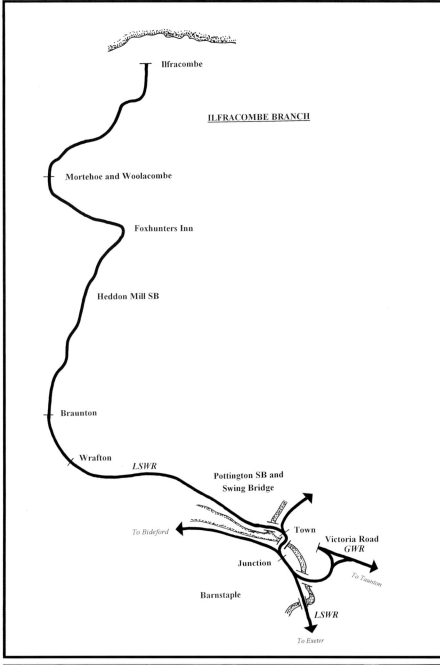

ILFRACOMBE BRANCH

Another view of the divergence of the divergence of the Torrington and Ilfracombe lines at Barnstaple Junction, taken before this 1874 signal box was replaced in 1912. *Irwell Press Collection.*

deck on stone abutments, No. 2. Next, on the right hand side, was an up signal, the Barnstaple Junction West home.

The short section of route so far had originally passed over salt marshes, but as Barnstaple expanded the area between the Ilfracombe branch and Sticklepath Road was built on, the roads of Signal Terrace, Clifton Terrace and Clifton Street dating from late Victorian and Edwardian days. To the left there was industrial development, originally leading down to Westcotts old shipyard on the River Taw. In later days it was taken over by the Devon Concrete Works. This was served by a long siding off the Torrington line, originally called Shipyard Siding, but later 'Saw Milling and General Supplies Siding'. In later years large concrete castings were moved around on the siding, on flat wagons propelled by the company's own steam crane.

By now the line had turned some 90 degrees from its original direction at Barnstaple Junction; on the left was a ground frame of two levers, unlocked by the single line tablet, giving access to Shapland and Petters Siding.

SHAPLAND AND PETTERS SIDING
In 1854 Henry Petter and Henry Shapland established their woodworking business, employing the best machinery of the period, in Bow Street, Barnstaple. In 1864 they moved to a factory at Pilton which sadly burned down on 5th March 1888, a terrible blow for one of the town's largest employers. However the firm had purchased Westacotts shipyard, adjacent to the Ilfracombe branch bridge across the Taw. The partners energetically set about the construction of their new Raleigh Cabinet Works, much of it in Marland brick, built to the highest standards of the period and within a year production was resumed and 300 jobs saved. In the earlier part of this century output included high quality domestic furniture, hand-carved church furniture, and fittings for ocean liners and Pullman carriages. It is believed that the body of the Lynton and Barnstaple Railway carriage No. 17 was built here. These days the company specialises in a wide variety of high quality doors used in all types of building and is a market leader, employing some 600 people.

The siding was inspected and approved by Maj.Gen. Hutchinson of the Board of Trade in his report of 2nd May 1890. Wagons were delivered and collected at the factory gate by the railway - inside they were moved by horse, and in later years by tractor. All raw materials, including different timbers from all over the world, were received by rail from the ports where the ships were unloaded or from timber merchants. Finished products were forwarded by rail to customers throughout the country. Three or four wagons were shunted in and out of the works at about 12.30pm every other day in later years, by a shunting engine from Barnstaple Junction. The siding was also booked for shunting by the late afternoon goods from Pottington Signal Box.

Passing the ground frame and the factory to the left, the line continued its

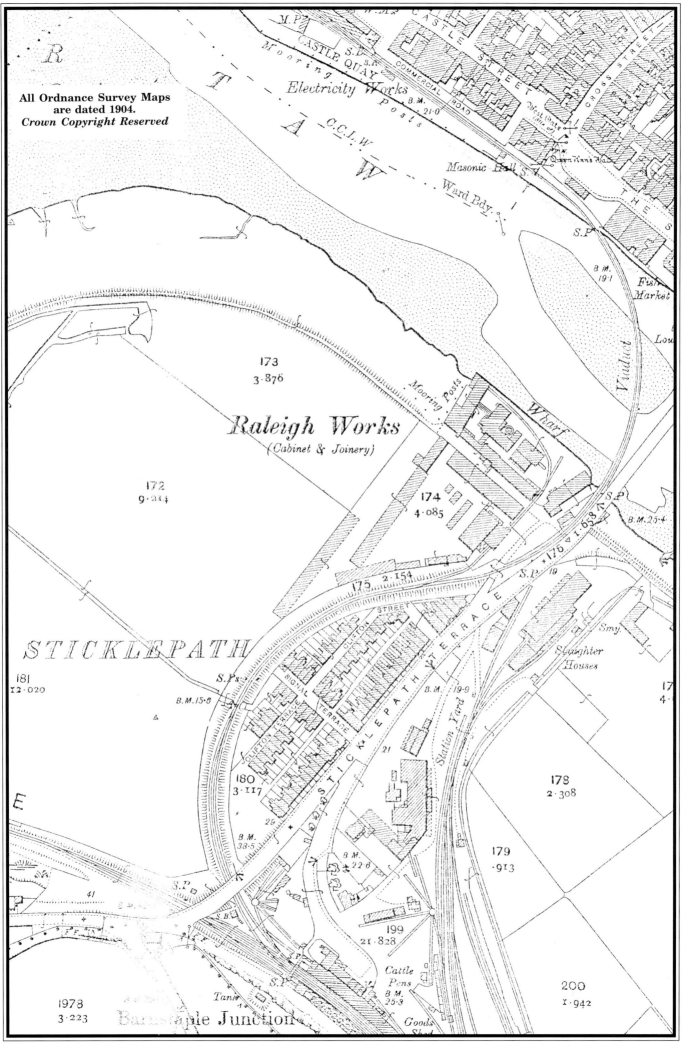

All Ordnance Survey Maps
are dated 1904.
Crown Copyright Reserved

The second Barnstaple Junction West, later Barnstaple Junction B, signal box can just be seen through the arch of bridge No.1 in 1964. The up and down tracks converge for the single track to Pottington, both being fitted with check rails on the sharp curve. *Author*

An undated aerial view showing the straight Barnstaple (road) bridge and the sharply curved railway bridge, No.3. Shapland and Petters factory and its siding is bottom left, and Westcotts Crossing just at the end of the bridge. *Lens of Sutton*

On 21st September 1954 Bulleid 4-6-2 No.34058 SIR FREDERICK PILE brings an up train over Barnstaple Bridge, the coaches being a Maunsell open third in red and cream livery, and a two coach Bulleid set in green . Details of the track laid over the viaduct can be seen. The site of Barnstaple Quay station was in front of the large white building at the far end of the bridge. *R.E.Tustin*

curve to the right until, having turned through some 120 degrees, the curvature suddenly reversed and the line ran adjacent to Sticklepath Road, which it had gone beneath less than a quarter of a mile previously. On the other side of the road was the end of Barnstaple Junction goods yard, where a siding ran into a two-storey warehouse just at the end of Barnstaple Bridge. Built by William Thorne, this dated back to 1848 - the oldest railway building in North Devon.

WESTCOTT'S CROSSING

There was a crossing for vehicles to Shapland and Petters works at 211m. 53ch. and one for pedestrians (with wickets), two chains further on, for 'Westcott's Footpath.' A cabin, normally staffed by two crossing keepers working early and late turns, was provided adjacent to the wicket gates. The cabin had bells and telephone to communicate with the adjacent signal boxes, and a lever to lock the wickets. Three minutes before departure of a down train from Barnstaple Junction West the signalman gave four beats of the bell and the keeper, acknowledging the bell signal by repetition, locked the gates across the roadway. The gates were unlocked after the train had passed. For up trains the Barnstaple Town signalman gave a signal of two beats.

Now turning sharply to the left the line bridged the estuary of the River Taw, just downstream of Barnstaple Long Bridge. This bridge, structure No.3, was the major engineering work on the line. It was made up of 15 main pairs of wrought iron girders 40ft in length and two other pairs, giving a total length of 213 yards on a curve of 7½ chains radius, requiring a continuous check rail. It approached the north bank of the Taw almost tangentially, affording excellent views of many of the principal buildings of the town, including the North Devon Athenaeum, before arriving at the site of Barnstaple Quay station.

BARNSTAPLE QUAY STATION
Chronology
Station and signal box opened as 'Barnstaple Quay' 20th July 1874
Renamed Barnstaple Town July 1886
Station and signal box closed 16th May 1898
The station was adjacent to The Strand and Queen Anne's Walk, between the Fish Market and Masonic Hall. It was the most convenient station for the town centre, but consisted of only one platform with single storey station building and a small awning. The signal box was equipped with a 6 lever frame which operated signals but no points, and controlled the level crossing and the interlocked bolt which, when released, permitted the opening of Pottington Swing Bridge. There were no sidings or loops, goods traffic being dealt with elsewhere. A handful of clerks, porters and signalmen worked under the supervision of the Barnstaple Junction stationmaster. Barnstaple Quay closed in favour of the new station, Barnstaple Town, built nearby to provide an interchange with the Lynton and Barnstaple

Commercial Road Level Crossing box in June 1958, built on the site formerly occupied by the original 1874 Barnstaple Quay signal box. The original Barnstaple Quay station had a single platform to the left of the line. The rail-built post at the end of the site, adjacent to the bridge, carries the Barnstaple Town up starting signal and, below it, the Barnstaple Junction West fixed up distant. The signal adjacent to the cabin is the Barnstaple Town down outer home, the rail-built post replacing an earlier South Western lattice post; the crossing box controlled only the gate locks, which were unlocked from Barnstaple Town signal box. *R.E.Tustin*

SOUTHERN RAILWAY STATISTICS 1928-36 BARNSTAPLE TOWN					
	1928	1930	1932	1934	1936
Passenger tickets issued	79,496	71,711	55,531	51,878	32,745
Season tickets issued	21	411	889	487	314
Tickets collected	149,934	141,819	110,917	116,273	74,269
Parcels forwarded	7,351	6,962	5,877	6,482	4,183
Parcels received	464	412	464	460	381
Horses forwarded	-	-	1	-	-
Horses received	-	-	1	-	-
Milk forwarded (cans) (gals from 1932)	-	5	-	-	69
Milk received (cans) (gals from 1932)	-	1	-	-	-
Fish, Meat forwarded(cwt)	2,421	2,274	1,253	1,244	722
Fish, Meat received (cwt)	131	486	27	7	13

line. The present bus station stands close to the site. In later days, on the right of the line, there was a double arm signal on a rail-built post. The upper arm was the Barnstaple Town up starting signal, the lower the Barnstaple Junction West up distant, whilst on the left was the Barnstaple Town down outer home signal, which protected Commercial Road Level Crossing.

COMMERCIAL ROAD GATES CROSSING

This level crossing was one of two, both under the control of Barnstaple Town, giving road access to Castle Quay from Commercial Road which ran parallel to it. The wooden gate box was built (probably in late 1898) on the site previously occupied by the 1874 Barnstaple Quay signal box. The Crossing Keeper operated the gates as instructed by the Barnstaple Town signalman; two beats of the bell to close the gates across the road for an up train, four to close the gates for a down train and a two pause two from Commercial Road to Barnstaple Town to release the gates. Signals were given two minutes before a train was due. Barnstaple Town signal box No.2 lever locked the Commercial Road gates.

Leaving Commercial Road Level Crossing the line continued straight on for a couple of hundred yards between Barnstaple Quay on the left and Commercial Road on the right, passing an unusual array of signals on a post to the left. The upper arm was the Barnstaple Town down inner home signal, next was the Pottington down distant signal, and the bottom arm was a calling on signal electrically controlled by Pottington, but operated by Barnstaple Town to admit trains to the station when Pottington Swing Bridge was open. These signals also protected Barnstaple Town level crossing adjacent to the signal box.

BARNSTAPLE TOWN STATION
Chronology
Station, signal box and level crossing opened 16th May 1898
Lynton line closed 30th September 1935
Interchange Siding closed 3rd April 1940
Station and signal box closed 5th October 1970

In many respects Barnstaple Town station was a railway modeller's dream, with the trains of three pre-grouping companies using its single platform. The standard gauge South Western and Great Western trains dwarfed the narrow gauge ones of the Lynton and Barnstaple, which were often mixed, with goods and passenger vehicles. Happily this was also a very useful station for passengers, and for many years more tickets were issued and

Barnstaple Town signal box in June 1952, with the up home signal. The signal box opened with the new station in 1898 and was the only block post remaining on the line when it closed in 1970. *R.E.Tustin*

Barnstaple Town station, probably early this century, showing Lynton and Barnstaple 2-6-2T 'Exe' built by Manning Wardle, on a 2ft gauge train for Lynton. The fine awning built to shelter the island platform can be clearly seen. *Irwell Press Collection*

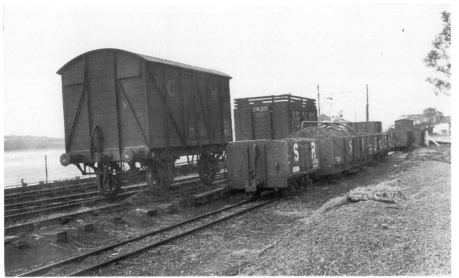

Above. A detailed view of the interchange sidings at Barnstaple Town in Southern days with both standard and narrow gauge wagons in view. Behind the wagons can be seen the roof of Pottington signal box, and apparently part of a coasting vessel sailing through the swing bridge into the Yeo. *Irwell Press Collection*

Left. Signals protecting the level crossing at Barnstaple Town. The up home is to the right, and to the left an unusual combination comprising, from top to bottom, Barnstaple Town down inner home, Pottington down distant, and a smaller calling on signal operated by Barnstaple Town but controlled by Pottington. This facilitated the entry into the station of a down train when Pottington swing bridge was open. *R.E.Tustin*

collected here than any other station in North Devon; indeed it was one of the busiest passenger stations on the Southern west of Exeter. It was very convenient for the town, the most important commercial, shopping and administrative centre of North Devon, so was used by many on a daily or weekly basis for local journeys from other conveniently situated stations, including Braunton. After 1925 when Ilfracombe became the main line for through trains from Exeter and beyond, the improved service increased the station's popularity further. It was very convenient for the famous Barnstaple Pannier Market held twice a week, and also for the bus station in the Strand. Barnstaple Great Fair was held in the adjacent North Walk for three days in mid-September and this brought much extra traffic, requiring excursion trains and extra platform staff.

The old Barnstaple Quay station also had some of these advantages, but Barnstaple Town replaced it in 1898 as a new interchange station with the 1ft. 11½in. gauge line to Lynton. For the 37 years of that line's existence there was considerable interchange across the platform between the two - not only passengers but also mail and a large quantity of parcels traffic carried in the guards compartments of passenger trains. This included newspapers, passenger luggage, wicker baskets of rabbits, and a wide variety of smaller consignments for both private and business customers. At the far end of the platform were two parallel sidings, one standard and one narrow gauge, used for interchange only.

Some full loads were exchanged between the two lines here, but much of the freight was carted between the South Western's extensive goods yard at Barnstaple Junction and the Lynton line's principal goods station at Pilton Yard, and also from the Great Western at Victoria Road. The Lynton line had its own siding on the Yeo and received much of its coal by sea from South Wales but some coal, forwarded direct from the colliery or from Fremington Quay, was transferred into narrow gauge wagons here. In a Southern Railway return in the 1920s the station master reported that the transfer dock was rarely used by the Traffic Department, but mainly by the Engineers Department. However, it is probably safe to assert that many construction materials used by the L&B contractor, Nuttall, would have been delivered here in the period 1895-98. These would have included gunpowder for blasting through the Exmoor rock, Marland brick used for Chelfham viaduct, timber, cement, iron rails, track spikes and signalling equipment. During 1898 the rolling stock arrived here, the locomotives from Manning Wardle at Leeds, and the coaches and wagons from the Bristol Wagon and Carriage Works. All appear to have came on flat wagons, and it seems that the South Western's Exmouth Junction steam crane was employed to lift the rolling stock on to the narrow gauge track. When more stock arrived in 1925, and LYN went to Eastleigh Works for heavy overhaul, the same method was used. After the sad clo-

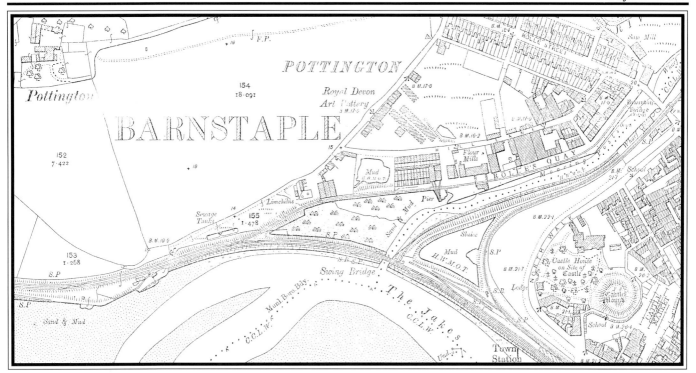

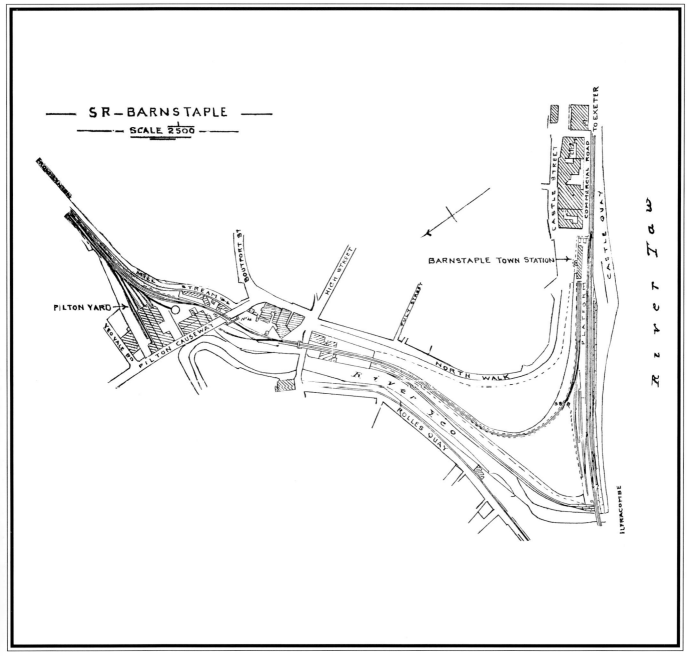

The level crossing gates at Barnstaple Town, operated by a wheel in the adjacent signal box, in August 1962. When open to road traffic the gates overlapped, because the width of the road was greater than the width of the single railway track. This, and Commercial Road Level Crossing, both gave access to Castle Quay from the Town. Shapland and Petters factory can be seen on the opposite bank of the Taw. *A.E.West*

When the signalman at the far end of the section depressed his plunger, the brass tablet for the section could be withdrawn, packed in a leather pouch attached to a large loop handle, and handed to the engine driver as his authority to enter the section. (This Barnstaple Junction - Barnstaple Town tablet has been preserved privately.) The tablets for the sections to Pottington and Barnstaple Junction had different configurations of notches to ensure that tablets could not be placed in the wrong instrument. *R.Lemon*

sure of the narrow gauge line, in 1936, steel rails and the locomotive LEW departed in the same way. The standard gauge siding was taken out of use in 1940, the points being retained as a trap for the swing bridge beyond.

On the standard gauge side there was a loop siding between the running line and the quay, which from time to time served for the storage of wagons destined for customers on Rolles Quay. With just a single platform it was not possible to cross passenger trains at Barnstaple Town, but a photograph exists of the down Devon Belle passing an M7 light engine in the loop.

The station building, constructed in local and Bath stone, was a substantial single storey structure, appropriate for the principal town in North Devon. The island platform boasted a long awning for interchange passengers and parcels work, although this was cut back after 1935. The 1920s return reported that accommodation included refreshment room, porters' room, parcels office, booking office, booking hall, general waiting room,

ladies waiting room, lavatories, and an office used by the District Inspector and Police Department, all lit by gas. Later, electric light was installed, but the refreshment room and several offices closed, probably after the closure of the Lynton line.

The signal box, between the station building and level crossing, was of a design typical of the later South Western period, built in brick with a central pillar in the middle at the front. Inside, the signalman had a 14 lever frame, a Tyers No.6 tablet instrument to control the single line section to Barnstaple Junction West and a No.3 tablet instrument for the single line section to Pottington Signal Box. There was also a tablet instrument for the narrow gauge section to Pilton Yard described variously in records as Tyers 'Hopper' or 'Hopper No.1', believed to be a rare example of the Tyers 7A design. The No.6 instrument enabled a Barnstaple Junction locomotive to shunt Shapland and Petters siding and return, whereas a No.3 instrument required the train to pass right through to the other end of the section. When the line was singled in 1967 the No.6 tablet to Barnstaple Junction West was replaced by an Electric Key Token, and the single line to Ilfracombe worked under 'One Engine in Steam' regulations using a round red wooden train staff. In the corner of the box overlooking the level crossing was a wheel to operate the gates.

The signalling diagram of 1935 includes a number of unusual features. There were fixed distant signals in both directions. In the up were two stop signals, the home of which protected both level crossings and the starting signal whilst in the down direction were three stop signals - the inner and outer homes each protected a level crossing and the starting signal, which was slotted by Pottington. Levers 1, 2, 3 locked the gates and wickets for the two level crossings. Levers 4, 9 and 14 were most unusual in that they controlled the Lynton line signals. A 1957 photograph of the interior shows these three levers painted white and out of use. Commercial Road Level Crossing Box was described as Ground Frame A, whilst Ground Frame B at the Pottington end controlled the points giving access to the transfer siding and the loop siding, and also locked the swing bridge. However, Ground Frame B was controlled by the Pottington signalman who was in charge of both sides of the swing bridge. The Barnstaple Town signalman was very busy indeed, particularly in summer with up to 20 trains each way daily. The passage of every train required co-operation with Barnstaple Junc-

By Saturday 15th August 1964, when ex-GWR 43XX class 2-6-0 No.5336 arrived with an Ilfracombe to Taunton train, the Barnstaple Town loop siding had been lifted. Through trains to the Great Western after 1945 ran only on summer Saturdays. Four newly installed sets of point rodding have now appeared but their purpose is not known. *E.Wilmshurst*

On 28th July 1951 a West County 4-6-2 arrives at Barnstaple Town with the down Devon Belle, passing M7 No.30247 in the loop siding. *R.J.Sellick*

tion West and Pottington signal boxes for the release of the Tyers tablets.

Perhaps surprisingly, Barnstaple Town did not have its own station master, the Barnstaple Junction station master being responsible for it. In common with all the other railways in North Devon the line was closed overnight and all signal boxes and stations were manned on two shifts, early and late turns, with two men to each box together with rest day reliefs. In 1891 Barnstaple Town (in latter days a class 4 box) had three signalmen, R. Ayre and relief men G. Hutchings and E. Jodram; in 1925 there was signalman W.H. Beer, and in the 1950s Mr Mills and Mr Ashby. The passenger station was manned by two men on each shift, classified over the years as clerks, senior porters or leading porters. Their duties included the sale of tickets and the administration of the parcels traffic in the booking office as well as collecting tickets from

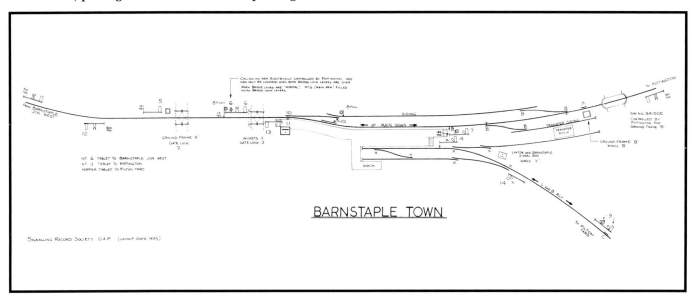

BARNSTAPLE TOWN

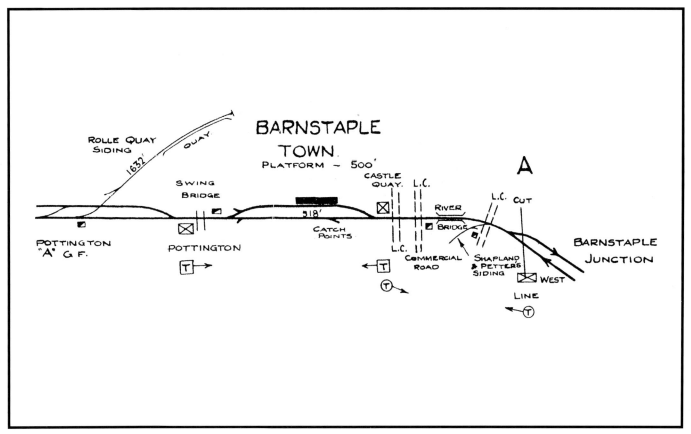

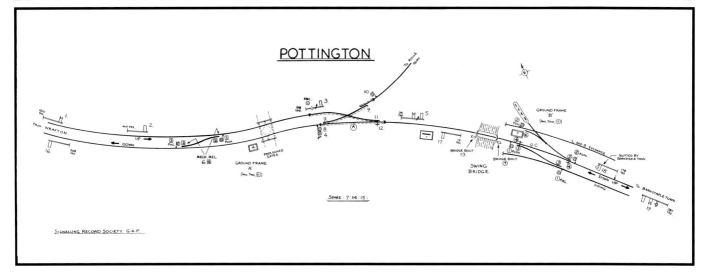

The 'country' end of Barnstaple Town in the late 1930s looking west showing, from left to right, the Taw estuary, the end of the loop siding, Pottington signal box and signals, the single main line running over Pottington Swing Bridge, Ground Frame B which was unlocked by Pottington box to control the points at this end of the layout, and the standard gauge interchange siding. The crossover boasts a South Western drop-flap ground signal, whilst the 2ft gauge line has been lifted. The premises of Squire and Co. can be seen on Rolle's Quay. *R.E.Tustin Collection*

Pottington signal box and swing bridge in 1952, looking down the River Yeo to the Taw beyond. The permanent way hut on the far bank was provided for the staff who had a capstan-like arrangement at the Pottington end to swing the bridge round through a right angle at high tide, providing access to the Yeo for small sea-going vessels. *R.E.Tustin*

passengers. Staff included William Jerrett in the 1900s, and in 1929 porter M. Bowles and joint Junction and Town Station Master Mr Sampson. Fridays were particularly busy throughout the year, with large numbers of passengers arriving for Barnstaple market day. The

only freight traffic handled here was in the 1898 to 1935 period at the interchange siding; in the 1930s a Mr Osborne was the porter employed to transfer loads between standard and narrow gauge wagons. At this time there was also a leading porter at the station, and it would ap-

pear that Commercial Road Level Crossing was operated by a member of the station staff.

POTTINGTON SWING BRIDGE AND SIGNAL BOX

Leaving Barnstaple Town the single track line continued to run along the north bank of the Taw estuary for a few yards, until it reached Pottington. The Yeo estuary was crossed on iron swing bridge No. 4. The Yeo is navigable at high tide for small coastal vessels and in earlier years the first road bridge, Braunton bridge, was also a swing bridge. Small coastal vessels berthed at wharves on both sides of the Yeo, including the Lynton and Barnstaple Railway wharf above Braunton Bridge (where coal brought over from South Wales was an important traffic) and Rolles Quay. The latter was served by a standard gauge siding, of which more later.

A few yards beyond the swing bridge was the Pottington down starting signal and then Pottington Signal Box, built on the side of the embankment with the single railway line in front and the Taw estuary behind, the Taw lapping its foundations at high tide. Next, on the opposite side of the line, was the post carrying the Pottington up starting and the fixed Barnstaple Town up distant signals. Just beyond here the line opened up to the double track which ran to Ilfracombe. Rolles Quay Siding came in across the up line to a trailing connection with the down line, next to the up inner home signal. Next came an occupation crossing giving access to the foreshore, the small wooden weatherboarded Pottington Ground Frame A, a trailing crossover used by the daily goods train, and beyond along the low embankment over the salt marshes the up outer home, down advanced starting and up distant signals.

Pottington swing bridge was an iron structure 59ft long and 14ft wide, pivoted towards the signal box end. Opening to shipping was a complicated job, beginning with the following signalling procedures, as detailed in Southern Region Instructions of 1961:
'The swing bridge cannot be opened after a tablet has been withdrawn at Barnstaple Town for a down train or after LINE

The double track to Ilfracombe began just beyond Pottington signal box, just visible in the distance, in the early 1950s. In the foreground is the entrance to Rolle's Quay siding, reached by a trailing connection from the down line. Beyond the siding gate can be seen some of the commercial buildings, and a van. *R.E.Tustin*

rotate the bridge through some 90 degrees, working the mechanism much like a ship's capstan. Because the bridge did not pivot about its centre, the Pottington end was counterbalanced. The whole weight was carried on three small wheels in a race. A standard South Western platelayers hut was provided adjacent to the bridge.

Vessels of up to 250 tons could navigate the Yeo, massive timbers installed on both sides of the channel protecting the railway bridge and its approaches. For many years the shipping comprised sailing vessels engaged in the coastal trade and a high level of seamanship was required to navigate the narrow channel. However, as we will see in Chapter Four, in 1891 a vessel grounded in the channel and blocked the line until the next high tide.

Pottington signal box dates from 4th August 1890 when the double line to Braunton opened. A wooden cabin on a masonry base, it was in the contemporary South Western style used all the way along the line. The main role for the signal box was control of the single line from Barnstaple Town (with the Tyers No. 3 tablet apparatus) and the double track on to Wrafton and Braunton. The up line from Wrafton was controlled by Sykes Lock and Block equipment, and the down line by Preece's Three Wire Block. In the up direction were distant, outer home, inner home and starting signals, and in the down home, starting and advanced starting signals, the down home being slotted by Barnstaple Town. The 19 lever frame also controlled the points and facing point lock, levers Nos. 11 and 12, for the commencement of the double track. Lever No. 9 operated the points giving a trailing connection from the down line to

CLEAR has been given by Pottington for an up train.

When the bridge is required to be opened the Signalman at Pottington must give a special BRIDGE OPENING signal of 6 pause 6 beats to Barnstaple Town and Wrafton (or Braunton) and on this signal being acknowledged by repetition he must give a special bell signal of 3 pause 3 beats to Pottington Ground Frame B and operate the bridge locking lever (No.13). He must then pull the side lever connected with the Sykes apparatus and plunge to release the bridge bolt lever at Pottington Ground Frame B. The man at Pottington Ground Frame B will then operate the bridge bolt lever and acknowledge the special bell signal by repetition. The bridge may then be opened.

After the bridge has again been closed the man at Pottington Ground Frame B will replace the bridge bolt lever, pull the side lever of the Sykes apparatus, plunge to Pottington signal box and give 3 beats on the bell; the Signalman must thereupon replace the bridge locking lever (No.13), acknowledge the bell signal by repetition and give the OBSTRUCTION REMOVED signal to Barnstaple Town and Wrafton (or Braunton) and on these signals being acknowledged normal working may be resumed. The key of Pottington Ground Frame B must be kept in Pottington box'

A team of platelayers had to remove the fishplates at each end of the bridge and insert four long iron handles into the top of the rack and pinion gearing, to slowly

Rolle's Quay in 1934, looking down the Yeo towards Pottington signal box and swing bridge in the distance. On the quay are the premises of several firms which made use of the long single track siding, with a number of vans in evidence. The Victoria Flour Mills of Stanbury and Son are an impressive example of nineteenth century industrial architecture. The sailing ships are *Democrat, Enid, Mary Stewart, Rossette,* **and** *Ocean Gem. D.J.Wroe Collection*

Rolle's Quay in 1934, looking upstream towards Braunton Road swing bridge. The Lynton line can just be glimpsed under the tree on the right. *D.J.Wroe Collection*

Rolles Quay siding. Ground Frame A was released by lever No.6 and controlled the trailing crossover, whilst Ground Frame B, on the opposite side of the Yeo, controlled the points on that side. There were a number of shunting bell codes in use between the signal box and each ground frame, examples being given previously for the swing bridge operation. The swing bridge was released by a bridge bolt on lever No.13 on the Pottington side and another on the Barnstaple Town side by lever No.7 in Ground Frame B. The box was operated by two men, latterly class 4 signalmen, working early and late turns. In 1925 one of these was A. Luggar, and in the 1960s Mr Lionel Short and Mr Bob Short. The box was reduced to a ground frame to control the swing bridge 'when required' when the line was singled throughout on 17th December 1967.

ROLLES QUAY SIDING
Also known as Rolle's Quay or Rolle Quay Siding
Chronology
Opened 23rd February 1881
Closed 7th September 1964

For many years the Working Timetable included a goods train from Barnstaple Junction to Pottington Signal Box, apparently something of an anachronism. This ran about teatime, past the signal box, and terminated at Rolles Quay Siding. This was single track, some 27 chains in length, with a capacity of about 80 wagons which ran across the salt marshes to serve Rolles Quay on the Yeo, terminating just short of Braunton Bridge. The quay was named after a prominent family of landowners, with a country seat at Stevenstone House near Torrington. Lord John Rolle had built the Rolle Canal to Torrington, opened in 1825.

There were a number of customers served by the railway here, but not necessarily all at the same time. One of the first was the Victoria Flour Mills of Stanbury and Son, millers and corn merchants. The magnificent brick built mill stood back from the Yeo but an enclosed sack hoist or conveyer ran over the siding to the quay where there was also a steam crane at one stage. Traffic to and from Stanburys included cattle feed, corn, flour, sugar beet, and coal. Other premises included Cardner and Perryman's wool, corn and seed stores, Mr Dalling, a coal merchant, and H.A. Scott & Son's haulage. By 1959 Messrs. John How and Co. (Bideford) Ltd. had a coal transporter about 50 yards from the buffer stops. Using tubs or grabs, this conveyed coal from wagons to the firm's adjacent storage area. Many of the wagons originated at Fremington Quay on the Torrington line, where South Wales coal was unloaded from coasters for distribution throughout North Devon. Another customer was Devon County Council which received bitumen in tank wagons. A 1963 wagon label on one of these read 'To BARNSTAPLE JCN LSW. ROLLES QUAY SDGS. via FELTHAM' - the wagon originating at Shell Haven Refinery, Thames Haven, L.T.&S.

Normally one railwayman was employed at Rolles Quay, where he was responsible for the labelling of wagons forwarded and liaison with the several customers. In 1957 for example, the

On 17th June 1958 an unidentified N class 2-6-0 shunts wagons on Rolle's Quay Siding. Since this was a long single track the train crew had to shunt wagons on to the main line, sometimes using the loop siding at Barnstaple Town. Beyond the end of the wagons can be seen the coal transporter, used by Messrs. How and Co. *R.E.Tustin*

4.25pm goods from Barnstaple Junction would arrive at Pottington Signal Box at 4.30pm, usually with the wagons in the correct order for the various customers on Rolles Quay. The outgoing wagons were shunted out of the siding and replaced with the arrivals, but shunting movements were constrained by the lack of any other sidings - the main line had to be utilised. The brake van was shunted to the other end of the train and on reversal on to the main line the locomotive ran round for the return using the crossover controlled by the Pottington A Ground Frame. This was operated by the shunter under the instructions of the signalman. The goods was then safely berthed in the siding, for before its return at 6.50pm, three down and two up passenger trains would pass. On its return journey the

goods shunted sidings at Barnstaple Town and Shapland and Petters 'if required'. At very busy times, such as the 1945-55 period, shunting might be going on as late as 10pm, after passenger trains stopped for the night.

Leaving Pottington and Rolles Quay Siding the double track main line ran in a north-westerly direction on a low embankment, following the north bank of the gradually widening Taw estuary. Across the estuary it would appear that the Ilfracombe branch train was having an unofficial race with a Torrington train on the opposite bank. The two frequently departed from Barnstaple Town and Barnstaple Junction at about the same time and ran almost parallel for a couple of miles until the Torrington train met a cutting and came to a halt at Fremington.

Passing the Pottington up distant signal, up trains were restricted to 40mph whilst down trains were permitted 55mph. After MP 213 the line, still on a low embankment over the salt marshes, passed over three culverts, 4A, 4B, and 5, the first accommodating Braddiford Water. Shortly after MP 214¼ came a stone overbridge, No.6, which gave access to the foreshore from the adjacent A361 Barnstaple to Ilfracombe road. Next, on the right hand side between the railway and the road, came Heanton Court, whose owner had been a major objector to the railway. Back in the 1860s Heanton Court and its 3,000 acres of land had been owned by Sir William Williams of Tregullow in Cornwall. He made himself very unpopular in North Devon when he opposed this line, but eventually came to

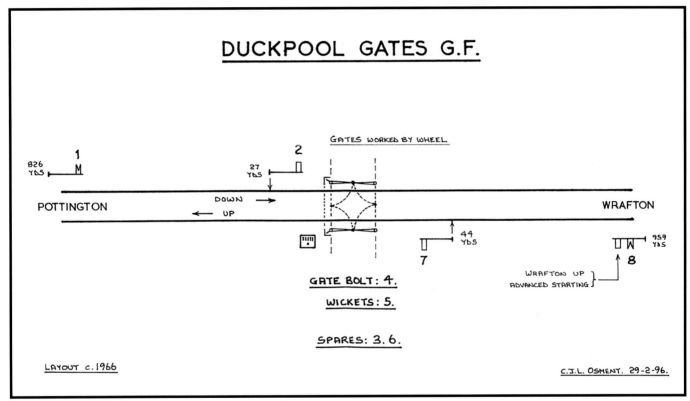

an agreement with the Barnstaple and Ilfracombe company.

Crossing another stream on the iron decked bridge No.7, the line passed milepost 215, followed by the down distant signal for Duckpool Crossing. It then ran under stone overbridge No.8 (which again gave access from the A361 to the salt marshes) and arrived at Duckpool Crossing.

DUCKPOOL CROSSING

Duckpool Crossing, sometimes known as Duckpool Level Crossing or Duckpool Gates, served a track which ran from the A361 at Heanton Punchardon to the small settlement at Chivenor. There was a crossing box with an 8 lever frame and a cottage for the resident keeper. Duckpool was typical of a number of level crossings from here onwards, all of them installed when the line was doubled in the 1889-90 period. The lever frame controlled distant and home signals in each direction, a gate bolt for the road crossing and (a later addition) wickets for pedestrians. This left two levers spare. Up to the 1930s the

A little down the line from Pottington signal box was Pottington A ground frame. When unlocked by the signalman it operated a trailing crossover behind the camera. This, together with the point at the end of the single line section at the signal box, provided a run round for goods trains from Barnstaple Junction which terminated here to shunt Rolle's Quay Siding. The occupation crossing gave access to the foreshore. *R.E.Tustin*

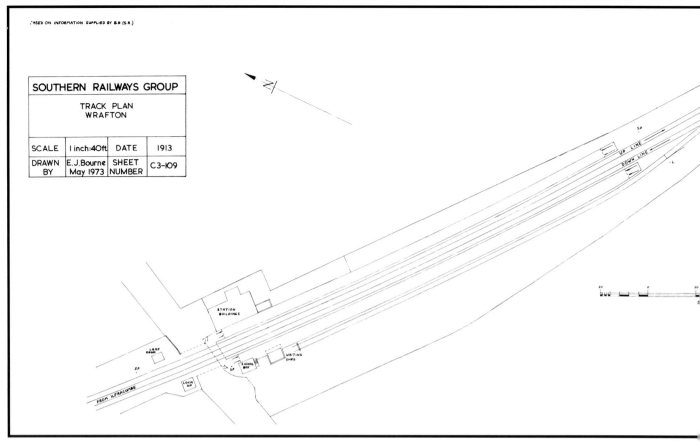

BASED ON INFORMATION SUPPLIED BY B.R. (S.R.)

SOUTHERN RAILWAYS GROUP			
TRACK PLAN WRAFTON			
SCALE	1 inch:40ft	DATE	1913
DRAWN BY	E.J.Bourne May 1973	SHEET NUMBER	C3-109

crossing was comparatively quiet, but that all changed with the opening of the RAF base.

The crossing box was supplied with relay bells which enabled the crossing keeper to know what trains were being offered or were in section between Pottington and Wrafton (or Braunton). The crossing keeper was authorised to keep the gates open to road traffic, but the gates had to be closed and locked against the road and signals pulled off at least three minutes before a train was due. The box was also equipped with a telephone, and during fog or falling snow the gates were normally shut against the road. They could be opened only after a telephone call

to Pottington signal box to seek permission from the signalman. The gates across the road were operated by a wheel in the crossing box. Accommodation was provided, so the crossing keeper was on duty throughout the opening hours of the line, except rest days, when a relief man was provided. In the 1950s the crossing keeper was a Mr Fisher.

Leaving Duckpool the line now continued westwards and inland, passengers getting a good view of RAF activities to the left. Wrafton down distant, in later years a colour light signal - unique on the line - was passed and then, on the up side, a post carrying the Wrafton up advanced starting signal, above the Duckpool

Crossing up distant. Passing milepost 216 the line arrived at Wrafton station, 216¼ miles from Waterloo.

WRAFTON
Chronology
Station and first signal box opened 20th July 1874
Line doubled, first signal box closed, second signal box opened 4th August 1890
Goods yard closed 7th September 1964
Line singled, signal box reduced to ground frame 17th December 1967.
Line closed 5th October 1970

It is perhaps difficult to understand why the little settlement of Wrafton, only a mile or so away from the small town of Braunton, should have merited its own station in 1874. It was a single-platform affair with a siding, and a level crossing giving access to the low lying land between the village and the River Taw. Nevertheless it was extended to two platforms with a new signal box when the line was doubled in 1890.

In 1934 the situation began to change when the North Devon Airport was opened at Chivenor, adjacent to the line at Wrafton. The original 'airport' comprised a large grass field, a clubhouse and a workshop, and from here the Lundy and Atlantic Coast Airline operated services to Lundy, Cardiff and the Channel Islands, advertised at Wrafton station accordingly. The Royal Air Force took over in 1939 and immediately set about its re-building into a major base; soon the short siding in the tiny yard was overwhelmed with wagons loaded with materials sent for the construction of the new runways, hangers and other buildings. The Southern Railway instituted single line working between Umberleigh and

The station buildings at Wrafton, in earlier BR days. They stood on the up platform and included accommodation for one of the porter-signalmen, together with the main station office. *Lens of Sutton*

SOUTHERN RAILWAY STATISTICS 1928-36 WRAFTON					
	1928	1930	1932	1934	1936
Passenger tickets issued	4,050	3,129	1,898	1,481	1,353
Season tickets issued	-	-	-	-	-
Tickets collected	5,090	4,313	1,608	1,562	1,880
Parcels forwarded	235	395	254	188	225
Parcels received	215	196	249	332	379
Horses forwarded	-	-	-	-	-
Horses received	-	-	-	-	-
Milk forwarded (cans) (gals from 1932)	1,527	1,292	14,895	6,058	6,567
Milk received (cans) (gals from 1932)	-	3	34	-	8,629
Fish, Meat forwarded(cwt)	-	149	4	34	4
Fish, Meat received (cwt)	-	-	-	-	-
General Merchandise forwarded (tons)	162	65	59	176	220
General Merchandise received (tons)	428	588	386	578	225
Coal forwarded (tons)	-	-	-	-	-
Coal received (tons)	260	117	231	157	71
Other minerals forwarded (tons)	172	365	139	267	215
Other minerals received (tons)	66,110	3,819	172	75	34
Livestock forwarded (trucks)	-	-	-	-	-
Livestock received (trucks)	-	-	-	-	-
Loaded wagons forwarded (not livestock)	83	53	36	79	83
Loaded wagons received (not livestock)	853	642	197	201	124

Barnstaple Junction and used the up line to store loaded wagons until space was available in Wrafton yard for their unloading. A second siding was brought into use later. The base was invaluable during the 1939-45 war, playing a major part in the anti-submarine campaign and in the transport of personnel overseas.

The two platforms were open, without any awning or other protection against the south westerly gales which sometimes swept across here. The main buildings were located at the western end of the platforms, the station building on the up platform and the signal box and a waiting shelter on the down. A lamp room and lock up shed were added in later years, on the other side of the level crossing (with Duckpool, the only road access to RAF Chivenor).

The signalling consisted of distant (colour light in later years), home and starter in the down direction, and distant, home, starting and advanced starting signals in the up. The Wrafton up distant was on the same post as the Vellator Crossing up home and the Vellator down distant was on the down starting post adjacent to the level crossing. The signal box, built to the contemporary South Western design when the line was doubled in the 1889-91 period, was a well-glazed wooden cabin on a stone base. Inside was a 17 lever frame for all the points, signals and level crossing (the gates were operated by a wheel). Apart from the block instruments and telephone there was also a 'closing switch'. This was a device whereby the box could be 'switched out', and therefore not manned continuously by a signalman. As we have seen at Pottington, the section then became Pottington to Braunton. This economy measure meant that Wrafton station

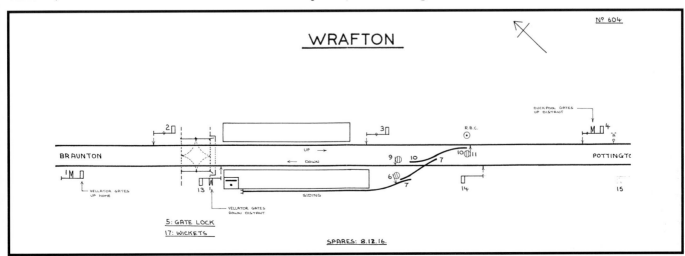

Down platform at Wrafton, looking east from the level crossing to the signal box, waiting shelter and goods shed. Beyond are several wagons in the yard and a hangar of the adjacent RAF Chivenor. Wrafton did not deal with a large volume of general merchandise and such consignments came in daily road box services, the goods train calling at the platform where they were unloaded directly into the small goods shed. *Lens of Sutton*

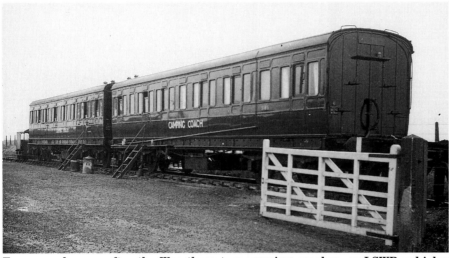

For several years after the War these two camping coaches, ex-LSWR vehicles Nos.S.18 and S.22, were regular features of the second (wartime) siding at Wrafton. They were built as 50ft composite coaches in 1901 and 1905, and converted for campers in 1936 and 1939 respectively. They are seen here on 19th June 1958, together with a motorised trolley used by permanent way staff. *R.E.Tustin*

could be staffed by only one man, and this was common practice at several Southern stations in the west country. The 'switched out' box at Wrafton was then operated in the same way as other crossing boxes, as previously described at Duckpool. It was 'switched in' for the half an hour each afternoon for the up goods to shunt the yard, and when the traffic was heavy on summer Saturdays.

The goods yard, on the down side, was reached by a trailing connection from the up line, crossing the down by a single slip. There was a small goods shed on the down platform, and down goods trains called here to unload parcels and small consignments from the road van (later road box) included in the train for the purpose. The lack of a second crossover meant that Wrafton yard could only be shunted by up goods trains, so wagons for Wrafton had to circulate via Braunton. In 1926 the 1.55pm goods from Ilfracombe shunted Wrafton yard between 2.52 and 2.59, whilst in 1957 it was the 3.14pm goods from Ilfracombe which was booked here between 4.24 and 4.33. The second siding in the yard was provided sometime after the opening of RAF Chivenor, and the stores traffic for the base was often considerable. Some of the most important items were replacement engines for the Hunter jet fighters, which the RAF unloaded with its own crane. Other traffic received included animal feedstuffs and fertilizers, whilst some sugar beet was forwarded in the season. After the closure of the yard some of this traffic remained on the railway, though it was brought by road from Barnstaple Junction yard.

One regular feature of Wrafton yard from the 1940s to the 1960s was a pair of camping coaches, converted LSWR vehicles, photographed by the author in 1964. These popular holiday homes were a feature of a number of Southern stations in the South West, but the only other example in North Devon was at Umberleigh.

Wrafton signal box on 28th May 1968. Opened in 1890, it had a 17 lever frame, a wheel to operate the level crossing gates and block instruments. Later a closing switch was fitted so that it could be 'switched out', but it was reduced to a crossing box in 1967 when the line was singled. *A.E.West*

Wrafton station was operated economically by two porter-signalmen working early and late turns. Their duties included all those necessary for the operation of the station including the issuing and collection of tickets, dealing with the parcels traffic by both passenger and goods trains, labelling any wagons forwarded from the yard, operating the level crossing gates and signals, and shunting the afternoon goods. For many years the Wrafton staff were supervised by the Braunton station master. Leaving Wrafton in a north-westerly direction, the line continued on a long right hand curve for a further mile or so. On a slight embankment it crossed over a couple of iron deck bridges constructed to take away flood water, Nos.9 and 10. Next came a stone underbridge, No.11, which took the line over Knowle Water, a stream flowing down from the hills which became tidal just below the bridge. Just after this the line reached Vellator Crossing.

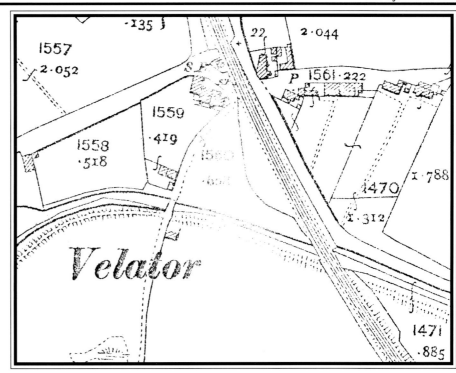

VELLATOR CROSSING

Vellator Crossing, sometimes known as Vellator Gates, was provided for a road which ran from Braunton and the A361 road out on to the lonely wetlands of Braunton Marsh. The first half mile of this road beyond the crossing ran alongside Knowle Water. Here, it was tidal, and in the old days sailing ships navigated up at high tide to reach a small quay at Vellator, just a mile from the centre of Braunton. It should be mentioned that an alternative spelling was Velator, but the railway used Vellator.

The crossing box and crossing keeper's cottage were provided on the down side of the line, and were to a design similar to that at Duckpool and others of the 1889-1890 era. The box had a frame with 5 working levers and 2 spares, there being distant and stop signals in both directions, and a wheel to operate the crossing gates. Adjacent to the crossing were two signal posts, both (for reasons of sighting) positioned on the down side, each with two arms, the four arms being operated from three boxes. The down post carried the Vellator home and the Braunton distant, whilst the up post carried the Vellator home and the Wrafton distant. The operation of Vellator Crossing was very similar to that already described for Duckpool. In the 1950s the crossing keeper was Mr Jack Perkins, and in the 1960s a Mr Chard.

Leaving Vellator the line continued its long right hand curve, with a built up area on the up side between the line

Vellator Crossing looking west on 28th May 1968 towards Braunton, showing the remaining up line after singling. The down signals on the left are the Vellator home and the Braunton distant, while the up signals in the distance are the Vellator home and the Wrafton distant. *A.E.West*

On 15th June 1957 West Country 4-6-2 No.34014 BUDLEIGH SALTERTON passes Vellator crossing with a down train. For sighting purposes, the LSWR lower quadrant up signals were located on the down side, the line running round a long curve between Wrafton and Braunton. Unusually, the Wrafton distant signal arm has a white rather than a black chevron, a practice discontinued in 1928. *R.E.Tustin*

and the A361 and the River Caen on the down side. During the Second World War there was a proposal to build an extra siding here on the up side for military traffic, but it did not materialise. The line passed MP 217 and arrived at Braunton Gates.

trailing crossover, and the Braunton down home and up advanced starting signals. On the other side of Braunton Gates were the pointwork and sidings of Braunton station.

The 1889 Braunton Gates crossing box, in the later British Railways period. *D.Nicholas*

BRAUNTON GATES

Braunton Gates was a level crossing provided for a minor road, Chapel Street, at the southern end of Braunton station. The ground level cabin, with a squat wooden top on a rendered base, stood on the up side of the line and had a 5 lever frame, only two of which were used. Being within Braunton Signal Box limits Braunton Gates was interlocked with it and so controlled no signals. When a train had departed the Braunton signalman unlocked the frame and enabled the Braunton Gates crossing keeper to pull his levers and unlock the crossing gates and wickets. On the Wrafton side of Braunton Gates were two trolley garages used by the permanent way gang based here, a

BRAUNTON

Chronology

Station and first signal box opened 20th July 1874

Line to Mortehoe doubled, first signal box closed, second signal box opened 1st July 1889

Line to Pottington doubled 4th August 1890

Goods yard closed 7th September 1964

Line singled, signal box reduced to ground frame 17th December 1967

Line closed 5th October 1970

At Braunton the line to Ilfracombe ran almost due north. The major part of the station lay between the two level crossings at Braunton Gates and Braunton

station. The latter accommodated Caen Street, a major road in the small town which was also part of the B3231 out to Saunton Sands, Croyde Bay and Croyde village. Braunton was the largest intermediate settlement on the line, with a population of several thousand. The station was very central for the town and as a result was well patronised by locals. The platforms ended at Caen Street level crossing, the signal box being on the down side. The down platform was significantly longer than the up. The main station building was on the down side with a spacious approach from Caen Street. On the up side, opposite, there was a waiting shelter and bookstall.

The goods yard was on the up side and comprised two sidings behind the platform, the nearer one serving a stone goods shed. The siding ran under an awning but there was no track through the shed. The outer siding ran under a gantry which could lift loads up to 10 tons. From this outer siding two short roads ran back to cattle pens and a loading dock, one for end-loading, the other for side-loading. In LSWR days there had been a third road. There were a number of buildings in the yard, including a lamp room, porters' room, trolley garage and permanent way hut.

From Barnstaple, as far as Braunton, the railway had been almost level, but from here on this changed completely, the line climbing to Mortehoe on gradients as steep as 1 in 40. For most of the year trains were sufficiently light for one engine to cope, but in the busy summer season all that changed and two or three engines were required for the heavier holiday trains. As we will see in Chapter Nine, assistance took various forms but, in general, a second locomotive was attached at the rear of the train and if necessary a third at the front. They assisted them up to Mortehoe station and then ran back to Braunton light for the next turn. To facilitate this there were two engine sidings at the rear of the down platform, with buffers at Braunton Gates, and one well in advance above Caen Street level crossing.

Locomotives required copious supplies of water for this heavy work, so four water cranes were provided, two at the end of the up platform and two on the down, one on each side of Caen Street level crossing. The water was pumped up from the River Caen to a tower from where it fed by gravity to the columns (as well as to the station for non-drinking purposes). As early as 1919 the water was pumped by electricity, supplied by the Braunton Electric Light Power Company.

The layout was completed with two trailing crossovers, one north of Caen Street level crossing, the other south of Braunton Gates (although in earlier years it had been just to the north). The whole layout was controlled from Braunton box, which also locked both Braunton Gates and Georgeham crossing boxes. Braunton had a 25 lever frame. In the down direction there were distant, home, starting and advanced starting signals, the distant being at Vellator, the home protecting Braunton Gates. The starter pro-

A fine view of Braunton station during the Southern period. The vans in the goods yard (several are of LBSC origin) are there for the heavy horticultural traffic, while the motor bus parked behind the signal box ran in connection with trains. The station has a number of Southern fittings including electric lights, and the earlier wooden signal post has been replaced with a lattice post, the distant having a yellow arm. The two water columns on the down side straddle the Caen Street level crossing, and are fed from the water tower along the line. The water was pumped up from the adjacent River Caen. *Knights Photographers*

Chapel Street level crossing, later known as Braunton Gates, in the early Southern period. Arriving from Barnstaple, these gates marked the start of the station area. The box controlled only the level crossing gates, when unlocked by the Braunton signalman who had charge of all the signals. The compact goods yard was quite busy, equipped with a gantry which could lift loads of up to ten tons. There were two water cranes on the up platform, often used by banking engines before they crossed over to the engine sidings to the left of the picture. Three level crossings on half a mile of railway can be seen here - the other two are Caen Street at the far end of the platforms and Georgeham in the distance. Later the crossover was moved to the other side of the crossing. *Knights Photographers*

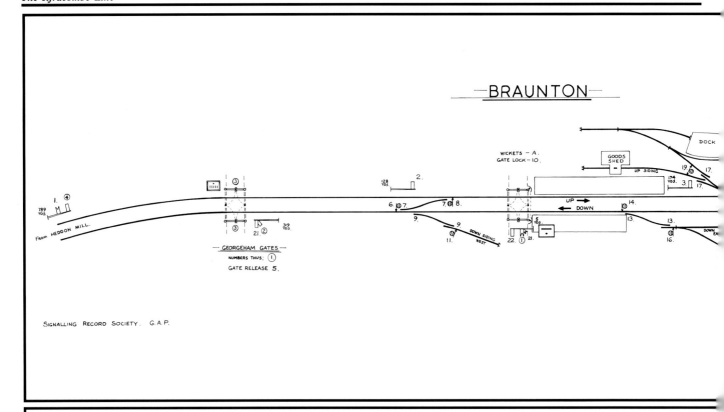

BRAUNTON

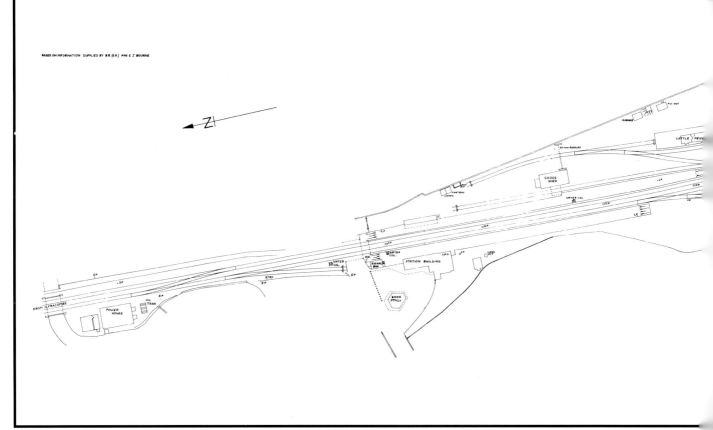

tected Caen Street level crossing and the advanced starter served for Georgeham level crossing. In the up direction were distant, home, starting and advanced starting signals at Georgeham, Caen Street, Braunton Gates and towards Vellator. Block instruments connected with adjacent signal boxes at Wrafton and Heddon Mill, or to Pottington and Mortehoe when these were switched out, and there was a wheel to operate the Caen Street level crossing gates. The Braunton signalman rang bells at Braunton Gates and Georgeham to instruct the crossing keepers to close their gates - two beats for up trains and four beats for down. On receipt of the message that this was done he restored his No.18 and 5 levers to normal, to lock these gates. After the train had passed he pulled these levers to enable the crossing keepers to open their gates to road traffic.

From the above it will be seen that the Braunton signalman was one of the most important men in the town, with the responsibility of cutting the town in half at three level crossings many times a day, sometimes for prolonged periods.

When an up goods shunted the yard, Braunton Gates had to be closed to road traffic for some time. For down goods it was worse - both crossovers were needed and Caen Street was also shut. When a long down passenger train arrived it would straddle Caen Street whilst extra engines were attached at the front or rear. In the meantime, road traffic was building up in Caen Street and the queues could stretch back for some distance, affecting the main Barnstaple to Ilfracombe (A361) road. The Braunton signalman would keep the crossing gates open for as

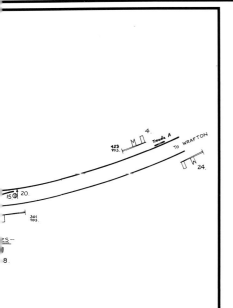

Caen Street, Braunton, probably in the 1930s, looking east across the level crossing. The station was very convenient for the town centre, but when the level crossing gates were shut to allow trains through, traffic queues soon built up. *Knights Photographers*

Braunton station in late South Western days, with equipment of the time including cap badges, oil lamps, notices, barrow, and wooden signal post. The lower signal arm, the Georgeham down distant, is painted red rather than the yellow of later years. This is the main station building on the down side, the 1889 signal box being adjacent to the Caen Street level crossing. It would appear that permanent way staff have prepared the track for re-ballasting. *Medina Gallery*

SOUTHERN RAILWAYS GROUP

TRACK PLAN
BRAUNTON

SCALE	1 inch : 40ft.	DATE	
DRAWN BY	E.J.Bourne	SHEET NUMBER	B3-215
	July 1973		

long as possible, but trains had priority and on a busy summer Saturday there were some frustrated motorists. As we will see in Chapter Four the Parish Council complained of delays to pedestrians as far back as 1919.

In the passenger station in the 1950s and 1960s there was a lot of traffic. Many local people bought cheap day returns to Barnstaple Town at 1s 6d, using the 7.15am and 8.34am departures, returning on the 5.15pm, for both stations were convenient for the town centres. Passengers with farther to travel could take a taxi which met every train - driven by Mr Braund and later by Mr Ken Lamprey - or a Western National bus, from the stop just outside the station. This ran on the Barnstaple - Braunton - Saunton - Croyde - Georgeham route. Extra buses ran on summer Saturdays in connection with holiday trains, in particular a double decker based at the station which ran to a NALGO holiday centre at Croyde. Important passenger rated traffics forwarded from Braunton for many years were flowers and mushrooms grown in a local nursery run by Seymour Cobley. Smaller consignments were loaded into the guards vans of through coaches to London, but the volume of traffic was at times enough to justify the presence of half a dozen luggage vans in the yard.

The goods yard was rather small, and there was a complication in that all wagons for Wrafton had to be worked here first and then up to Wrafton. The main traffic was coal, the local merchant for many years being Mr Arnold Comber of North Street who had a depot in the yard. In the 1920s W.H. Smith had a store and other customers included builders' mer-chant Mr Arthur Kingdom (who received bricks and other materials) and Mr Stan Simmonds, who dealt in basic slag for the use of local farmers. At one time there was a private owner wagon lettered 'ISAAC WILSON, Braunton No.3', painted black with red corners, probably owned by a local coal merchant. Traffic forwarded included sugar beet in the season, scrap metal, and a wide variety of livestock including cattle, donkeys, sheep, bulls and horses. Mr Eric Perryman owned a collection and delivery service and had a contract to serve Croyde, Georgeham and outlying districts. The vehicle was driven by Mr Jack Worth.

There was a considerable number of railwaymen employed in the Braunton area, under the supervision of the station master. In 1891 they included signalman F. Snell and relief signalmen J. Wonnacott and W.D. Hodges. In 1925 the station master was Mr Lucas, in charge of signalman C. Holman, porters J.H. Beer and F. Cooper, and crossing keepers W. Heale and J.J. Jones. By 1929 Mr Labdon was station master. In the 1940s and early 1950s Mr Stan Lilley (who had been the

N class 2-6-0 No.A857 awaits the next banking turn in the engine sidings opposite Braunton Gates box. In the foreground is the River Caen, to the left a group of wagons in the goods yard, and in the background East Hill and the town. The private owner wagon belongs to Evans and Bevan of Neath, painted black and lettered in white with red shading. *Knights Photographers*

After a cloudburst one day (during the Southern period) the River Caen burst its banks and flooded the centre of Braunton. These are the tracks, awash, over Caen Street level crossing with an M7 class 0-4-4T. *Lewis Andrews Collection*

A general view of Braunton station looking north in 1954. British Railways fitments, including the enamel station nameboard, have now appeared. The water tower can be seen just behind the level crossing. *R.E.Tustin*

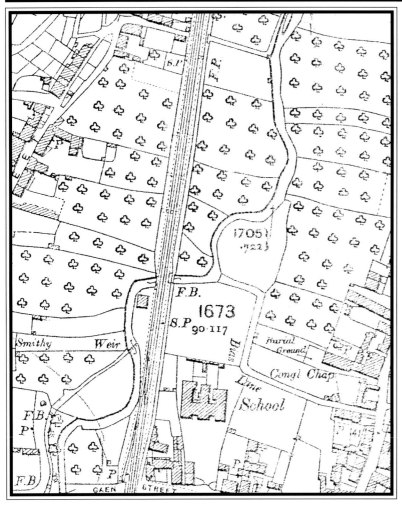

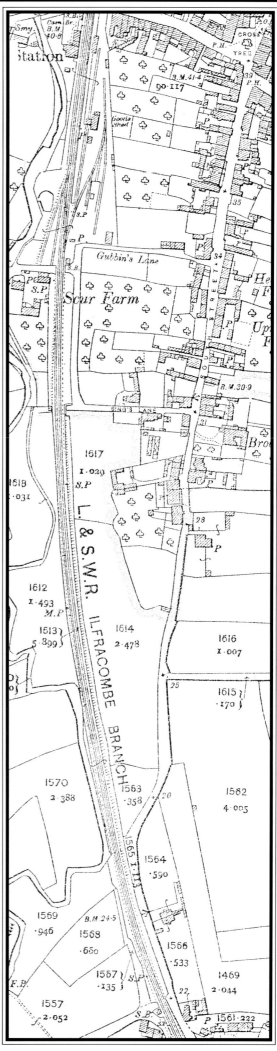

station master at Lynton when the line there closed) was in charge. He was followed by Mr Gregory. There were two signalmen in the early 1950s, Mr P. Rich and Mr F. Winter, the latter followed by Mr W. Crook who remained until the signal box closed. There were four porters working in the passenger station and goods yard in the early 1950s, F. Woodley, K. Almond, Lakeman and Mock and, in the late 1950s, F. Woodley and B. Fox. There was also a clerk, D. Cox - the post was later held by Mrs I. Smith. There were two permanent way gangs at Braunton, led by Gangers H. King on the Ilfracombe side and P. Mock on the Barnstaple side. The Braunton station master also

Braunton signal box in later British Railways days. Opened when the line to Mortehoe was doubled in 1889, the box contained 25 levers, block instruments and the level crossing gate wheel. The lattice post has the Braunton down starting and the Georgeham down distant signal arms, the latter also being back-slotted by Braunton's down advanced starting signal. After the line was singled in 1967 the box lost its block instruments and all its point levers became spare, but basic signalling was retained to protect the level crossing. *D.Nicholas*

SOUTHERN RAILWAY STATISTICS 1928-36 BRAUNTON					
	1928	**1930**	**1932**	**1934**	**1936**
Passenger tickets issued	40,213	45,096	26,629	22,764	22,175
Season tickets issued	66	110	141	157	110
Tickets collected	49,227	59,224	37,031	33,029	31,835
Parcels forwarded	4,851	6,010	6,382	5,378	5,253
Parcels received	8,561	9,818	10,474	11,978	12,683
Horses forwarded	22	5	2	11	-
Horses received	25	19	12	13	
Milk forwarded (cans) (gals from 1932)	-	-	-	1001	1807
Milk received (cans) (gals from 1932)	-	219	-	727	1231
Fish, Meat forwarded(cwt)	3,365	4,508	3,748	5,062	5,710
Fish, Meat received (cwt)	120	176	162	83	1,039
General Merchandise forwarded (tons)	1,401	1,122	742	1,024	1,629
General Merchandise received (tons)	2,677	3,002	2,253	2,725	2,777
Coal forwarded (tons)	-	-	-	-	21
Coal received (tons)	1,822	2,589	3,121	3,025	3,067
Other minerals forwarded (tons)	567	384	187	493	346
Other minerals received (tons)	2,668	2,714	2,558	3,627	3,290
Livestock forwarded (trucks)	11	19	21	37	80
Livestock received (trucks)	20	22	-	9	11
Loaded wagons forwarded (not livestock)	358	298	293	495	975
Loaded wagons received (not livestock)	1,540	2,135	1,807	2,175	2,430

Braunton was the only intermediate station on the line to have its own goods shed and siding in the yard. The siding ran outside the shed under an awning where one wagon at a time could be dealt with. This is the yard side of the goods shed in 1968, four years after its closure. *A.E.West*

supervised Wrafton station and all the crossing keepers from Duckpool to Heddon Mill. The establishment also included two relief crossing keepers - in the late 1950s these were R. Batten and K. Almond. When the conductor guard scheme was introduced in 1968 the remaining staff were signalman W. Crook, porters F. Woodley, K. Almond and J. Lakeman.

Leaving Braunton station the line headed due north and commenced its climb to Mortehoe, six miles away but 600 feet higher. Initially the gradient was 1 in 74. The line passed the pump house on the left and crossed the River Caen on an iron girder bridge, No.12. To the right a footpath ran alongside the line as far as Georgeham Crossing.

GEORGEHAM CROSSING
Georgeham Crossing was provided for a minor road which ran from the main A361 adjacent to the line to part of Braunton and on to the picturesque village of Georgeham some three miles away. The crossing box and gatekeeper's cottage were adjacent on the up side of the line, the box containing a 5 lever frame, tel-ephone and bells to communicate with the Braunton signalman. Georgeham had up and down distant and home signals, but in the down direction these were slotted with Braunton signal box. The Georgeham down distant signal (at Caen Street level crossing) was operated by Georgeham No.1 and slotted by Braunton No.22 levers, and the down home signal by Nos.2 and 21 respectively. This was not the case in the up direction but the Georgeham home and Braunton distant signals were together, on a post 206 yards away.

When a train was due at Georgeham the Braunton signalman would send a bell signal, 2 beats for up, 4 beats for down. After acknowledgement of the signal the crossing keeper opened each of the four gates by hand, there being no wheel in the box, and locked them with No.3 lever. He then phoned Braunton where the signalman also locked the crossing gates with his No.5 lever, and the stop and distant signals were pulled off. The crossing keeper lived in the adjacent cottage and was on duty whenever the line was open, except on his rest day when two shifts of relief crossing keepers were provided by Braunton. In the late 1950s the crossing keeper was Mr A. Grove and in the 1960s Mr Cooper.

At the crossing the gradient eased to 1 in 96 and the line ran along the valley of the River Caen, closely following the main A361 road. A minor road crossed over the line on a skew stone-built bridge, No.13. It then crossed and re-crossed the River Caen on culvert No.13A and an iron deck bridge No.14, past milepost 218 and over a minor stream on iron deck bridge No.15. Here the gradient steepened slightly, to 1 in 87, and ran in a cutting under stone-built bridge No.16, which carried a minor road. Adjacent to this, on the up side, were a couple of cottages built to the standard South Western design, together with the Georgeham distant signal. By the adjacent A361 was the small settlement of Knowle. The gradient eased to 1 in 128 , but then steepened to 1 in 82 on a slight embankment. Here the line crossed the River Caen,

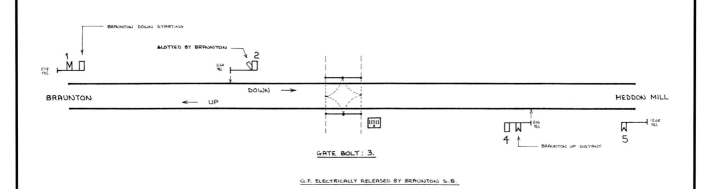

GEORGEHAM GATES G.F.

BRAUNTON DOWN STARTING

SLOTTED BY BRAUNTON

DOWN →

BRAUNTON ← UP

HEDDON MILL

GATE BOLT: 3.

BRAUNTON UP DISTANT

G.F. ELECTRICALLY RELEASED BY BRAUNTON S.B.

Georgeham level crossing, a short distance beyond Braunton, in 1968. The box, built adjacent to the crossing keeper's cottage, dated from 1889. *A.E.West*

again on an iron deck bridge, No.17, and passed the Stoney Bridge distant signal. Next came milepost 219 and the gradient changed twice, first to 1 in 73 and then 1 in 83, before reaching Stoney Bridge Gates.

STONEY BRIDGE GATES
Stoney Bridge Gates, or Stoney Bridge Crossing as it was also known, accommodated a minor road which ran from the main A361, adjacent to the line, to small farms at Nethercott and Upcott and thence towards Georgeham. The crossing box and gatekeeper's cottage stood on the up side of the line above the crossing. The box contained a 6 lever frame, with one spare, and repeater bells for the Braunton to Heddon Mill (or Mortehoe) block section, the operation of the crossing being similar to that described already at Duckpool and Vellator. There were distant and home signals in each direction, the down signal post carrying the Stoney

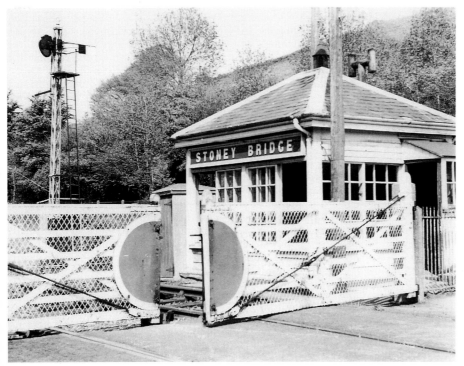

Stoney Bridge level crossing in 1968, with a fine example of a South Western lower quadrant signal on a lattice post. *A.E.West*

In the last years of the line the Stoney Bridge crossing keeper was Mr W.Darke, seen here opening the gates by hand, there being no gate wheel provided in the box. *W.Darke Collection*

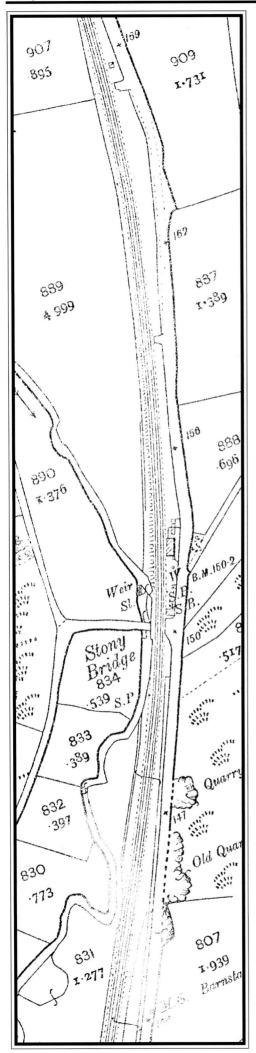

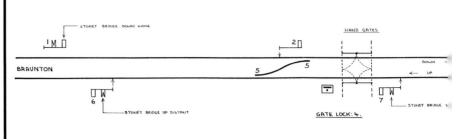

HEDDON MILL

Interior of Heddon Mill box in 1968, showing the 8 lever Stevens knee frame.
A.E.West

Bridge home and the Heddon Mill distant arms. The Stoney Bridge up distant was at Heddon Mill. The four crossing gates at Stoney Bridge were each opened by hand, there being no gate wheel. The *Southern Railway Magazine* in 1929 reported the retirement of signalman Manning from Stoney Bridge after 47 years service. In the late 1950s the crossing keeper was Mr A. Travers, later it was Mr J. Rhodes and the last, from 1963 to 1970, was Mr W. Darke. The crossing keeper was on duty from 6am to 10pm. The usual bell codes were 3-1 for a passenger train, 3-2 for goods, 4-1 for light engines and 6 for signing off.

Leaving Stoney Bridge the line curved up the valley alongside the A361; on the down side was the first catch point on the bank. This protected the line below in the event of any vehicles breaking loose from an ascending train. A coupling on a goods train did break once, farther up at Hunters Inn, although this was a very unusual event in steam days. The errant wagons were fitted only with hand operated brakes; unlike the vacuum brake fitted to passenger rated vehicles, it did not automatically come on in the event of a breakaway and they finished up in the adjacent meadow. The gradient eased slightly to 1 in 100 as the line arrived at Heddon Mill Signal Box.

HEDDON MILL SIGNAL BOX

At first sight Heddon Mill seems identical to the other crossings on this section, but it was established as a signal box (with a closing switch) when the line was doubled in 1889. There were two block sections, Braunton to Heddon Mill and Heddon Mill to Mortehoe, with the Heddon Mill signalman responsible for offering and accepting trains into his sections. When the box was switched out the section was Braunton to Mortehoe and Heddon Mill operated as a crossing box like the others. Heavy summer holiday trains took 16 minutes or more to climb from Braunton to Mortehoe, so without Heddon Mill signal box trains would have to wait at Braunton until the preceding one had left Mortehoe. With Heddon Mill signal box open there could be two trains ascending the bank, one in each section, and extra paths were available for engines descending light to Braunton for their next banking duty. On a busy summer Saturday there were as many as 20 trains in each direction, with another 10 light engines descending the bank, but on other days the box was switched out, reverting to a crossing box.

The signal box and signalman's cottage lay on the up side, just below the crossing which accommodated another minor road, running from the A361 towards Georgeham. There were distant and home signals in each direction, the down distant being at Stoney Bridge. The Stoney Bridge up distant was on the same

A 1968 view of the exterior of Heddon Mill box and the keepers cottage adjacent to it. *A.E.West*

Mortehoe, and a closing switch to switch out the signal box, allowing it to revert to a crossing box. There was no gate wheel so the four crossing gates were opened by hand. In the 1950s and 1960s the crossing keeper was Mr Martin, a passed signalman who could operate the signal box. If he was not available a relief signalman was sent instead. After the singling of the line in 1967 it became a crossing box, operated by Mrs Harris.

Leaving Heddon Mill the gradient stiffened, first to 1 in 50, and then to 1 in 40 for almost all the next four miles to Mortehoe. The River Caen was crossed over a culvert, No. 18, and then the line followed the A361 up a different valley, towards Pines Dean. A minor road crossed the line on stone arch bridge No.19 and the line curved up the valley past milepost 220 and Heddon Mill up distant signal, to Pines Dean.

South Dean accommodation level crossing, at 220 miles 19 chains, was the subject of considerable correspondence in 1938-39, following a complaint from a farmer, Mr W. Avery of South Dean Farm.

post as the Heddon Mill up home signal and slotted the Heddon Mill up distant. Originally there were also starting signals, and a trailing crossover was provided just below the crossing, but these were taken out about 1922. When the crossover was in use there was an advantage in that single line operation could be instituted on the shorter sections if engineering work was going on. After 1922 the whole section from Braunton to Mortehoe had to be worked as a single line in such circumstances, though the work was normally done outside the busy summer period.

Inside the box was an 8 lever frame, 6 levers for signals (later reduced to 4), one for the crossover and one for the gate lock. There were block instruments for the sections to Braunton and

A fine view of Heddon Mill, centre, in Southern days. The railway and road climb alongside each other up the beautiful wooded valley, with Heddon Mill signal box adjacent to the level crossing. The signal posts carry the Heddon Mill down home and the Heddon Mill up home, with the Stoney Gates up distant below it. Traffic on what is now the A361 road is light. *Knights Photographers*

Above left. Heddon Mill crossing gates and signals in 1968. *A.E.West*. *Above right*. In 1968 the Heddon Mill crossing keeper was Mrs Harris. *A.E.West*

On Saturday 27th July 1963 N class 2-6-0 No.31838 with the five coach portion of the 1.0pm from Waterloo to Ilfracombe ascends the bank, having just passed Heddon Mill level crossing. *Peter W. Gray*

On Saturday 1st September 1962 ex-GWR 2-6-0 No. 7333 ascends the bank past Heddon Mill level crossing with the five coaches of the 10.55am from Wolverhampton Low Level to Ilfracombe banked by West Country 4-6-2 No.34002 SALISBURY. *Peter W. Gray*

He was concerned at the danger in taking cattle over the crossing due to the frequent passage without warning of both trains and light engines. On the up line, trains coming down the bank could be seen for only 90 yards due to the curvature of the line. A telephone was suggested, or a whistle board, but the Southern Railway felt that as there had been no change in conditions over a number of years, no action need be taken. No mishap had been reported, and the company saw no need to provide any special arrangements.

There were a number of minor foot crossings. A stream was crossed on culvert No.19A, a track on iron bridge No.20 and a stream on culvert No.20A. Here the locomotives of ascending trains really had to work hard, particularly on the sharp 120 degree left hand curve near milepost 221, adjacent to the *Foxhunters Inn* on the A361. On Christmas Eve 1889 an Ilfracombe Goods engine descending the

On Saturday 27th July 1963 ex-GWR 2-6-0 No.6346 hauls the four coaches of the 8.50am from Taunton to Ilfracombe, banked by Ivatt 2-6-2T No.41298 on the 1 in 40 near Pines Dean. *Peter W. Gray*

On Saturday 27th July 1963 ex-GWR 2-6-0 No.7333 coasts down the 1 in 40 bank with the five coaches of the 9.20am Ilfracombe to Taunton train, passing Heddon Mill up distant signal. *Peter W.Gray*

On Saturday 7th July 1962 the five coach portion of the 8.35am train from Waterloo to Ilfracombe comes off the long curve at *Foxhunters Inn*, hauled by Battle of Britain class 4-6-2 No.34067 TANGMERE, and banked by N class 2-6-0 No.31856, tender first. On summer Saturdays banking engines were employed in the mornings on heavy up trains from Ilfracombe to Mortehoe, and in the afternoons from Braunton to Mortehoe; in between there was little opportunity to turn them on the Ilfracombe turntable. *Peter W.Gray*

On the same day at the same location as the two photographs opposite the four coach 1.57pm from Taunton to Ilfracombe is hauled by ex-GWR 2-6-0 No.6327, banked by Ivatt 2-6-2T No.41298. *Peter W.Gray*

These two photographs taken on Saturday 27th July 1963 show the 11am 'Atlantic Coast Express' from Waterloo to Ilfracombe, hauled by Battle of Britain class 4-6-2 No.34079 141 SQUADRON, banked by N class 2-6-0 No.31846, approaching Willingcott, near milepost 222. The train, which usually comprised the maximum eleven coaches for the line, has here about a mile of the 1 in 40 bank remaining before reaching the summit at Mortehoe station. *Peter W.Gray*

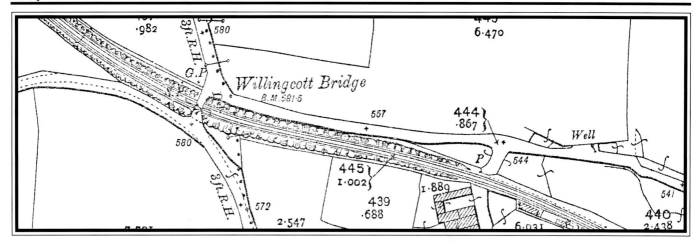

The only available photograph of Willingcott Crossing was taken on 4th August 1951, from a GWR B set of a down train hauled by a 45XX GWR 2-6-2T. The crossing keeper's cottage was on the down side and the crossing box opposite. The two down signals pulled off are the Willingcott home and the Mortehoe distant. *R.J.Sellick*

tion crossing, since road vehicles could cross the line on the next overbridge, No.24, at the expense of only a quarter of a mile. The hut was on the up side of the line and operated in the same way as other crossing boxes, as described at Duckpool. There were distant and home signals in each direction. The down home signal also carried the Mortehoe distant, and the Willingcott up distant was on the same post as the Mortehoe up advanced starting signal. A couple of railway cottages in standard South Western style stood on

bank with a train was derailed here on the sharp curve of 16 chains radius; full details are in Chapter Four. Just before here the gradient eased briefly to 1 in 366 and then 1 in 100 before resuming at 1 in 41 over an iron deck road bridge, No.21.

Now running a little to the north of west, the line climbed up a lonely valley, crossing a minor road on iron deck bridge No.22 whilst on a long embankment. After a foot crossing came milepost 222, and then the down distant signal for Willingcott Crossing. The gradient eased slightly to 1 in 45, but soon reverted to 1 in 40, just before a stone bridge, No.23 carrying the line over a minor road. At the end of a long section on an embankment the line reached Willingcott Crossing.

WILLINGCOTT CROSSING
This accommodated a minor road which connected with others leading to the B3231. It was not mentioned in the 1889 Inspection Report nor were the buildings to the same design as at other crossings on the line, so it would appear to be a later addition. Early in BR days, it was downgraded to an occupa-

SOUTHERN RAILWAY STATISTICS 1928-36					
MORTEHOE					
	1928	1930	1932	1934	1936
Passenger tickets issued	20,806	17,798	14,158	12,138	11,553
Season tickets issued	99	113	93	95	71
Tickets collected	52,145	43,440	29,598	30,116	29,698
Parcels forwarded	1,356	1,422	1,324	1,178	1,026
Parcels received	6,548	6,422	5,502	7,317	7,800
Horses forwarded	7	7	10	21	21
Horses received	9	7	11	26	23
Milk forwarded (cans) (gals from 1932)	-	-	-	-	10
Milk received (cans) (gals from 1932)	290	90	1154	2752	4596
Fish, Meat forwarded(cwt)	23	44	32	72	42
Fish, Meat received (cwt)	442	746	369	166	467
General Merchandise forwarded (tons)	188	272	117	267	299
General Merchandise received (tons)	2,055	1,844	1,163	1,299	1,450
Coal forwarded (tons)	-	-	-	-	-
Coal received (tons)	1,449	1,659	1,641	1,790	1,770
Other minerals forwarded (tons)	6	12	-	-	-
Other minerals received (tons)	1,270	963	1,370	954	994
Livestock forwarded (trucks)	23	33	16	18	15
Livestock received (trucks)	7	32	2	-	-
Loaded wagons forwarded (not livestock)	59	79	53	169	142
Loaded wagons received (not livestock)	937	763	858	798	921

Mortehoe and Woolacombe station looking north in British Railways days. *Irwell Press Collection*

the down side. In the 1950s the crossing keeper was Mr H. Clarke.

Leaving Willingcott Crossing the line entered a cutting and passed under stone built bridge No.24, which carried the B3231 from Ilfracombe to Georgeham. At the end of the cutting came another embankment, and the line ran over bridge No.25, a stone built skew structure built for a farm track. Just past here was a set of catch points on the down line, provided to take care of any runaways from

Mortehoe station. On the up side was a post carrying the Mortehoe up advanced starting and the Willingcott distant signals. By this stage the line had completed a long right hand curve to head almost due north into Mortehoe station.

MORTEHOE AND WOOLACOMBE
Chronology
Station and first signal box opened 20th July 1874

Line to Braunton doubled, first signal box closed, second signal box opened 1st July 1889
Line to Ilfracombe doubled 1st July 1891
Goods yard closed 7th September 1964
Line singled, second signal box closed 17th December 1967
Line closed 5th October 1970

Originally named Morthoe, in 1902 the station was renamed 'Mortehoe for Lee and Woolacombe'. In 1950 it became Mortehoe and Woolacombe; it was 223¼ miles from Waterloo and a lonely 600 feet above sea level, at the summit of the line.

The small settlement of Morthoe (later spelt Mortehoe) was two miles away to the west near Morte Point, the headland which separated Bideford Bay from the main Bristol Channel. The slightly larger resort of Woolacombe, with its three mile beach, developed after the arrival of the railway and lies just south of Mortehoe, at the end of the B3343 road which runs from the A361 at Mullacott Cross, past Mortehoe station.

When the line opened there was little here except the station, but the large *Fortescue Hotel* was subsequently opened opposite; long distance travellers may have previously passed the *Fortescue Arms Hotel* at South Molton Road station 25 miles away. Earl Fortescue owned extensive estates in North Devon and, as we shall see in Chapter Two, was a prominent supporter of the broad gauge route from Taunton. There were three railway cottages adjacent to the yard and the station house, but apart from these there was

On Saturday 27th July 1963 ex-GWR 2-6-0 No.6346 departs from Mortehoe with the 8.50am from Taunton to Ilfracombe. There are a couple of wagons in the yard indicating a little freight traffic. *Peter W. Gray*

On Saturday 1st September 1962 ex-GWR 2-6-0 No. 7326 departs from Mortehoe with the 2.17pm Taunton to Ilfracombe train. *Peter W.Gray*

The station buildings at Mortehoe in May 1968. The signal box was now closed and the track reduced to a single line. *A.E.West*

The entrance to Mortehoe station in May 1968 was rather dilapidated even before the staff were withdrawn in the conductor-guard scheme, introduced the following autumn. *A.E.West*

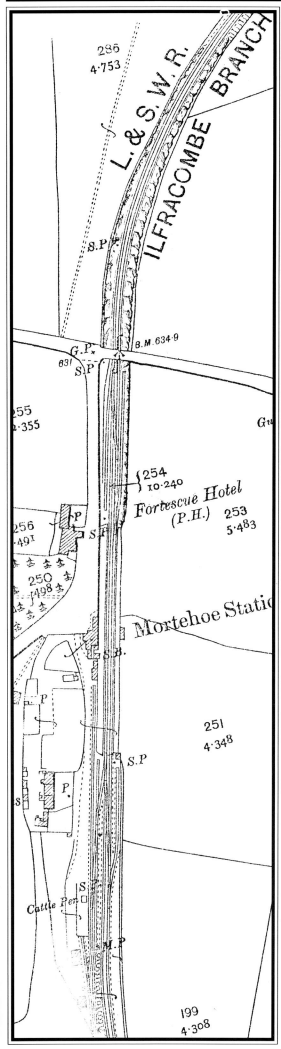

no other habitation. The place could seem even more isolated than ever when a cold Atlantic mist rolled in from the sea, even in midsummer, restricting visibility to a hundred yards or so.

At the summit of the line, with gradients of 1 in 40 up from Braunton and 1 in 36 from Ilfracombe, the operation of the station on a summer Saturday was something very special. It was arranged so that assisting engines, both pilots and bankers, could be taken off and sent quickly back ready for their next turn. To expedite this, at each end of both up and down platforms there was a trailing connection to a siding - four in all, where the engines could be held until dispatch. The main part of the station was on a gradient of 1 in 288 falling towards Braunton, but the 1 in 40 started at the end of the trailing crossover at the south end. The bank down towards Ilfracombe, starting at 1 in 190, commenced just beyond the trailing crossover at the north end, just under the stone built overbridge No.26, carrying the B3343.

The goods yard was reached by the trailing crossover at the Braunton end of the down platform. The yard was rather short but the complex of pointwork within it enabled wagons to be expeditiously shunted to the cattle pen, side and end loading dock and under the 2 ton crane. The sidings were on the level, and the severity of the gradient on the main line was vividly illustrated at the far buffer stops, where the siding was about 12 feet above the running lines. There were a number of stores in the yard, including a Shell Mex depot, but no conventional goods shed. Instead, as at Wrafton, the goods shed was on the down platform and goods trains paused here for a few minutes for consignments for Mortehoe to be unloaded from a road van (later road box). Practically all freight arrived and departed in the Barnstaple direction, so wagons arrived on down goods trains, and departed on up trains, most of these going away empty. Goods traffic here was light but included coal, animal feedstuffs, fertilizers, building materials, and oil, with some livestock and sugar beet forwarded.

The passenger facilities were mostly on the down platform where there was a substantial station house and offices. The second building on the site, it had replaced the original, burnt down a month after opening. The signal box and goods shed were here too. There was a waiting shed on the up platform, and both plat-

forms were provided with awnings to a rather severe steel and asbestos Southern Railway design. In the station approach the Southern National green single decker bus provided a connecting service to Woolacombe, which was particularly well-patronised in the summer holiday period. Up to 1925, all tickets for down trains were collected here, for Ilfracombe was then an open station. In the early 1960s this isolated wayside station boasted its own restaurant car express to Waterloo on summer Saturdays. The empty train was worked up from Ilfracombe and filled rapidly, here and at Braunton, with holidaymakers holding reserved seats. An associated traffic was passenger luggage in advance, and a lorry sent up from Ilfracombe operated a collection and delivery service to the resorts.

The signal box on the down platform had a 20 lever frame to control the station. There were distant, home, starting and advanced starting signals in each direction, and within the station limits ground signals to control shunting movements. There were strict regulations for the shunting of goods trains, to minimise the risk of any runaway wagons, but in case of failure there were catch points on both sides of the summit. The block sections were to Ilfracombe and to Heddon Mill (or Braunton) and the Mortehoe signalman was very busy indeed on a summer Saturday with some 20 trains in each direction, and some 10 banking and pilot engines in each direction coming off their trains and returning to the foot of the bank. A number of changes were made in 1936 to facilitate the use of the 'Section Clear but Station Blocked' signal on the up line between Ilfracombe and Mortehoe, to overcome delays to following trains when assisting engines were detached here; details are given in Chapter Five.

The original station master here was Mr Rice. In 1891 staff included porter W.H. Slater and relief signalman M. Kerslake, and in 1925 station master R.H. Holmes, signalman C. Lambert and porters E.R. Bransgrove, W. Mallett and B.M. Long. In the 1930s the station master was Mr G. Dark and later Mr Somerfield, their duties including the supervision of Willingcott Crossing. In later years it was supervised by the Ilfracombe station master, and the establishment was two signalmen and two porters, who attended to all station business. On busy summer Saturdays relief staff were sent to assist with the greatly increased work.

As previously indicated, the descent to Ilfracombe began under bridge No.26, first at 1 in 190 and then after a few yards, 1 in 76. Here was the summit cutting, which had caused considerable difficulties during construction; the line curved round to the north east, passing the down advanced starting signal; on the up line was a catch point to derail any vehicles which might run away from Mortehoe. There was an occupation crossing for a farm track and then the Mortehoe up distant signal. Adjacent to this signal was a fogman's hut, a reminder of the Atlantic mists which swirled in to obscure the footplatemen's view. During such conditions the Mortehoe station

Mortehoe yard in 1962, this time looking towards Braunton. The main line fell away steeply away from the level goods sidings and there were strict regulations for the shunting of goods trains. This is the end loading dock, with some evidence of recent traffic in coal and minerals. Traders' sheds are still here but the Shell Mex depot has gone. *A.Shelley*

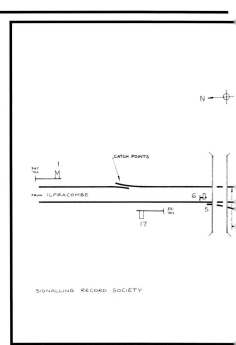

SIGNALLING RECORD SOCIETY

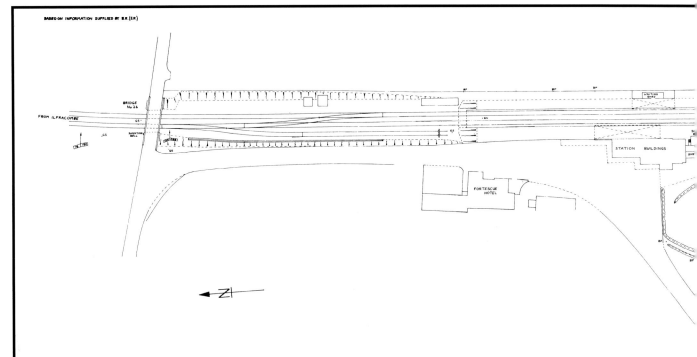

master sent a man out with a supply of detonators which would be placed on the line when the signal was at caution. As locomotives passed over them the detonations would warn the crew that they were approaching Mortehoe and that the distant signal was at caution. The problem was not made any easier by the noise and steam generated as the engine worked very hard up the bank. The line here was on a slight embankment and the downhill gradient changed several times to 1 in 133, then 1 in 445, 1 in 1330, 1 in 68 and then 1 in 36, the gradient all the way down to Ilfracombe station.

An empty goods yard at Mortehoe in 1962 showing the cattle dock, yard crane and down home signal on a concrete post. The run-round in the yard was useful in earlier years when certain freight trains terminated here. *A.Shelley*

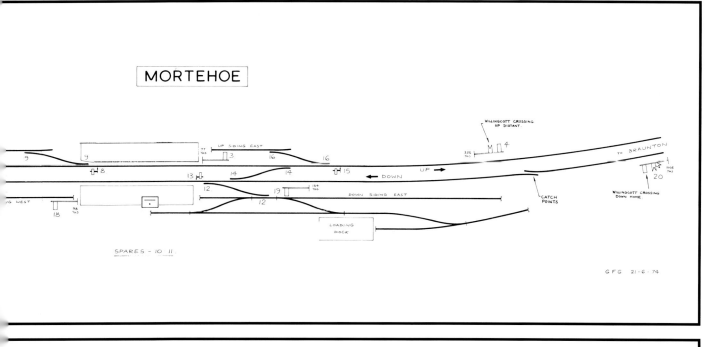

MORTEHOE

UP SIDING EAST

TO BRAUNTON

WILLINGCOTT CROSSING
UP DISTANT.

DOWN   UP

CATCH
POINTS

WILLINGCOTT CROSSING
DOWN HOME

DOWN SIDING EAST

LOADING
DOCK

SPARES - 10 11.

G F G 21-6-74

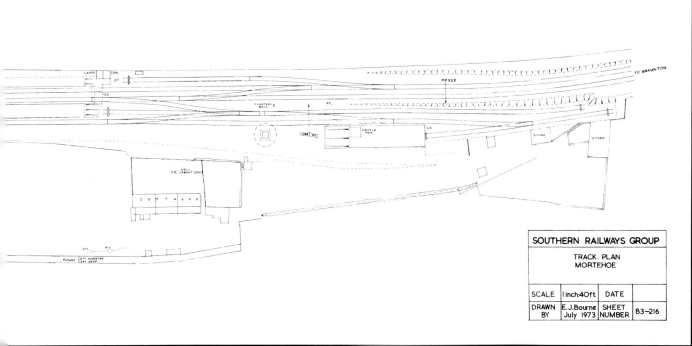

TO BRAUNTON

SOUTHERN RAILWAYS GROUP			
TRACK PLAN MORTEHOE			
SCALE	1inch:40ft	DATE	
DRAWN BY	E.J.Bourne July 1973	SHEET NUMBER	B3-216

The line passed under the B3231 road on stone built bridge No.27 and entered a long cutting running almost due east. Milepost 224 was passed and then a farm track crossed the line on stone built overbridge, No.28. Emerging from the cutting the line headed north east down the east side of the Slade valley, crossing a minor stream in culvert No.28A. Here the line ran above the two Slade Valley reservoirs which provided the water for Ilfracombe. It was a photogenic location, and a justly popular one for recording trains work-

Adjacent to Bridge No.26 was the shunting bell, used in conjunction with the coupling, uncoupling and shunting of banking engines. The standard Exmouth Junction concrete gradient post marked the summit itself. *A.E.West*

A South Western period photograph, in October 1907, of the then Mortehoe for Woolacombe and Lee station, with the main buildings on the down side and a couple of wagons in the yard. The small wooden building between the wagons and the signal box is the goods shed, which catered for general merchandise unloaded from road vans running in goods trains through to Ilfracombe. Other features are the standard South Western oil lamps and the wooden signal posts. *F.E.Box courtesy National Railway Museum*

Above. On Saturday 7th July 1962 the four coaches of the 6.37pm train from Ilfracombe to Taunton are hauled up the 1 in 36 bank towards Mortehoe station by 2-6-0s, N class 31875 piloting ex-GWR 7337. *Peter W. Gray*

Below. On Saturday 1st September 1962 the 11.5am Ilfracombe to Wolverhampton Low Level train storms up the 1 in 36 bank near milepost 225, hauled by 2-6-0s N class No.31847 and ex-GWR No.7311. Slade reservoir is in the background, and the Ilfracombe (fixed) distant signal can be seen near the rear of the train. *Peter W. Gray*

Above and top right. On Saturday 27th July 1963 the 5.57 train from Ilfracombe to Taunton climbs the 1 in 36 bank past the Slade reservoirs, hauled by Battle of Britain class 4-6-2 No.34079 141 SQUADRON and ex-GWR 2-6-0 No.6346. *Peter W.Gray*

On Saturday 27th July 1963 the 2.55pm train from Ilfracombe to Waterloo is hauled up the 1 in 36 past the Slade reservoirs, hauled by Battle of Britain class 4-6-2s No.34075 264 SQUADRON and 34069 HAWKINGE. *Peter W. Gray*

The twin bores of the 69 yards of the Slade tunnels looking towards Ilfracombe in 1963. The up (right hand) tunnel was the original of 1874, and the down opened in 1891. When the line was singled in 1967 it utilised the up line, on recently re-laid track. *J.Scrace*

West Country class 4-6-2 No.34015 EXMOUTH emerges from Slade tunnel in May 1964 with an evening train from Ilfracombe to Barnstaple. *G.F.Heiron*

Above. West Country class 4-6-2 No.34020 SEATON emerges from the 'down' bore of Slade tunnel with a train bound for Ilfracombe in May 1964. *G.F.Heiron*

Below. On Saturday 27th July 1963 Battle of Britain class 4-6-2 No. 34072 257 SQUADRON climbs out of Ilfracombe with the 2.10pm train to Waterloo. *Peter W.Gray*

SOUTHERN RAILWAY STATISTICS 1928-36 ILFRACOMBE					
	1928	1930	1932	1934	1936
Passenger tickets issued	69,218	46,245	30,628	26,406	23,943
Season tickets issued	44	413	492	743	448
Tickets collected	151,641	125,717	99,736	105,314	98,929
Parcels forwarded	6,669	5,681	4,846	4,597	4,054
Parcels received	54,572	56,854	56,080	65,195	53,304
Horses forwarded	1	1	-	2	61
Horses received	4	1	-	5	50
Milk forwarded (cans) (gals from 1932)	-	3	504	648	-
Milk received (cans) (gals from 1932)	1,797	1,599	18,033	13,802	15,493
Fish, Meat forwarded(cwt)	898	1,154	991	1,543	911
Fish, Meat received (cwt)	4,248	3,962	3,393	3,515	3,731
General Merchandise forwarded (tons)	1,265	1,346	1,018	965	1,075
General Merchandise received (tons)	7,026	7,705	6,645	6,594	6,753
Coal forwarded (tons)	1,876	1,919	1,916	1,547	965
Coal received (tons)	1,474	2,740	3,518	4,010	4,419
Other minerals forwarded (tons)	387	430	315	432	463
Other minerals received (tons)	2,232	3,912	1,380	3,225	1,992
Livestock forwarded (trucks)	8	5	1	-	14
Livestock received (trucks)	30	73	10	1	-
Loaded wagons forwarded (not livestock)	2,159	2,221	2,363	2,309	2,210
Loaded wagons received (not livestock)	4,093	4,356	3,779	4,139	4,007

ing up the bank. A minor track passed under the line by means of stone built bridge No.29, then passed milepost 225 and the (fixed) Ilfracombe distant signal. The line then curved to the right and passed through Slade Tunnels, No. 30 on the line. There were two bores, one for each line, 69 yards long, with stone portals lined with masonry and brick. The up line used the original 1874 bore, the second being built on doubling in 1891.

Emerging from Slade tunnels the line slowly curved round from east to north, clinging to the side of the valley, and providing the expectant traveller with the first views of the open sea. A farm track swept by under bridge No.31, an iron deck structure carried on stone abutments. The Ilfracombe down outer home signal was passed, then the up advanced starting signal, then the final bridge, No.32, again an iron deck under bridge,

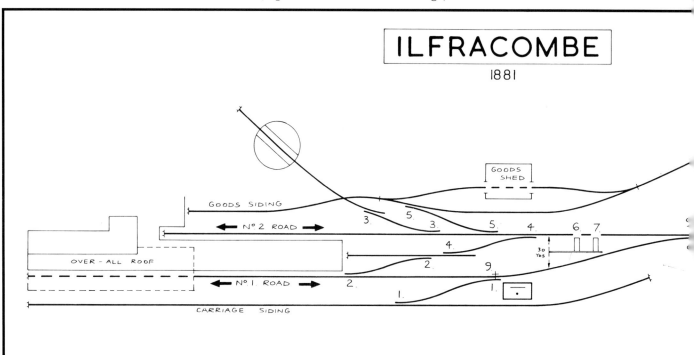

ILFRACOMBE

1881

In May 1961 Battle of Britain class 4-6-2 No.34066 SPITFIRE departs from Ilfracombe with the 10.30am 'Atlantic Coast Express' for Waterloo, fighting for adhesion on the 1 in 36 bank which commenced at the terminus. The array of inner home signals were installed in 1929. *G.F.Heiron*

and the line entered Ilfracombe station 226 miles from Waterloo and some 225 feet above sea level.

ILFRACOMBE
Chronology
Line and first signal box opened 20th July 1874
Line to Mortehoe doubled, second signal box opened 1st July 1891
New enlarged turntable installed 1925
Second engine shed opened 1929
Third signal box opened 7th April 1929
Goods yard closed 7th September 1964 Line singled, signal box closed, new ground frame opened 17th December 1967
Line closed 5th October 1970

1874 - 1889 PERIOD
Over its 96 years the station at Ilfracombe saw many changes so we will consider the major stages of its development. For its first fifteen years the terminus, at the end of a single line, had a short island platform with a track either side. On the ar-

rival side was a short train shed at the buffers, and an adjacent carriage siding. There was a short run round beyond the platform, a two road goods yard with a small shed on a loop, and a short stone built engine shed approached via a 40ft. turntable, between the departure platform and the approach road. Opposite the goods shed there was a signal box of the South Western style of the period, a weatherboarded wooden cabin on a stone base. It had a 12 lever frame, the up starting and down home signals having two arms, one for the arrival platform and one for the goods yard, on the same vertical post, rather than the bracket signals used later. The whole layout was on a difficult hillside site above the town, approached (according to the 1887 gradient manual) on a 1 in 36 bank which eased to 1 in 55 and then to 1 in 300 into the station.

1891 - 1928 PERIOD
The double track line from Mortehoe opened on 1st July 1891, together with an enlarged station at Ilfracombe. This extra capacity was the South Western's response to increasing traffic, not only its

WN   UP ➡   TO MORTEHOE

12

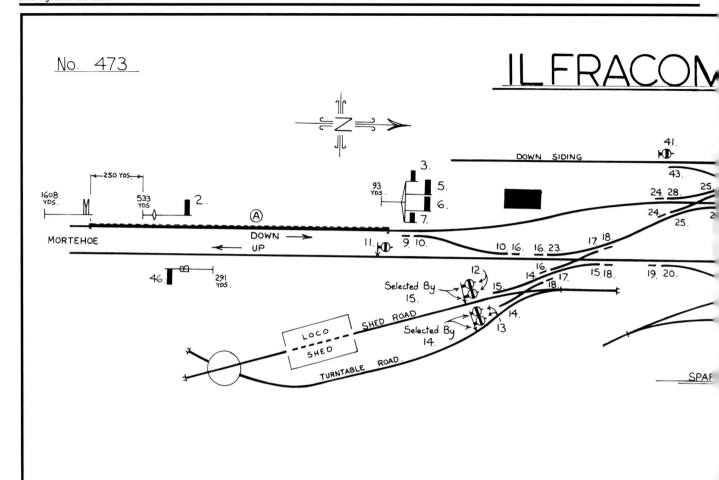

No. 473

ILFRACOM

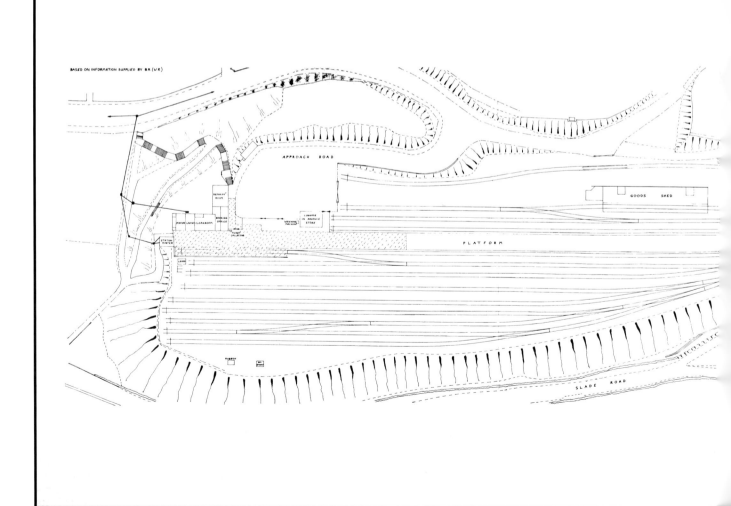

BASED ON INFORMATION SUPPLIED BY B.R.(W.R.)

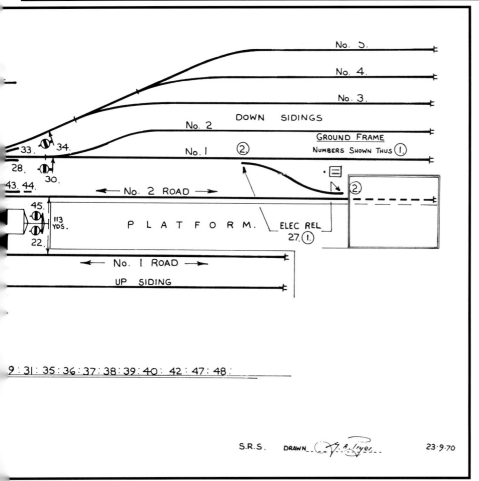

No. 5.

No. 4.

No. 3.

DOWN SIDINGS

No. 2

GROUND FRAME

No. 1 ② NUMBERS SHOWN THUS ①

33. 34.

28.

43. 44. 30.

← No. 2 ROAD →

45.

113 YDS. P L A T F O R M. ELEC REL

22. 27 ①

← No. 1 ROAD →

UP SIDING

9 : 31 : 35 : 36 : 37 : 38 : 39 : 40 : 42 : 47 : 48 :

S.R.S. DRAWN *J. A. Pryor* 23·9·70

own but also from the Great Western, which had commenced on the opening of the Barnstaple Junction Railway in 1887. The island platform was extended in the direction of Mortehoe, the goods yard enlarged and some carriage sidings with a headshunt provided, on a site extended with considerable earthworks. Not all these works may date back to 1891, though a second signal box certainly did. It contained 50 working levers and 10 spare ones, provision having been made for two more platform lines if required.

By 1902 there were five carriage sidings, all of which could be shunted from the headshunt. This was level and the running lines climbed quickly above it. Halfway along their length a series of connections gave access from the carriage sidings direct to the running lines. Photographs about this time show a considerable number of coaches stabled here, mainly South Western but also Great Western. The original 40ft turntable was replaced in 1895 with a 42ft turntable recovered from Okehampton. About 1911, a new 60ft siding with pit appeared, running off the turntable.

1929 - 1965 PERIOD
As traffic increased the Southern Railway had to solve a number of problems at Ilfracombe. Holiday trains were getting longer and heavier, and at the terminus it

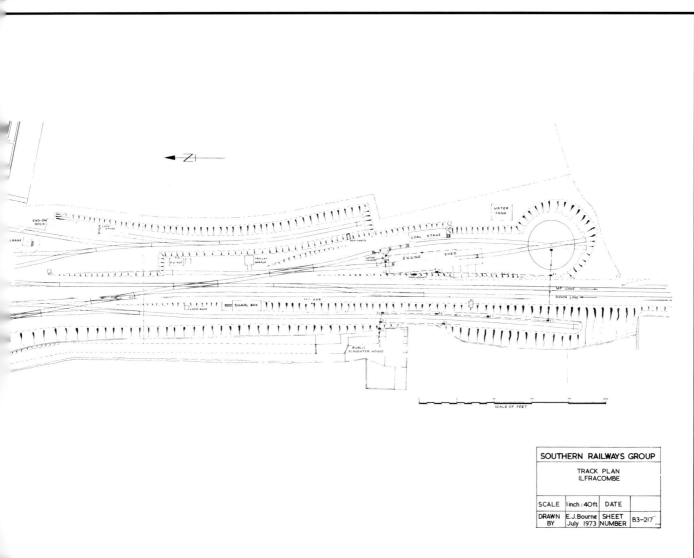

SOUTHERN RAILWAYS GROUP		
TRACK PLAN ILFRACOMBE		
SCALE 1 inch : 40 ft	DATE	
DRAWN BY E.J.Bourne July 1973	SHEET NUMBER	B3-217

Apparently recorded in the late South Western period M7 0-4-4T No.251, recently arrived on the Ilfracombe Branch following electrification of Waterloo suburban services, departs from platform 2 with a Barnstaple train comprising a mixture of South Western coaches. Many of the feature seen here were swept away during re-building in the 1920s. *Irwell Press Collection*

became the practice that passengers travelling in the rear coaches of longer non-corridor trains beyond the platform end had to climb down on to the ballast and walk to the platform. The shed had been designed for the short Ilfracombe Goods and tank locomotives, and the 42 ft turntable precluded the regular use of even the medium sized tender locomotives of the period. The advent of Maunsell N class 2-6-0s on a new Exeter - Ilfracombe service in the summer of 1925 required far better provision, and the first step was the excavation of a large volume of rock on the up side (opposite the headshunt) to form a site for a new engine shed. A new 65ft turntable - 'the best in the west' according to some crews, for it was long enough to balance any locomotive easily - was installed here in time for the new service, though there was no building at first.

By 1929 it was time to replace the old engine shed with a modern building alongside the new turntable, and a single road shed was built on one of the tracks leading to the turntable, with a second track behind. The new building was in concrete blocks, together with toilet, mess room and stores, with a corrugated asbestos roof, and a pit throughout the length of the building. A large capacity water tank was built at the top of the adjacent cliff to supply the water column below An ash pit was conveniently located close to the buffer stops of the goods yard headshunt which was at a lower level, so a chute was provided to load ash into a wagon below. During the 1950s a second water tank, adjacent to the original, was installed to provide extra capacity.

The removal, first of the turntable and then the first engine shed, allowed the extension of the goods yard into this area and a simplification of the rather complex pointwork, although a short headshunt had to be cut into the hillside. The carriage sidings headshunt on the down side was extended further, and the spoil produced from all these excavations enabled the carriage sidings to be extended and simplified. In 1929 the arrival platform was provided with a release crossover worked from a ground frame near the buffer stops. Previously, a shunting locomotive was required to release the train locomotive, or gravity shunting was employed. In 1926 and 1931 there were accidents when vehicles ran down the gradient into Platform Two out of control; full details are given in Chapter Five. Beyond the engine release road there were now seven long carriage sidings, which could be shunted from the carriage headshunt or from either running road.

A new, third signal box was provided in 1929. It had a 50 lever frame, of which 15 were spare, reduced to 14 when the release lever for the crossover at the end of Platform 2 was provided. The old platform was raised and considerably extended in length, the awning extended, station buildings improved and electric light installed. When Colonel Trench of the Board of Trade made his inspection and reported on 25th May 1929 the new trackwork and signalling had been completed, station building improvements were in hand but work on the new engine shed had not yet started.

Ilfracombe station had now reached the stage of development which

lasted for the next forty years, and which many people will remember. The station throat incorporated four successive double slips which saved space and allowed for considerable operational flexibility. The two running lines climbed up at 1 in 36, above the level carriage headshunt on the down side and the engine shed on the up. There was a slaughterhouse adjacent to the headshunt but apparently any traffic for it had to come by road from the goods yard opposite. On summer Saturdays the station pilot, often an M7 0-4-4T, could easily collect empty stock from Platform 2 (usually used for arrivals), draw the stock back into the headshunt and put it into one of the seven carriage sidings. When empty stock had to be shunted to or from Platform 1, which usually served for departures, the headshunt could not be used and the stock had to be hauled up the 1 in 36 on the up running line clear of the station throat. This caused considerable difficulty on occasions, particularly in wet conditions with heavy trains, and several attempts might be needed to clear the points before setting back.

The goods yard was on the east side of the station, with a reception/departure siding adjacent to Platform 1. The short headshunt was cut into the rock to give access to a short siding (serving an end loading dock) and two long sidings. The outer one of these served a loading bank and a 10 ton crane, adjacent to the Anglo American Oil Co. depot, whilst the inner siding ran through the substantial stone built goods shed. This had its own internal 40 cwt crane, and a crossover connection to the reception road. All shunt-

SOUTHERN RAILWAY STATISTICS 1928-36 ILFRACOMBE TOWN OFFICE					
	1928	1930	1932	1934	1936
Passenger tickets issued	-	2,513	2,451	2,141	2,263
Season tickets issued	-	69	82	70	103
Tickets collected	-	-	-	-	-
Parcels forwarded	-	733	1,149	1,185	1,080

turn, coming back out through the shed ready for its next turn of duty, without conflicting movements with other locomotives. This was particularly valuable on a busy summer Saturday when there was a steady flow of locomotives, many on turns from Barnstaple, Exeter, Taunton and even further afield, together with bankers and pilots. The turntable was also used for the observation car of the Devon Belle. Once balanced it was fairly easy to turn a locomotive by hand, but this occasionally caused its own problems when a very strong sea breeze took over - the 'table could then only be lined up to the track by throwing a sleeper into the pit.'

The signal box, at the station throat between the down road and the carriage sidings headshunt, controlled almost all movements in the station. Exceptions were hand point levers in the goods yard and carriage sidings and a ground frame, released by lever 27, which controlled the engine release crossover at the end of Platform Two. Short or medium length trains stopped here, the fireman climbed down to uncouple the engine, the driver moved forward clear of the crossover which was pulled over by the fireman, and reversed when the engine had passed on its way to the shed. On the down line traffic was controlled by a fixed distant signal, an outer home (with a track circuited section), and an inner home with four dolls. These indicated, from left to right, carriage sidings (No.3 lever), Platform 2 (No.5), Platform 1 (No.6) and goods reception (No.7). In the up direction there was a bracket signal at the platform end,

Ilfracombe station with a diesel multiple unit signalled for departure. This was apparently taken after the goods yard had been closed in September 1964, but before the singling of the line and abolition of signalling in December 1967. *Irwell Press Collection*

ing at Ilfracombe had to be done with care: in 1924 the Southern Railway instructed the station master that shunting by gravitation should only be resorted to when absolutely necessary, and after 1929 the use of gravity for shunting coaching stock was prohibited. If wagons were drawn up the incline a manned braked

vehicle was required at the station end. The short headshunt ensured that only a few wagons at a time could be worked in the yard.

The engine shed was designed so that once a locomotive was released from its train it would reverse directly into the depot, take water, coal if necessary and

Ilfracombe station throat showing the complex pointwork installed. *Philip J. Kelley*

Ilfracombe station on 17th April 1954 with N class 2-6-0 No.31832 awaiting departure with a Bulleid three coach set. *B.K.B.Green*

train before the weekend. These were delivered to the resort's many hotels and guest houses by railway lorry, ready for the guests arriving on Saturday, and returned in similar fashion. There was a weighing machine on the platform, and tall iron railings with a couple of gates on to the approach road. These were normally only brought into use on summer Saturdays, to cope with the large number of passengers. The rather nondescript main station buildings were arranged in an L shape. Adjacent to the ticket collector's booth was the booking office and hall, parcels and left luggage office, ladies room, porters room, gents' and station master's office. On the other side of the L, by the approach road, was the generously appointed refreshment room. The top of a long series of steps gave pedestrian access towards the town and there was a small office, once belonging to the station master but used in later years as a rest room for taxi drivers. Opposite here were the gates of the goods yard, on to the ap-

A general view of Ilfracombe station, 30th July 1951. The well-filled goods yard was shunted from the short headshunt in the foreground, and a Bulleid Pacific is working the carriage sidings behind the platform. In the foreground is an SR Theatrical Scenery van, used by companies of actors performing at the town's theatre, and in the carriage sidings is a rake of Pullman cars for the Devon Belle. *R.J.Sellick*

the starting signals being on levers Nos. 50 and 49 for Platforms 1 and 2 respectively, and an advanced starting signal. The control of the pointwork at the station throat was complicated, with several levers controlling two sets of switch blades for crossovers and slip points. There were also numerous facing point locks; several levers actuated two of them and Nos.16 and 18 actuated three. There were also a number of ground signals to control shunting movements.

About 300 feet of the platform was sheltered from the elements by a rather grand awning, part South Western, part Southern Railway. Adjacent to the buffer stops at the end of Platform 1 was a substantial concrete block building, the 'luggage in advance' store, which had two wide doors on to the platform and on the other side two similarly wide doors on to the approach road. In a typical summer holiday week a thousand or more trunks and heavy items of luggage would arrive by

proach road which wound its way down the hillside to the town below.

The goods traffic dealt with at Ilfracombe was varied and justified two trains daily for many years, although loads were limited by the gradients. A major 'import' was coal, some originating in South Wales, shipped to Fremington, unloaded, screened, and distributed by rail. Other wagonloads came direct from the collieries including Abernant, Rufford, Lydney, Lightmoor, Parkend, Silverhill,

Above. General view of 1963 showing the engine shed and two water tanks. The nearest was installed in the 1920s and the other in the 1950s. The four adjacent double slips at the station throat can be clearly seen, together with the cramped but level goods yard layout. *J.Scrace*

Above. Ilfracombe shed employed three pairs of railwaymen early in British Railways days, including Driver Bert Johns and Fireman C.T.Nott, seen here with Battle of Britain No.34059 SIR ARCHIBALD SINCLAIR, carrying its Devon Belle headboard and ready for departure at 12 noon. *C.T.Nott collection*

Left. From Ilfracombe platform in 1952, a view of the fouling bar on No.1 platform road which was usually used for departures, the goods reception road, and its connection to the yard headshunt cut deep into the rock to achieve a level alignment. The crane had a capacity of 10 tons, but its use meant hard manual work for the goods yard staff. *R.E.Tustin*

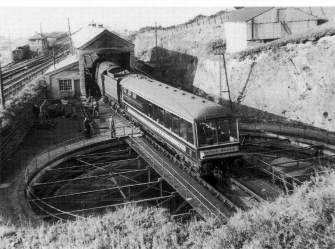

These two photographs illustrate the procedure for turning the Pullman observation car of the Devon Belle, after its arrival about 5.30pm. Whilst the N class 2-6-0 shunts the other Pullman cars in the carriage sidings the train engine propels the observation car through the engine shed on to the turntable where it is balanced and then turned by hand before re-joining the other cars in the carriage sidings. Southern locomotive crews regarded the Ilfracombe turntable as the 'best in the west' due to its ease of operation. *B.Wright*

Above. **Two N Moguls at Ilfracombe in the 1950s together with Bulleid and Maunsell coaches, including a dining car in the carriage sidings. In the foreground is the crossover connecting the goods reception and goods shed roads.** *Lens of Sutton*

Clydach Merthyr and Bolsover. Coal merchants included Mr Harris, Mr Dutton, Mr Boudier, and Mr Laramy. Other traffic included flour from Avonmouth loaded (in sacks) in vans for the Co-op, sacks of fertilizer for local farmers, arriving in vans, sackloads of basic slag in vans or sheeted open wagons, oil for the Anglo American Oil Co. depot, and a wide variety of general merchandise including building materials, timber, steel girders and telegraph poles. There was also some livestock. Local hauliers collected and delivered to the goods yard - Mr Hancock had a number of lorries, Mr Lake had a horse van at one time and Mr Willis was the carrier for the Coombe Martin area. In later years the railway took over collection and delivery, using two lorries for the goods and one for passenger luggage in advance, with three extra in the summer season.

Apart from the goods trains there was a regular vacuum fitted van (a road box) which ran overnight from Nine Elms,

the huge Southern goods station in London, arriving about 8.40am on a passenger train. This carried perishables including meat, bacon, fish, fruit and vegetables as well as general merchandise. The Ilfracombe Goods staff gave this a high priority, so that most consignments had been unloaded and delivered to customers in the town by 10.30am. Other regular vans scheduled to run to Ilfracombe were from Exeter Queen Street and Plymouth Friary. They were not usually vacuum fitted, but were 'road box vans' carrying small consignments and running to regular schedules. The 'road box van' system is covered in more detail in Chapter Seven.

Each summer a circus, in later years Bertram Mills, made a visit to Ilfracombe, the entire company travelling by train. After unloading the circus made its way down the approach road to Slade and Lamb Park towards the town. One summer there was a gale which blew the big top tent down. On another occasion,

in the 1930s, an elephant which had been unloaded chased the signalman, Joe Chamberlain, all the way along the platform. There was some speculation that the elephant, who is supposed never to forget, had some bad memory of a previous visit to Ilfracombe... Theatrical companies performing at the town's theatres arrived by train with all their props.

Goods traffic forwarded from Ilfracombe was not great, and many wagons left empty - though there was a little livestock. Some consignments of rabbits in hampers went to Nine Elms in the return vacuum fitted van/road box that went out on the 3.20pm goods. Empty fish boxes were returned to the fishing ports of origin by goods train. Other general merchandise went out in the Exeter and Plymouth road boxes. From time to time a wagon positioned under the chute in the goods yard headshunt would be loaded with ash and clinker from the shed and forwarded for engineering use. Apart from passenger luggage in advance, further traf-

Left. **Ilfracombe goods shed in 1968, after goods services ended. About four men worked there, assisted by up to four railway lorry drivers and several other carriers, dealing with a wide variety of merchandise. Up to the 1950s practically all merchandise used in the town arrived by train.** *A.E.West.* *Right.* **A general view of Ilfracombe goods shed, 1968. The track through the building was level whilst the running lines were on a gradient. Approximately 140 feet in length, it could hold 6 or 7 wagons, and a 40 cwt crane was available inside. The design was similar to other North Devon goods sheds of the 1870s, at Bideford and Torrington.** *A.E.West*

The interior of Ilfracombe station from the end of platform 2, showing the extensive awning and train shed provided to shelter passengers from the elements. *Lens of Sutton*

Left. A similar view from Ilfracombe platform 2 buffer stops with an Ivatt 2-6-2T on a train arrived in platform 1. Irwell Press Collection

Below. Looking towards the buffer stops of platform 2 in 1952 there is a wealth of detail both under the awning and in the main station offices beyond. The crossover was operated from a ground frame released by No.27 lever in the signal box. *R.E.Tustin*

fic carried in luggage vans included general merchandise (in great variety) and fish from Hull, Grimsby and Lowestoft. Some locally caught fish was forwarded for the London market.

Passengers arriving at Ilfracombe station had a choice of transport available for the final part of their journey. Horse-drawn cabs and omnibuses ran from the station to the town in connection with every train, and there were services to Coombe Martin and Lynton. Later they were replaced with motor vehicles, including Copps silver bus and Clatworthys town bus - Southern National buses came in later years.

Although within the town boundary, the station was not convenient for the town centre, so both the South Western and Great Western maintained a town office. Indeed, the companies had established such premises early on, well before the physical arrival of the railway, when passengers and parcels were conveyed to the respective stations at Barnstaple by horse drawn coach. In Edwardian days the South Western had its office at 96, later

The main station buildings, seen from the station approach about 1960 and showing, from left to right: entrance gates to the platform, booking office, refreshment room and gate to the steps leading directly down to the town. *Reg Spurway courtesy David Watts*

108, High Street and the Great Western at Clock Tower, High Street. In BR days there was just the one office, in the High Street, where passengers could make enquiries about train services, buy tickets and make seat reservations, and arrange for luggage to be collected from hotels and sent in advance by train. Parcels could also be collected and delivered there. At this time the office was run by Mr Norman Wheeler; before him it was Mr Douglas Ackland.

The first station master at Ilfracombe in 1874 was Mr King, who had spent the two previous years as the first incumbent of the new station at Torrington, and his staff included Mr Alfred Hearson. Staff numbers increased over the years but fluctuated greatly from season to season. In winter there was a permanent staff, but in summer they were augmented by a combination of men taken on in the spring and laid off in the autumn and others who were drafted in from all over the Southern Railway. Indeed many railwaymen in North Devon found themselves working at Ilfracombe over a summer season, and also at Fremington Quay when freight traffic there was heavy.

In 1891 staff included relief signalman R. Kerslake and porters J. Arthurs, F. Short and W. Chapple. In 1925 the station master was Mr Balch and the signalmen A. Chamberlain and S. Hatchley. The porters are listed as A. Causley, S. Martyn, J.S. Norman, F. Cooper, G. Luggar, S. Mort and a Mr Paul, with goods porter S.A. Lovell and coaler E. Dart. Mr Sluman was station master in 1929 and in 1931 staff included signalman Arscott and shunter Bowerman. In the 1950s the establishment under the station master was usually two signalmen, two booking clerks (three in summer) and two platform porters (four in

Rear view of the station buildings facing platform 2, about 1960. *Reg Spurway courtesy David Watts*

The pedestrian access to Ilfracombe station was by mean of this steep flight of steps. At the top to the left is the taxi drivers' rest room and to the right the refreshment room. A 1961 view. *Peter Swift*

An early view at Ilfracombe station looking up the formidable bank towards Mortehoe after a heavy snow fall. Irwell Press collection.

Right. Ilfracombe about the turn of the century, before the awning was extended along the platform with a group of railwaymen, many wearing South Western uniforms with distinctive cap badges. On right of those seated is Mr Joseph Hatchley, signalman here for many years. Both his son and grandson also worked here. *William Hatchley collection*

Right. Posed outside the goods shed in September 1928 with a carriage destination board for identification is a group of 40 railwaymen. Here we see not only the Ilfracombe men but also a number drafted in from elsewhere to cope with the heavy summer season traffic. A Great Western guard is included in the second row seated at the right end. *William Hatchley collection*

summer). In the goods station were a checker, three goods porters and a pair of lorry drivers (four in summer). Permanent way staff comprised a ganger and six or seven men. At the engine shed were three drivers, three firemen and a night shift man who lit up the one or two locomotives stabled overnight. Around 1950 the men included S. Hatchley and J. Burrows (signalmen), W. Hatchley (checker), B. Norman (guard), G. Gregory (porter), T. Knight (clerk), J. Dryver and J. Swindells (lorry drivers), B. Johns, R. Ackland, G. Tucker (engine drivers), G. Hooper, G. Knill, C.T. Nott (firemen) and W. Hill (shed man).

As often happened on the railways, at times there were members of the same family working at Ilfracombe. Mr Joseph Hatchley, born in 1855, started on the South Western at Bow and came to Ilfracombe as a signalman. His son Sidney started at Plymouth Friary in 1911 but later came here, retiring in 1956. In turn, his grandson, William, started at Ilfracombe in 1943 as checker in the goods yard, and also passed as a guard and signalman. In 1925 Sidney, at that time a shunter, was involved in the accident when three coaches ran away and demolished the buffers at the end of Platform Two. Photographs in the family collection include one in late South Western days of a group of 16 railwaymen including Joseph and Sidney, and another in September 1928 of a group of 40, including a Great Western guard and probably a number of men drafted in for the summer season.

Mr Joe Chamberlain started work on the South Western in 1889 at Exeter Queen Street, moved to Barnstaple (where he is recorded in a 1911 group photograph) and came to Ilfracombe as signalman in 1924. He retired in 1938, succeeded by Mr Eric Kipling, but returned to work during the war as a relief signalman on the Exeter - Barnstaple line, and in Ilfracombe Goods, completing some 55 years of work for the railway. A memory of his grandson is of Christmas Day 1936

when he and his mother, Joe's daughter, went to Ilfracombe signal box to deliver Joe's roast Christmas. It was, after all, an age when the train service never stopped.

Some Ilfracombe railwaymen reached positions of responsibility within the community. In the 1930s Driver H. Roulstone played a leading role in the work of the Ilfracombe Urban District Council, and eventually became its Chairman. There is a photograph of him wearing his chain of office on the footplate of N 2-6-0 No.1407.

William Hatchley also served on the Ilfracombe Urban District Council from 1965 onwards and became Chairman of its Industrial Planning Committee in 1967. On the closure of Ilfracombe goods he moved to Barnstaple Victoria Road; he served as a magistrate on Barnstaple Bench, becoming its Deputy Chairman, and in the New Years Honours list of 1973 was awarded the British Empire Medal 'for outstanding service to the community'.

Up to September 1964 a staff of about 30 were employed at the station, but this was rapidly reduced on the closure of the goods yard, dieselisation, and rationalisation of the passenger services. Over the next couple of years the staff had been reduced to seven under the supervision of the foreman. Singling of the line, closure of the signal box and introduction of the conductor/guard scheme with the closure of the booking office reduced them even further. For the last couple of years the foreman was George Facey who was responsible for the station and the parcels traffic and, on summer Saturdays, seat reservations and shunting movements too! By this time the single platform had just a run round loop, for almost all services were multiple units with conductor/guards, apart from one or two locomotive hauled summer Saturday trains.

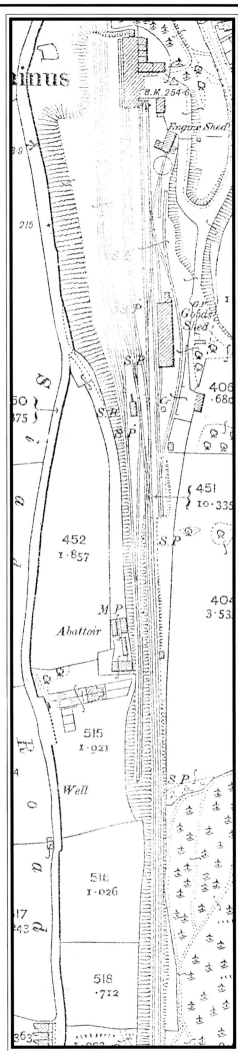

Presentation to guard W. Lethaby, in December 1906, on reaching forty years of service to the Company. *Irwell Press collection*

The 12 noon departure from platform 2 at Ilfracombe on 30th July 1951 was the Devon Belle hauled by Battle of Britain class Pacific No.34059 SIR ARCHIBALD SINCLAIR. Both locomotive and observation car had been turned on the Ilfracombe turntable. *R.J.Sellick*

Steamships, propelled both by paddle and screw, provided regular services between Bristol, Ilfracombe and other Bristol Channel ports as early as the 1820s. Before 1874 the Great Western and Midland Railways routed their passengers for Ilfracombe via Portishead and the steamer service. This later scene at Ilfracombe harbour was photographed on 18th June 1894. The steamers at the end of the pier are *P.S.Westward Ho* (inside) and *P.S.Broderick Castle*, whilst the four moored together, from the inside, are *P.S.Velindra*, *P.S.Scotia*, *P.S.Ravenswood* and *P.S.Bonnie Doon. Medina Gallery.*

CHAPTER TWO

EARLY RAILWAY SCHEMES 1845 - 1868

THE RAILWAY MANIA 1845 - 1847
The first recorded schemes to build a railway to Ilfracombe came during the Railway Mania of 1845-1847. The Bristol and Exeter Railway had opened in 1844, and whilst one group of promoters sought to build lines linking it with North Devon, starting at Exeter or Tiverton, others proposed a more direct central route, direct from London to Exeter and Cornwall, with a North Devon branch from Exeter. The various projected routes into North Devon all ran to Barnstaple, often with branches to Bideford, South Molton and Ilfracombe.

First in the field was the North Devon Railway which, after several local newspaper advertisements, published its prospectus on 30th June 1845, for a line from the Bristol and Exeter's Tiverton branch terminus *to or near Bampton, Dulverton, Southmolton, Barnstaple, and Bideford, with a branch to Ilfracombe, if deemed expedient, or to some other avail-* *able harbour on the Bristol Channel.'* The engineer was Brunel and the scheme was backed by numerous influential local landowners, the Great Western, Bristol and Exeter and South Devon Railways. A Bill went forward to parliament for the 1846 session, but it failed Standing Orders on 12th May because of the late delivery of the engineer's plan and sections. Substitute the M5 motorway for the Bristol and Exeter, and the North Devon Link road for the North Devon and we see how the road builders of the late 20th century used almost the same routes.

On 25th September 1845 the 'Great Western Extension Atmospheric Railway' published its prospectus for a line from Exeter to Barnstaple and Ilfracombe, with branches to Bideford and Southmolton, together with improvements to the port and harbour of Ilfracombe, the engineer being John Taylor. A meeting at the *Britannia Inn*, Ilfracombe, on 23rd October received a deputation from the directors; they were very supportive, but no more was heard of the venture. Another short-lived scheme of 1845 was a London, Salisbury and Exeter Railway, which included a branch to Ilfracombe. There was, however, competition for the port facilities at Ilfracombe in a prospectus published on 23rd October, for a 'North Devon Extension Railway' from Barnstaple to Coombmartin, and Coombmartin Harbour of Refuge. If these schemes seemed somewhat implausible then the projectors of the 'Somersetshire and North Devon Junction Railway', from Bridgwater along the coast to Ilfracombe with a branch to Barnstaple' were 'profoundly ignorant of the country', according to the editorial of the *North Devon Journal* of the same date.

Having considered the unsuccessful schemes, we now move on to the Taw Vale Extension and Dock Company, which

Outside Sam Colwill's Coach Office at 96, High Street, Ilfracombe in Edwardian days with a well-laden coach about to depart. The three horses had a difficult journey ahead of them over the hills out of the town. The South Western Railway opened its first Ilfracombe Town Office near the *Clarence Hotel* in the 1860s, before the railway arrived. It was later moved to 97, High Street (seen here on the left) and 108, High Street, and the Great Western also had its Town Office in the High Street. *Ilfracombe Museum*

on 18th September 1845 published its prospectus for a line from Barnstaple to Exeter with branches to Bideford, Ilfracombe and Southmolton. The original Taw Vale from Fremington to Barnstaple had gained its Act in 1838, with an Amendment Act in 1845 to extend the construction period. The Taw Vale Extension got its Act on 7th August 1846, but only for a line from Crediton to Barnstaple. Powers for the Bideford and Southmolton branches were gained in another Act, of 22nd July 1847 but the branch from Bishops Tawton, two miles south of Barnstaple, to Ilfracombe was dropped. However, the aftermath of the Railway Mania was a depression during which many of the lines authorised were not built.

THE NORTH DEVON RAILWAY
Following financial reconstruction and contraction, the Taw Vale was re-named the North Devon Railway in a new Act of 24th July 1851, and opened from Crediton to Barnstaple on 1st August 1854. Barnstaple to Fremington, open for goods since 1848, gained a passenger service on 2nd November 1855 when the independent Bideford Extension Railway opened. Broad gauge services ran from Exeter St Davids along the Exeter and Crediton Railway (operated by the Bristol and Exeter), and thence to Barnstaple and Bideford on the North Devon and Bideford Extension Railways (leased and operated by the eminent railway contractor Thomas Brassey).

Within a week of the opening of the North Devon it was reported that Ilfracombe was so full of visitors that there was no lodging to be had. Visitors arriving by train at Barnstaple and thence coach to Ilfracombe augmented those coming by the well-established paddle steamer services from numerous ports on the Bristol Channel, including Swansea, Cardiff and Portishead.

THE BARNSTAPLE AND ILFRACOMBE RAILWAY OF 1854
On 11th November 1854 Robert Wreford, an Exeter solicitor, published a prospectus for the Barnstaple and Ilfracombe Railway. The broad gauge line was to start at Fremington, three miles west of Barnstaple on the North Devon Railway. From there it would cross the Taw estuary and follow more or less the course of the line as it was eventually built, terminating near Ilfracombe harbour. The line was to be built by Thomas Brassey and Robert Ogilvie, his manager on the North Devon. Brassey was prepared to build the line if there was no opposition, and to this end the North Devon, Exeter and Crediton and Bristol and Exeter Railways would be authorised to take shares in the line. Meetings in favour of the line were held at Ilfracombe and at *Elliots New Inn*, Braunton.

The line would have used the North Devon's Barnstaple station, which was inconvenient for the town centre, and the crossing of the Taw estuary at Fremington would have required a long bridge with a lifting or swinging section for shipping

bound for the port of Barnstaple. Although the scheme came to nothing it brought together a number of people who subsequently worked on several projects to bring the railway to Ilfracombe, in particular Robert Wreford and the Rev. Benjamin Price of Ilfracombe.

THE LONDON AND SOUTH WESTERN RAILWAY
As long ago as 1847 the then far-off London and South Western Railway had - illegally - gained control of the Exeter and Crediton, and had a substantial stake in the North Devon. Eventually, in 1860, the South Western completed its own standard gauge line from Waterloo through Salisbury and Yeovil to Exeter Queen Street, and then set about extending its services along these lines. On 2nd March 1863 South Western standard gauge trains from Waterloo and Exeter to Barnstaple and Bideford were inaugurated. The South Western amalgamated with the North Devon and Bideford Extension in 1865, although the broad gauge survived until 1877. A minor but significant innovation came in June 1863, when some coaches on the Waterloo to West of England express carried destination boards 'Exeter and Ilfracombe', the final stage of the journey being by coach from Barnstaple. It was about this time, it would appear, that the first railway facilities were opened at Ilfracombe. This was the South Western Railway office near the *Clarence Hotel*, where the staff provided information about train services, sold tickets and dealt with parcels traffic, which was conveyed by road to and from Barnstaple station.

THE ILFRACOMBE RAILWAY OF 1864
In late May 1859 a party consisting of James Taylor, contractor on the Yeovil and Exeter line, his son, also James Taylor, contractor on the Exmouth Line, and Robert Wreford arrived at the *Clarence Hotel*, Ilfracombe and made a reconnaissance of the line by the Slade Valley and Braunton route. A local committee was established and together with Robert Wreford, courted all the parties mentioned in the Barnstaple and Ilfracombe project five years previously, together now with the South Western.

Notice was given to Parliament for a Bill for the 1861 session, but this came to nought when a board of directors could not be formed. Notice was then given for a Bill in the 1862 session but the South Western felt unable to support it until delicate negotiations for the purchase of the North Devon were completed, which indeed they were in July 1862. An Ilfracombe Railway Bill was presented to Parliament for the 1863 ses-

sion, for a line starting from a junction with the North Devon at Bishops Tawton, two miles east of Barnstaple station and east of the Taw, skirting the east of the town and then via Braunton to Ilfracombe. Despite parliamentary support from the South Western, North Devon and Bristol and Exeter companies, this Bill was rejected by the House of Lords Committee on 25th April, as a result of the opposition of Sir William Williams. He did not want the line passing through his estates at Heanton Punchardon and his petition asserted that a cheaper and better line could be made farther to the east via Bittadon rather than Braunton, an opinion not shared by the South Western's engineer Mr Galbraith, who costed the Bittadon route at £220,000 against £160,000 for the Braunton line. Although the Lords reported that an Ilfracombe Railway was required, news of the Bill's rejection set off ugly scenes between railway supporters and opponents, at Braunton and Ilfracombe.

Encouraged by the South Western, the promoters went back to Parliament in the 1864 session with a new Ilfracombe Railway Bill, again starting at Bishops Tawton but this time taking the eastern Bittadon route to avoid the opposition of Sir William Williams. The opposition this time, however, came from the Devon

A wonderful view of the line winding its way out of the station and up the bank towards Mortehoe. *Irwell Press collection.*

and Somerset Railway Bill in the same session, and its line from Taunton to Barnstaple with an extension to Ilfracombe - in many respects another attempt at the 1845 North Devon project. The Ilfracombe Harbour Company backed the Devon and Somerset, but local opinion favoured the Ilfracombe Railway. After much negotiation and horse-trading the Ilfracombe Railway got its Act on 25th July 1864, and the Devon and Somerset on 29th July for the Taunton to Barnstaple line only.

The Ilfracombe Railway Act 1864 contains a wealth of detail. The capital was £210,000 in £20 shares, with powers to borrow another £70,000. There were six directors; three to be appointed by the shareholders, initially Benjamin Price, William Huxtable and William Stanney, and three by the South Western, initially Charles Mangles, Ralph Dutton and Edward Hutchins. The South Western would take £50,000 worth of shares with powers to subscribe for up to £60,000 more. There were to be twelve road overbridges and six road underbridges but no level crossings. The single line was to be built to mixed gauge, with land for a second line of rails. Connections were specified to both the North Devon and Devon and Somerset, and at Ilfracombe there was to be a tramway running down to the harbour. Five years were allowed for construction, and details were given of a Bill for the 1865 session in which the Devon and Somerset and South Western would become joint owners of the Ilfracombe Railway. This Act was passed on 2nd June 1865. Sadly, the company solicitor Robert Wreford, died in November 1864.

The two Acts had been passed as a result of complicated and protracted negotiations between the Devon and Somerset promoters and the South Western Railway (both of whom looked to Ilfracombe for through traffic) and the Ilfracombe Railway promoters, who had become pawns in the contest. Ilfracombe would certainly be the winner, for it would gain a railway paid for by and connected to the other two. Braunton would lose completely because of the opposition of Sir William Williams, but Barnstaple's position was unclear, with the junction at Bishops Tawton hardly conducive to the interchange of traffic. The South Western seemed to have come out of it rather badly, having conceded access to Ilfracombe to a rival line, albeit one yet to be built.

The old dictum 'if it looks too good to be true it probably isn't' was soon clear at Ilfracombe. The Ilfracombe Railway made its first call of £2 per £20 share and by July 1865 the South Western had paid up on its 5,250 shares, but the Devon and Somerset defaulted on its 5,250. Although the Ilfracombe Railway Act had treated the two as equals, they were not; the South Western had been running trains and paying dividends for a quarter of a century and was one of the largest railways in the south of England. Construction of the Devon and Somerset had only just started and was to drag on for nine years, for the company was plagued with financial problems. Construction of the Ilfracombe Railway never started but there was much legal activity. An 1867 Bill for more time was withdrawn, but a Devon and Somerset Act of 12th August 1867 allowed it to shed its commitments to the Ilfracombe Railway. So, on 25th June 1868 the Ilfracombe Railway gained an Abandonment Act, which required discharge of all its debt before dissolution. Legal judgement against the Devon and Somerset for its share of the debt was gained in 1877, but this was not paid until 1901, when the Great Western acquired this impoverished line. The Ilfracombe Railway gained its final dissolution on 21st November 1901.

The result of this debacle was the postponement of the railway's arrival at Ilfracombe for several years.

A provision of the Barnstaple and Ilfracombe Railway Act of 1870 was that the ten southernmost piers of the bridge over the Taw should be in line with those of the Long Bridge, in order to minimise the obstruction to navigation. This 1951 photograph of the bridge with an N class 2-6-0 on an up goods shows how this was done. *R.J.Sellick*

CHAPTER THREE

THE BARNSTAPLE & ILFRACOMBE RAILWAY 1868 - 1874

THE 1870 ACT

A few months after the Ilfracombe Railway Abandonment Act the South Western Railway wrote to the Ilfracombe promoters, in October 1868, suggesting that the new Regulation of Railways Act 1868 might be used to build the line. At the request of the promoters Mr Galbraith again surveyed the line and found that the Braunton route, as selected by Mr Errington in 1860, was indeed the best. To avoid the opposition of Sir William Williams the route bridging the Taw at Fremington was again suggested. It was, in the event, found wanting, and at a meeting in February 1869 a tunnel was considered instead. The Rev. Price told the meeting that a line with South Western support would shortly be announced, and a local committee was again formed.

Up to now the promotion of the railway had essentially been an Ilfracombe matter with some involvement of others; Barnstaple interests had not been involved even though the town had obvious concerns in the project. Ilfracombe railways starting at Fremington, or at Bishops Tawton and passing to the east could count on little support at Barnstaple, which was after all the principal town of North Devon. Wisely the promoters now sought its backing, and during 1869 negotiated with Barnstaple Corporation the line which was later built. The Corporation gained a number of improvements, including new quay walls on the north bank of the Taw, and a new passenger station very close to the town centre. In November 1869 the Barnstaple and Ilfracombe Railway published its prospectus and deposited its plans. The line could now count on the support of Barnstaple, Braunton and Ilfracombe, and the South Western; the near bankrupt Devon and Somerset was out of the reckoning, leaving Sir William Williams as the only serious opponent.

The Bill went before Committee on 15th, 16th and 17th March 1870. The principal witnesses supporting the line included prominent citizens of Barnstaple, Braunton and Ilfracombe and officers of the South Western. Following their overwhelming evidence in support of the line, Sir William withdrew his opposition and the Bill passed the committee stage; Sir William died a few days later. The Bill passed unopposed through the Lords and the Barnstaple and Ilfracombe Railway Act 1870 gained the Royal Assent on 4th July.

The Act of 69 clauses and 2 schedules authorised a railway (No.1) of 1 mile and 1 furlong from Barnstaple station to Pottington Marsh, and railway (No.2) of 13 miles and 5 furlongs thence to Ilfracombe. The capital was £105,000 in £10 shares, half of that of the 1864 Ilfracombe Railway, and there were powers to borrow another £35,000. The first directors were Ilfracombe residents or businessmen, Thomas Pain, Philip Stoneham, Thomas Fry, William Gould, and Benjamin Price, together with Joseph Beattie, the Mechanical Engineer of the South Western. The line was to be constructed and worked as a light railway according to the Regulation of Railways Act 1868. There were to be 3 level crossings in the parish of Heanton Punchardon and 7 in Braunton, together with 5 road overbridges and 2 road underbridges. There was a clause for the protection of Mr William Westacott's shipyard, and three clauses for the protection of the Long Bridge at Barnstaple, in response to a petition from the Feoffees - the trustees of the bridge. The ten southernmost piers of the railway bridge over the Taw were to be in line with those of the Long Bridge, so as to minimise the obstruction to navigation. Five years were allowed for construction. A number of clauses empowered the use of the South Western's Barnstaple station and facilitated through traffic to and from the South Western.

The First Schedule included full details of the agreement made on 9th March 1870 between the railway company and Barnstaple Corporation. It included details of the embankment and retaining wall along the Taw, including sewer and other outlets, for two cranes, mooring rings and posts, weighbridge and level crossing access to the new quay. There was provision for a path along the east side of the Yeo for men and horses towing vessels on the river. It is of interest to mention that the Mayor of Barnstaple at this stage was Mr William Thorne, who had played a leading part back in 1847, in the (illegal) take-over of the Exeter and Crediton by the South Western, when he was the Chairman of the Taw Vale.

The Second Schedule covered the agreement of 11th November 1869 between the company and the South Western. The Ilfracombe company would pay for the necessary improvements at Barnstaple station. The South Western would have running powers, subject to a maximum of eight tons weight on any pair of wheels, and there were arrangements for payment for this. Alternatively, the South Western could work the line for fifty per cent of gross receipts, and the Ilfracombe company had the power to insist on this. Although the Ilfracombe line could permit a junction between itself and any other company, South Western agreement would be required (the Devon and Somerset, then under construction, was not specifically mentioned).

The first half-yearly meeting of the Barnstaple and Ilfracombe Railway was held on 14th October 1870, when the directors reported that 'It is a matter of notoriety that the amount of subscriptions forthcoming from the district is so exceedingly small that it would be useless to attempt the construction of the line unless some substantial subsidy can be obtained from the LSWR'. On 16th February 1871 at the half-yearly meeting of the South Western Railway there was discussion of a number of extensions in North Devon including those to Okehampton, Torrington and Ilfracombe. It was reported that South Western traffic from Barnstaple was £56,000 a year, besides another £10,000 from Ilfracombe (presumably the town office). The South Western directors reported that the proposed agreement to work the line, for 50% of gross receipts subject to a rebate of £2,000, made it impossible for the Barnstaple and Ilfracombe to raise its capital, and proposed instead a rent of £6,000 per annum, which the shareholders agreed. The public was now attracted by a return of more than 5% on capital invested and the shares were fully subscribed.

The contract for the construction of the line at £90,000 was let to James Taylor, who was at the time also building the Torrington extension from Bideford, and as we have seen in Chapter Two, had looked over the route back in 1859. The 5½ miles of the Torrington extension cost the South Western £100,000; the 14¾ miles of the Barnstaple and Ilfracombe eventually cost £135,000 - a bargain in comparison. Apart from the lightweight track the main economy was the provision of a large number of level crossings rather than bridges under or over roads. But a century later this feature made the line very expensive to operate and came to be a significant factor in its closure. Whilst the chosen route through Barnstaple and Braunton necessitated level crossings in the town centres, most of the others could have been replaced by bridges at this stage.

CONSTRUCTION

Much of the information available on the construction of the line comes from the reports given by the directors and engineer to the half-yearly company meetings,

For the opening of the Barnstaple and Ilfracombe Railway a triumphal floral arch, one of many in the town, was erected in the High Street. Supplied by the South Western Railway, it had previously been used at Windsor for the visit of the Czar and Czarina of Russia. *Ilfracombe Museum*

together with reports given in the local press, in particular two Barnstaple papers, the *North Devon Journal* and *North Devon Herald*, and the Ilfracombe *Gazette*.

Construction started in 1871 once the shares were fully subscribed. Anticipating this, on 2nd February it was reported that the engineers had nearly finished staking out the line, and Messrs. Drew of Exeter, the company's surveyors, had prepared the plans required for negotiation with landowners. On 27th September at 11 o'clock, in pouring rain, a lengthy procession formed up outside the *Ilfracombe Hotel* and wound its way through the streets up to the site of the station on the hillside above the town. The procession included directors of the company, officials of the South Western, the contractor, a portrait of Robert Wreford, and three bands. At one o'clock the first sod was cut by Thomas Pain, the company chairman, and others followed his example. This was followed by a luncheon for 150 at 3 o'clock in the Town Hall. On both occasions plenty of speeches were delivered. At the same time there was a ceremony at Braunton where George Hartnoll cut the first sod. On 7th December it was reported that several navvies were at work on the line near the reservoir, a couple of miles up the Slade valley from Ilfracombe, and hopes were expressed that the line would open in mid-1873.

More substantial progress was made during 1872. At the half-yearly meeting on 21st February the engineer,

Galbraith, reported that '*...the possession of the land has been obtained at various points along the course of the railway, and operations commenced by the contractors in the parishes of Pilton, Mortehoe and Ilfracombe. In the first named parish the line is being formed through the property of Mr Rolle by side cutting and in Mortehoe and Ilfracombe wagon roads have been laid in; and the contractor is opening out the cutting at the summit where, altogether, about one mile of railway has been formed. The land where possession has been obtained is being fenced off; about a mile of fencing has been erected, and materials for three miles more are on the ground. 130 men and 20 horses are now at work on the railway and an ample supply of contractor's plant is provided for further operations. It is hoped that in a short time the contractor will be able to enter the Heanton property....*' It was reported that one of the directors, Joseph Beattie, had died, and another, William Thorne, had resigned through ill health, their places being taken by Archibald Scott and Charles Mortimore, General Manager and Director, respectively, of the South Western. In early August 1872 a navvy working on the line near *Foxhunters Inn* was completely buried by an earthslip. When rescued he was found to have two broken arms and severe back injuries, and was taken to Ilfracombe Cottage Hospital under the care of Mr Burroughs, the medical attendant of the company. On 15th August it was reported that at Barnstaple and Pottington the embankment was in an

advanced state, and at the Ilfracombe end from Cairn Top to Score Tunnel a good bank had been made and the tunnel was well advanced. On 31st August an 11 year old boy, James Matthews, employed to grease the axles of wagons on the works at Heanton Punchardon, was crushed between two wagons and died from his injuries. Meanwhile, James Taylor's other local contract was completed, when the Torrington Extension opened in August.

At the half-yearly meeting on 14th August 1872 the Engineer, Galbraith, reported:- '*Earthworks. There are 23 cuttings on the line, of these 7 have been finished, 15 are in progress, and 6 still remain to be commenced. Out of a total quantity of 400,000 cubic yards of earthwork to be moved, 140,000 have been shifted, leaving 260,000 to be done. The heaviest single work is the summit cutting, from which about 80,000 cubic yards have still to be excavated. About 4½ miles of railway have been formed and partially ballasted. Masonry. Good progress has been made in this department of the work; 13 road, river and other bridges have been completed, leaving 17 still to be built. The culverts are well advanced, and none of large dimensions remains untouched. The heavy river wall at Barnstaple has been commenced, and notwithstanding the floods it has advanced rapidly, and, if anything like the same rate of progress be maintained, there will be no reason to apprehend delay from this work. There is now a strong force of masons employed on the line. Tunnels. Near Ilfracombe a short but very deep cutting* had to be made on side lying ground. The contractor proposed to substitute a short tunnel, and as I considered the alteration would expedite the work and involve less risk in future maintenance, I assented to the change. About two thirds of the heading have been driven, and a favourable progress is still maintained. Permanent Way. A considerable quantity of sleepers are on the ground, and a cargo of rails is daily expected....'

On 14th August 1872, at the half-yearly meeting of the South Western, the directors reported on the agreement with the Ilfracombe company, including the purchase of the entire £30,000 of debenture stock. On 21st August there was a meeting of the Local Government Board to discuss the borrowing of £1,500 for new works for the Barnstaple sewerage system, in consequence of the agreement with the railway for the provision of sewer outlets through the new embankment into the Taw.   There were more accidents in 1873 including a navvy injured by a falling wheelbarrow at Willingcott, another who badly damaged a hand when trying to stop a moving wagon, and in July John Crich was killed by a fall of earth. At the half-yearly company meeting on 20th August the directors reported delays to the anticipated opening that autumn. The engineer, Galbraith, wrote: '*In January last I reported that the works were very much behind at one or two points, and I am sorry to say that the time then lost has not been recovered. The summit cutting is still progressing very slowly, and thirty nine thousand cubic yards remain to be moved, but the contractor has arranged to put in an extra gang of men at this point, to run a portion of the cutting to spoil. The embankment on the foreshore at Barnstaple also requires to be pushed, but less anxiety is felt concerning this than about the summit cutting, as labour can more readily be obtained there. The masonry, we are glad to observe, is said to be well advanced. The bridges which remain to be built are of no great magnitude, and will be completed in the course of the autumn. The quay wall at Barnstaple, which has been carried on in a more satisfactory manner than any work of similar magnitude on the line, will be finished in about four or five weeks. The whole of the piles of the iron bridge over the River Taw at Barnstaple have been driven, but the wrought iron girders which are to form the superstructure are much behind and the engineer has had to call the contractor's serious attention to the delay which has occurred in the delivery of the ironwork. The report on the permanent way is very satisfactory. Out of a total of 15 miles of railway 13 have been formed, 9½ ballasted, and the permanent way laid over 8½, the rest being pushed forward rapidly. The station houses at Barnstaple and Wrafton are about half built, the Braunton station house and goods shed are finished, and the goods shed at Ilfracombe is well advanced .....*'

On 13th October 1873 after heavy rain, three men were working in a cutting in the Slade valley near Borough Corner when their 15ft high platform collapsed, throwing them into a deep pool of water and covering them with earth and rock. One, Ben Sellick, died two days later from his injuries. By 30th October it was reported that half the iron bridge was ready, with temporary rails, the new piece of road at the south end of the long bridge was being metalled, the bridge over the Yeo was started, but that there were still delays with the earthworks at the Ilfracombe end. Meanwhile, on 1st November the Devon and Somerset Railway was opened to Barnstaple, nine long years after it gained its Act.

On 8th January 1874 considerable progress was demonstrated when a locomotive and some trucks ran along 12 miles of the line from Pottington to Mortehoe, about 10 miles of this being laid with permanent track. On 20th January a young man tried to derail an engine at Braunton by placing stones on the rails, but the engine driver stopped short of the obstruction. The perpetrator was taken to Braunton police station where he was found to be insane, and sent to the Devon Asylum. On 24th January it was reported at Ilfracombe that the tunnel was finished for half its length, although progress on the summit cutting was slow, but on 7th February a man was seriously injured during blasting in the tunnel.

At the half yearly company meeting on 18th February 1874 the engineer, Galbraith, reported '*I hoped ere now to be able to report that the railway had been completed and inspected, but I regret to say that a considerable amount of work still remains to be done. The summit cutting, which from the first has caused anxiety, is still unfinished, and even with favourable weather cannot be got through before the end of March. The river embankment at Barnstaple is also much behindhand, and a considerable quantity of earthwork has still to be deposited. The swing bridge over the River Yeo, after many months of delay, has at last been delivered, and is now being fixed, but 13 of the wrought iron girders for the viaduct over the River Taw have not yet been supplied. The station buildings are well advanced, and can all be got ready by the end of March. The masonry of the whole line, including the tunnel near Ilfracombe, will be finished at or before that date. Thirteen out of a total of 15 miles of permanent way have been laid, and the ballasting is now being pushed forward with two locomotive engines, while a third engine is at work in the summit cutting. The approach road to the Ilfracombe Station has been commenced and will be ready in good time. Having just returned from an inspection of the works, I am of the opinion that they cannot be completed before the month of May*'.

The directors reported that the contractor had met with great difficulty in obtaining the requisite labour, and ironwork, and that the South Western was preparing a Bill for parliament to authorise the merger of the two companies. The 'great difficulty in obtaining the requisite labour' must be questioned since Taylor himself had employed numerous navvies on the Torrington extension up to July 1872, and more were available after the opening of the Devon and Somerset three months previously; perhaps the difficulty was in the pay offered?

More progress was apparent at Ilfracombe on 16th March when the contractor's four wheel coupled tank engine 'Gnat', coupled to ten loaded ballast wagons, came down from near the summit, through the completed tunnel to the terminus. By 19th May the volume of material to be removed from the summit cutting had been reduced to an estimated 1,300 cubic yards, the spoil being taken by train from each end of the cutting. Ships pumps were used to remove water from the Mortehoe end of the works. At the end of their shift men returned to Ilfracombe in wagons running down the 1 in 36 gradient, which on occasions caused minor accidents when they ran out of control. On 9th June a ballast train from Mortehoe almost ran down a man on the line despite the engine's whistling, the man being completely deaf. It was then reported that the summit cutting had been opened up and that many of the points, signals and other equipment were ready. Gas pipes were being laid from the town to the station.

At Ilfracombe a new approach road was built, illuminated by gas lamps. A triumphal floral arch inscribed 'United in Bands of Iron' was erected for the ceremonial opening just before the right hand bend into the station yard. Cairn Top can be seen through the arch. *Ilfracombe Museum*

On the evening of 16th June hundreds of Barumites witnessed the passage of the first locomotive over the Taw iron bridge, and the next morning an engine and tender, weighing about 80 tons, passed over it with a group of officials going on to Mortehoe. Later the same day a train of South Western trucks, laden with rails, girders etc., became the first to run the entire length of the line from the South Western station at Barnstaple right through to Ilfracombe, though the tracks through the summit cutting were only temporary. On Tuesday 30th June a special train consisting of Ilfracombe Goods 0-6-0s Nos. 283 and 282, one first, four second and one third class carriage ballasted with iron chairs, and two brake vans, left Barnstaple at 4 o'clock with a party of South Western officials on an inspection of the new line, which included stations, signal boxes and brakes. At Braunton one of the engines was detached and followed the train up the incline, while between *Foxhunters Inn* and Mortehoe the other engine was detached, the carriages allowed to run down the incline and then brought to rest by their own brakes. Ilfracombe was reached at 6.20pm and after an inspection of the station, where several sidings, the turntable, railings and gates were still unfinished, the special left at 7.10pm.

Speculation as to the opening date was now rife, not least because Ilfracombe had to prepare its celebrations. On 2nd July it was reported that more men had been put on and that everything was near completion. The ballast engine 'Whitmore' which had been working at Braunton, came through the summit cutting with more trucks to assist with the completion of the works.

TOWN OFFICES AND COMPETITION

As we have seen, the South Western already had its own Ilfracombe office, near the *Clarence Hotel*. On 19th March 1874 it was reported that the office was to be moved to the High Street, opposite the Post Office. At the same time the sudden death of the general manager and booking clerk, Mr Christopher Bowles, was reported; he had run the South Western office for the previous five years.

Shortly afterwards, the Devon and Somerset Railway opened its office at the Clock Tower, also in the High Street, for goods and passenger traffic conveyed by road to and from its newly opened station at Victoria Road in Barnstaple. They also took stabling for 15 horses, which from 1st June 1874 were employed in running three coach services daily from the *Royal Clarence Hotel*, calling at the Booking Office in High Street, to Barnstaple station in connection with the principal trains to Taunton and beyond, with four services in the opposite direction. The splendid new coaches, hauled by a team of four horses, were booked to cover the 12 miles in 1¼ hours, and initially were well patronised. Previously, passengers from the Great Western line had been booked by train to Portishead and thence by paddle steamer to Ilfracombe. Passengers from the Midland Railway system continued to be booked via Portishead, and it was believed that the London and North Western was routing its passengers via Swansea and paddle steamer to Ilfracombe. The new Barnstaple and Ilfracombe Railway certainly did not lack for competition.

BOARD OF TRADE INSPECTION

On 13th July 1874 Col. Hutchinson came to inspect the line, arriving at Barnstaple accompanied by company officials in a special train. He started at 8am, looking at the arrangements there for the Ilfracombe trains. His special train of five carriages and a brake van hauled by two locomotives, one in front and one behind, started along the new line and spent two hours on the Taw iron bridge. Considerable time was also spent on the Yeo swing bridge, and inspecting all stations, signal boxes and other equipment right through to Ilfracombe, to arrive back at Barnstaple about 6pm. He reported as follows:

Railway Department
Board of Trade
16th July 1874
I have the honour to report for the information of the Board of Trade that in compliance with the instructions contained in your minute of the 7th instant I have inspected the Barnstaple and Ilfracombe Railway.

This is a single line of railway 14 miles 65.8 chains long which forms a junction with the North Devon Line of the London and South Western Railway at Barnstaple and runs thence to Ilfracombe.

By Section 29 of the Barnstaple and Ilfracombe Railway Act of 1870 it was authorised to be constructed and worked as a Light Railway and in consequence about 5¼ miles have been laid with a flat bottomed rail weighing 60lb per yard, and an iron swing bridge has been constructed with girders of sufficient theoretical strength to bear only the light class of engines which are intended to run on the line. In other respects the works are all of sufficient strength to remove it out of the category of a 'Light Railway'.

No provision has been made for a future doubling of the line. The width at formation level is 15 feet. Stations have been provided at Barnstaple Town, Wrafton, Braunton, Morthoe and Ilfracombe; at the first of these there are no sidings whatsoever, at Wrafton there is a siding but no passing place; at Braunton and Morthoe there are passing places and sidings and at Ilfracombe a large station yard. In places where the line is double there is a 6ft interval between the lines of rail.

The sharpest curve on the line has a radius of 7½ chains and the steepest gradient (of which there is 2¼ miles near Ilfracombe) has an inclination of 1 in 36, besides which there are 3¼ miles of 1 in 40 between Braunton and Morthoe stations.

The permanent way consists of about 5¾ miles of flat bottomed rail weighing 60lb per yard, of about 3 miles of the same description weighing 72lb per yard and the remainder (about 6 miles) is a double headed rail weighing 75lb per yard. This latter has been

An old print of Ilfracombe station in its early state. Artistic licence has been employed in many details, but the signal, signal box, station building, engine shed and general layout appear to be consistent with later photographs. However, the train is unconvincing, the goods shed far too small and the location of the town is wrong. *Ilfracombe Museum*

used principally upon the steep gradients. The 60lb rails are in 24 feet lengths, fished at the joints and fixed by a fang bolt on the inside and a spike on the outside to each sleeper, the 72lb rails are in 5 and 6 metre lengths fished at the joints with only bolts (a French custom) and similarly secured to the 60lb rails. The 75lb rails fished at the joints in 24ft lengths are fastened by outside oak keys in cast iron chairs weighing 32lb each, the chairs are fixed to the sleepers by spikes passing through oak trenails; the sleepers are 9ft long and half round some 10 x 5 others 9 x4½ ins; they are laid 3 feet apart from centre to centre at the joints and from 2ft 9 in to 3ft elsewhere. The ballast is of broken stone and hard shale and is one foot thick beneath the sleepers, as returned in the details. There are Engine Turntables at Barnstaple and Ilfracombe. The fencing is for the most of post and rail.

The most important work on the line is a wrought iron viaduct of 17 spans ranging between 30 feet and 40 feet in width across the River Taw at Barnstaple constructed on a curve of 7½ chains radius. The girders are supported on Hughes wrought iron piles braced together with timber. The main girders are plate girders 4 feet deep and the flanges are curved on plan, a construction I have never before seen adopted. The ribs have accordingly in consequence been made somewhat thicker than usual. The structure possesses (so far as I have calculated it) ample theoretical strength for the passage of ordinary heavy engines; under a rolling load of which it behaved very well and gave only moderate deflections. I have therefore no doubts as to its being amply strong for the weight it will have to carry, but at the summer time I would recommend a careful watch being kept upon the gauge particularly where any effect arising from the curvature of the flange would be most likely to show itself.

The next most important work is a wrought iron Swing Bridge of 110ft opening across the Yeo. This (to avoid unnecessary weight) has been constructed only of sufficiently strong theoretical strength for light engines and under the passing of these it gave only moderate deflections. The opening arrangements are safe in character but rather slow in operation. Besides these two bridges there are 4 bridges over the line constructed entirely of masonry or brick and 26 bridges or viaducts under it 17 of which have timber tops resting on masonry abutments largest span 10¾ feet and four are built entirely of masonry, the largest span being 21 feet. There is also a tunnel lined with masonry and brickwork 69½ yards long and 1 large culvert. These appear to be all substantially constructed and in the case of the timber topped bridges the deflections were minimal. There are 8 authorised level crossings of public roads. The sharp curves have been constructed with check rails.

The following are the requirements which I observed during the course of Inspection:
Barnstaple Station (old) Points Nos.10 should precede Nos.8 and 9.
Barnstaple Town Station. The fencing should be extended to opposite the end of the verandah. The positions of the levers in the cabin should be reversed so that they may stand next the signals to which they refer.
Wrafton Station. Levers Nos.4 and 5 should interlock and the putting in of an interlocked catch siding should be completed.
Braunton Station. Shelter is required on the up platform and the level crossing gates should be prevented from opening outwards.
Morthoe Station. Shelter is required on the up platform.
Ilfracombe Station. Fencing is required on the left side of the down line. The turntable road requires interlocked catch points. The lower arm on the arriving signal should apply to the goods line. The level crossing gates at 6 miles 17 chains require an up distant signal. The bridges at 7. 26 and 10. 15 require tie rods, the straps on the viaduct for preserving the gauge require completion; some ties to preserve the gauge are required at the swing bridge, the flooring of which and of the viaduct required. Covering as a precaution against fire, some of the fencing requires completion. An interlocked bolt worked from the Barnstaple Town Station cabin is required to give the signalman command of the Swing Bridge, which has been provided with telegraphic apparatus.
These requirements are all to be at once proceeded with and there is no reason they should not be substantially completed by the end of this week. The line is to be worked by the London and South Western Railway Company upon the train staff system and I enclose an undertaking to that effect.

In consequence of the very steep gradient on which Ilfracombe is approached the L and S W Company have provided special break vans which are to run in addition to the ordinary vans with every train between Braunton and Ilfracombe. These appear to be ample by themselves to hold trains of a reasonable length such as one engine can manage and I should strongly recommend double trains never being run on the line. The special engines have now been provided with engine as well as hand breaks.

Subject to the completion of these requirements above enumerated and my re-inspection of them at an early period I can recommend the Board of Trade to sanction the opening of Barnstaple and Ilfracombe Railway for passenger traffic on the 20th instant.
C.S.Hutchinson Lt. Col.

OPENING

After months of eager anticipation and planning by the local committee, Ilfracombe celebrated the opening of its new railway on Monday 20th July 1874. The first train of two locomotives and twelve carriages left Ilfracombe at 6.35am, on time, to the ringing of the bells of the parish church. A four horse bus from the Ilfracombe Hotel and a bus from the Clarence Hotel ran in connection with the trains. During the day the railway brought hundreds of passengers to the town; there was an Oddfellow's Fete, and a tea in the Market for aged people and school children. Many more had arrived by the paddle steamer Prince of Wales and the number of visitors reached several thousands.

The first up train arrived at Barnstaple a few minutes early, greeted by detonators on the rails and volleys fired from Westacott's shipyard, opposite the Quay station. The first down train, scheduled to leave Barnstaple Junction (as it had now become) at 8.50am, after the departure of the Torrington train, consisted of two engines and thirteen coaches which left at 9.10am. Large numbers of Barumites were waiting at the Quay station, and more again at Wrafton and particularly Braunton, and at Morthoe, where a fog hid Morte Bay from view.

The organising committee had ensured that Ilfracombe was well decorated for this most important event in the town's history. The South Western had assisted by sending down decorations used previously at Windsor for the visit of the Czar and Czarina of Russia, including at the end of the platform awning 'V. Welcome R', and on the approach road a triumphal floral arch 'A. Welcome M' (Alexander and Maria), and another 'Waterloo to Ilfracombe', 'United in Bonds of Iron'. All the way down the road from the station to the town were more flags, banners and arches, and the town centre, including the South Western Railway Office, was decorated in style.

The organising committee chose Tuesday 21st July for the formal celebrations, when at 2.30pm a civic procession formed up at the Ilfracombe Hotel and wended its way up through the town to the station where they greeted many more guests on the arrival of their train. The enlarged procession then returned to the town centre where at 6 o'clock a Public Banquet for a hundred gentlemen was held at the Ilfracombe Hotel. After a five course meal there was a very large number of speeches, as was the custom on these occasions, with toasts to the directors, solicitor, surveyor, engineer, contractor, the South Western, mayors of other North Devon towns and so on. There were illuminations in the town that night, and next day a cold collation was provided in the Market for 150 navvies who had worked on the line; they were addressed by the Rev. Benjamin Price who, as we have seen, had been very active over many years in promoting the railway.

AMALGAMATION

The South Western Act of 16th July 1874 authorised its amalgamation with the local railway, with £30,000 of 4¼% debenture stock and £105,000 of 4½% Ilfracombe Rentcharge Stock being exchanged for Barnstaple and Ilfracombe Railway stock of the same value. This yielded a dividend totalling £6,000, exactly the rent the South Western had agreed to pay for the line. As a result, shareholders in the Barnstaple and Ilfracombe Railway were almost unique amongst investors in North Devon railways in getting all their money back. Only Bideford Extension Railway shareholders were equally fortunate.

Rolle Quay Siding opened in 1881 and one of the major customers was the Victoria Flour Mills of Stanbury and Son, Millers and Corn Merchants. This is their premises, with a South Western wagon in the siding, apparently in the later LSW period. *Medina Gallery*

CHAPTER FOUR

THE SOUTH WESTERN ERA
1874 - 1922

EARLY YEARS, 1874 - 1889

When opened, the line was single throughout, with passing loops only at Braunton and Morthoe. Wrafton had a siding and Barnstaple Quay just a platform; Shapland and Petters and Rolles Quay sidings came later. The rather sparse train service, as originally provided, was first four, then five, up, and five down trains daily, with no Sunday service. All trains were restricted to a maximum speed of 25mph under the Light Railway regulations.

Motive power was provided exclusively by the 0-6-0 Ilfracombe Goods locomotives for almost 20 years, and it would appear from the Working Timetables and accident reports that trains were mixed, for there were no 'passenger' or 'goods' train designations for some years. By the end of July 1874 traffic was exceeding the South Western's expectations and the majority of passengers travelled first or second class; more than twenty first class passengers from beyond Exeter arrived at Ilfracombe on the last train one evening. A request for cheap excursion tickets to the resort was deferred until the summer of 1875. However, the Devon and Somerset Railway coach service continued in competition until that company's

own trains arrived in 1887, and as late as 1894 the London and North Western Railway advertised at the harbour its direct train services from Swansea to Shrewsbury, Chester, Liverpool, Manchester and Leeds - Ilfracombe passengers reaching Swansea by paddle steamer.

An early incident occurred on 7th August 1874, when Morthoe station was seriously damaged by fire. About 3am that Friday morning the station master, Mr Rice, his wife and daughter were woken by detonators exploding in a fire in a store room. The alarm was raised and local people helped to put the blaze out eventually; surprisingly it was found that there was no shortage of water at the station to extinguish the flames. The booking office, porters' room, office equipment and the electric telegraph were completely destroyed; the damage estimated at £150. Replacement buildings were soon provided. Later that summer, the summit cutting at Morthoe (it had proved a major obstacle during construction) caused further problems when on 11th September the 8.35pm train from Barnstaple ran into a landslip there, fortunately without causing injury or serious damage.

There was a serious incident on

Friday 3rd August 1880, and once again it occurred to the last down train, now the 8.25pm from Barnstaple, consisting of Ilfracombe Goods 0-6-0 No.282, a wagon loaded with bricks, and five coaches heavily laden with passengers. About three quarters of a mile beyond Barnstaple Quay station the engine hit some stones, left the rails, and ran on about 70 yards before overturning. Driver Whitehome, trapped under the cab, was rescued uninjured but Fireman Davolls was scalded by escaping steam. The wagon stopped the locomotive from running down the embankment and saved the coaches and passengers from injury. The stones had been placed on the track by some boys, who were apprehended and thrashed by their fathers in front of the Barnstaple station master, Mr Heather.

ROLLE QUAY SIDING 1881

On 11th March 1881 Major F.A. Marindin reported to the Railway Department as follows: '*I have the honour to report for the information of the Board of Trade that in compliance with the instructions contained in your Minute of 9th ultimate, I have inspected the new connection with the Barnstaple and Ilfracombe branch of the London and South Western Railway at Rolle Quay Siding , Barnstaple - The line is single and the points of the new connection are locked by a key attached to the Train Staff, and also by an Annetts Key which locks the signals in the signal cabin at Barnstaple station - This station is not a staff station and lies between Barnstaple Junction, the Staff Station, and the Connection, so it has been thought advisable to have both the locks mentioned, the points remaining locked up unless both are opened - I do not myself see any necessity for more than the key attached to the Staff, but there is no reason for objecting to the use of this new connection.*'

Anticipating Major Marindin's approval for the works, the South Western's Instruction No.36, 1881, for Rolle Quay Siding was dated Wednesday 23rd February, and is here reproduced. An interesting feature of the operation in these early years was that no facility existed for an engine to run round the train, so that the return journey from Rolle Quay Siding to Barnstaple Junction, almost a mile including sharp reverse curves, was performed with the engine propelling the wagons. This practice ended in 1890 when the Pottington Signal Box to Braunton section was doubled and a crossover provided for running round. Goods trains between Barnstaple Junction and Rolle Quay Siding ran 'as required' for some years and did not appear in the Working Timetable.

Ilfracombe Goods 0-6-0 No.283 leaves Ilfracombe with a passenger train headed by LSWR 6-wheel brake third and a bogie third. Two GWR coaches are in the level headshunt to the carriage sidings, and the up running line is laid with the standard South Western 24ft bullhead rail as described by Col. Hutchinson in his 1874 report. No.283 was 'duplicated' in 1899 so the photograph can be dated in the 1891-99 period. The sign decrees a speed of 4 mph. *R.C.Riley collection*

Barnstaple Quay station, re-named Barnstaple Town in 1886, consisted of a single platform with station buildings at the end of Barnstaple bridge, and was very convenient for the town centre. A signal box opposite the down end of the platform was unusual in that it controlled no points but only signals, protecting Pottington Swing Bridge. This closed in 1898 when the new Barnstaple Town station opened just down the line. *Medeva Gallery*

SOUTH WESTERN RAILWAY.

INSTRUCTION, No. 36, 1881.

2999 R

BARNSTAPLE & ILFRACOMBE LINE.

Instructions to Superintendents, Station Masters, Inspectors, Enginemen, Guards, Signalmen, and all concerned as to the Opening of the

ROLLE QUAY SIDING

ON

WEDNESDAY the 23rd February, 1881.

The above-named Siding is situated on the North side of the Ilfracombe Line, about half a mile from the Barnstaple Quay Station, towards Braunton, the points being facing for Up Trains.

There are two Annett's Locks fitted to the points leading into the Siding, the key of one Lock is the Barnstaple and Braunton Train Staff, and the key of the other fits a Lock in the Barnstaple Quay Signal Box, and cannot be withdrawn from there till all Signals (except the Up Starting Signal) worked from that Box are locked at Danger.

The mode of working will be as follows :—

An Engine or Train can only be sent to Rolle Quay when the Train Staff for the Barnstaple and Braunton Section is at Barnstaple Station.

Whenever there are any Trucks at Barnstaple to be taken to Rolle Quay, or at Rolle Quay to be brought away, Mr. Heather will send an Engine from Barnstaple for the purpose, accompanied by two men in charge, one to act as Guard, and the other as Shunter.

On leaving Barnstaple for Rolle Quay, the Guard in charge will take with him from Barnstaple Junction the Barnstaple and Braunton Train Staff, and will stop at Barnstaple Quay Station and take from the Signal Box there the key of the Annett's Lock fitted in that Box.

[TURN OVER.

2

On arriving at Rolle Quay the points will be unlocked by the Guard with the two keys above referred to, and the Train or Engine admitted by him on to the Quay, and he will remain at the Junction in charge of the points until the work on the Quay is completed and the Train or Engine has again passed over the points on to the Main Line, when he will lock the points with both keys, and on his return will hand the key belonging to the Barnstaple Quay Station Signal Box to the Signalman there, and will take the Barnstaple and Braunton Train Staff to Barnstaple Junction Station in order to open the Line again for the ordinary traffic.

ELECTRIC SIGNALLING.

The Warning Signal from Barnstaple Junction to Barnstaple Quay for a Train or Engine going to Rolle Quay will be four beats given twice, and the Departure Signal will be four beats ; but the Ordinary Signals only will be used for Trains or Engines returning from Rolle Quay to Barnstaple Junction.

Before any Train or Engine is allowed to leave Barnstaple Quay Station for Rolle Quay, the obstruction Danger Signal, six beats, must be given to and acknowledged by Wrafton, and on the return of the Train or Engine to Barnstaple Quay Station this Signal will be cleared by the Error Signal, viz. : seven beats given and acknowledged, and the usual all clear Signal sent afterwards.

RATES for Haulage from Barnstaple Junction Station to Rolle Quay, and vice versa.

For Bricks, Tiles, Lime, Coal and Coke	4d. per ton.
For Grain, Oil Cake, Artificial Manures, Timber, Slates, and other such like Goods	6d. ,,
For General Merchandise	1s. ,,

No less charge in any case for one consignment than as for one ton, at the above respective rates.

All Goods must be loaded and unloaded on the Quay Siding by and at the expense of the Consignors or Consignees.

These Rates will be in addition to the Ordinary Rate from or to Barnstaple Station.

BY ORDER.

[TURN OVER.

Distant view of Ilfracombe station in late LSW days, probably the summer season, to judge by the large numbers of coaches in the carriage sidings, both South Western and Great Western four and six wheelers and bogies. By this time the station awning has been extended along the platform. *Lens of Sutton*

THE BARNSTAPLE JUNCTION RAILWAY 1887

As we have seen, the Great Western camp had ambitions to reach Ilfracombe as long ago as 1845, and the Devon and Somerset had opened throughout between Taunton and Barnstaple in 1873, with its own Ilfracombe office and connecting coach service thereto following in 1874. The line, worked by the Bristol and Exeter until its amalgamation with the Great Western in 1876, then by the Great Western until the latter purchased it outright in 1901, was converted to the standard gauge between 15th and 17th May 1881, after only eight years on the broad gauge. In 1884 the Great Western proposed to build a supposedly independent line from the Devon and Somerset, by-passing Barnstaple, to Ilfracombe. Alarmed by this, Barnstaple Corporation urged the South Western to 'make a junction line between the two railways at Barnstaple in preference to the proposed new line', and on 21st October the South Western

agreed not to oppose a Great Western Bill for a junction line. On 3rd July 1885 the two companies reached agreement over junction arrangements. The GW would pursue no other route to Ilfracombe, but would gain the use of Barnstaple Junction for Ilfracombe traffic; certain of their staff would be allowed on the line, but not to work trains.

The Great Western Act of 31st July 1885 authorised the loop line, only 1 mile 27 chains in length, which opened on 1st June 1887. Through carriages between Taunton and beyond and Ilfracombe were worked by the Great Western into its terminus, and reversed out, until the Barnstaple East Curve was opened on 1st July 1905, facilitating a direct route from Taunton to Barnstaple Junction. The loop line, the Barnstaple Junction Railway, was of great benefit for both passengers and goods traffic linking up the South Western and Great Western routes in North Devon, although initially the Great Western stipulated that 'The Through

Carriages must be reserved for Passengers going to the Ilfracombe Branch, and Passengers for other Stations on the L and SW must not be allowed to use them .....'

For about forty years, Great Western coaches were worked over the Barnstaple Junction Railway by one of that company's own locomotive and attached to an LSWR Ilfracombe branch train for the final part of the journey. When the Great Western service to Ilfracombe began on 1st June 1887 the competing coach service from Victoria Road ceased, after precisely 13 years. Great Western guards accompanied their carriages for protection, but the train was worked by South Western men. The Great Western office at the Clock Tower, High Street, gained in importance for the sale of tickets and for parcels traffic, but Ilfracombe station offices remained a South Western preserve.

The Great Western and South Western now competed for the long distance traffic to Ilfracombe almost as equals, the South Western running all the trains from Barnstaple over the branch, which it was now improving. Lt Col. Hutchinson visited the line and reported to the Board of Trade on 12th February 1887 that it had been re-laid, partly with steel and partly with wrought iron double headed rails, weighing 82lb and 75lb per yard, carried in 40lb and 32lb chairs, and was in good order. The Swing Bridge had been strengthened for heavy engines. His five requirements were that Braunton up distant signal should be placed under the Georgeham level crossing up home, check rails be provided on reverse curves, Barnstaple Quay bridge bolt lever (which released Pottington Swing Bridge) be made easier to operate, timbers on two bridges were to be moved, and wall plates on 7 underbridges required strengthening. He returned and on 12th November reported the completion of these requirements, and sanctioned the use of the line as an ordinary railway. The South Western anticipated this in the new Working Timetable dated October 1887 which announced that 'This line has now been converted from a Light Railway into the Company's standard type for every class of traffic'.

In the summer of 1887 there were three passenger trains each way over the new Barnstaple Junction Railway, timed to allow attachment to or detachment from LSW Ilfracombe services. From 1st July 1889 the Great Western put on a through train from Paddington to Ilfracombe in 6hrs 55mins, running via Bristol, whilst the South Western service from Waterloo took 6hr 22mins. This was the start of real competition between the two, particularly in terms of the journey time and the convenience of the service.

DOUBLING THE LINE 1889-1891

Traffic grew during the 1880s, and by summer 1887 there were nine trains each way daily. It became clear that a single track branch with two passing places lacked the capacity to handle the volume of traffic anticipated in future years, particularly the extra Great Western services. The

An early view of Ilfracombe from Cairn Top, showing the station built high above the town. The layout is that following the doubling of 1891, with the second signal box opposite the goods shed, no less than four wooden post bracket signals, the short turntable and original locomotive shed. The little four or six wheel coaches suggest the 1890s period. In the valley to the right is a field with a fairground roundabout, which was used for the circus when it visited Ilfracombe in its train. *Ilfracombe Museum*

A group of South Western railwaymen at Barnstaple Town early this century. This distinctive enamelled station nameboard faced the Ilfracombe line, and a different version faced the Lynton line. Both were later replaced by a standard Southern concrete version. The man on the extreme right is William Jerrett, and it is believed that the Station Master in the centre was a Mr Riley. *Cynthia Sheppard collection*

this part of the line. There are 4 authorised level crossings of public roads provided with proper arrangements. There is no intermediate station between Braunton and Morthoe and these are provided with the necessary accommodation. New signal boxes have been erected at these stations and also at Georgeham, Stoney Bridge and Heddon Mill Level Crossings; these cabins contain the following levers:-

1. Braunton	*19 working levers, 5 spare levers*
2. Georgeham	*3 working levers, 2 spare levers*
3. Stoney Bridge	*5 working levers, 1 spare lever*
4. Heddon	*8 working levers, 0 spare levers*
5. Morthoe	*16 working levers, 4 spare levers*

I observed the following requirements:-
1. Braunton Station. Nos. 5 and 22 levers should not be interlocked.
2. Morthoe Station. The platforms should be made of a uniform level throughout, and boarded crossings provided at the ends of the platforms.
No.3 lever should not lock No.4 back and front.
No.18 lever should not lock No.17 back and front.
Runaway points should be provided a full train's length below the down home signal.
3. Heddon Mill Crossing. The same remark as to levers not locking applies as at Morthoe. The runaway points should be moved back a full train's length below the down home signal.

upgrading from Light Railway to standard track lifted the restriction on motive power, although the Ilfracombe Goods engines were still in evidence for some years. The South Western decided to double the line from Pottington to Ilfracombe, the cost of doubling the short section from Barnstaple Junction to Pottington with two major bridges being too expensive. The contract, with Lucas and Aird, was for £40,000, the work being carried out in three stages, each being completed for the start of the summer season.

Work started in August 1888 and the first section, from Braunton to Morthoe, was ready the following year. Maj.Gen. Hutchinson made his inspection and reported on 7th June 1889: '.....*I have inspected the doubling of the (single) line between Braunton and Morthoe stations on the Barnstaple and Ilfracombe branch of the London and South Western Railway.*

*The additional line, which is about 6 miles in length, has been laid with the standard type of permanent way now in use on the London and South Western Rail-*way; *it has been well laid and well ballasted.*

The curves and gradients are the same as those of the original line, the latter being 1 in 40 for more than half the distance. The works are not important and consist
1. Four overbridges entirely reconstructed (except one of the abutments of each) with stone abutments and brick arches, widest span 30½ft.
2. Nine road and river under-bridges, the original abutments have been lengthened and the tops of both new and old lines formed with wro't iron troughs, widest span 13 ft except in one case, span 12 ft., where the top is a lengthened stone arch.
3. Seven culverts, widest 7ft., all built of stone, except one (4 ft. wide) which has a top of old rails.

These works appear to have been substantially constructed and to be standing well. The wro't iron troughs have sufficient theoretical strength and gave moderate deflections under test. There are no tunnels on

Subject to the prompt completion of these requirements, the Board of Trade being informed of the same, I see no objection to the additional line of rails between Braunton and Morthoe being used for passenger traffic.'

The South Western attended to these details and on 1st July 1889 this double track section was brought into use, although it was not until 26th April 1890 that Maj.Gen. Hutchinson returned to report that his requirements had been complied with. His next observations are dated 2nd August 1890 '....*I have inspected the additional line of rails which has been laid between Barnstaple Swing Bridge and Braunton, on the Ilfracombe Branch of the London and South Western Railway. This additional line, which is about 5 miles in length, is laid with the company's standard type of permanent way; it is in good order and well ballasted. The curves and gradients are those of the original single line.*

An unidentified Adams 0-4-4T ascends the 1 in 36 gradient past the Slade reservoir with the 12 noon Ilfracombe to Barnstaple train of four South Western bogies, the first two being an arc roof two coach set. *Frank Box courtesy National Railway Museum*

In October 1907 Frank Box visited the line, taking a number of excellent photographs and recording the formations and timing of trains. Here we see an unidentified O2 class 0-4-4T on Barnstaple Bridge on a down train of four-wheelers, the first four being South Western and the last two Great Western. *Frank Box courtesy National Railway Museum*

The works on the line consist of the re-construction in masonry and brickwork of two overbridges of 25½ft span, of the widening in masonry and brickwork of a river bridge of 20¾ft span and of the widening of 4 underbridges maximum span 13 ft, having stone abutments and wrought iron trough girder tops, and the lengthening of a 3½ft culvert.

These works appear to be of a substantial character and to be standing well. The trough girders gave only slight deflections under test. There are no tunnels; there are 4 public road level crossings provided with proper gates. The only station on the line is Wrafton where a second platform has been provided.

The signal arrangements have been carried out as follows:-

Pottington (Swing Bridge)	*17 working levers, 2 spare levers*
Pottington (Level Crossing)	*6 working levers, 0 spare levers*
Duckpool (Level Crossing)	*5 working levers, 3 spare levers*
Wrafton (Station)	*15 working levers, 2 spare levers*
Vellator (Level Crossing)	*5 working levers, 2 spare levers*
Braunton (Level Crossing)	*2 working levers, 3 spare levers*
Braunton (Station)	*21 working levers, 3 spare levers*

The arrangements for securing the safety of the Swing Bridge which is situated between Barnstaple Town Cabin and the new cabin at Pottington are carried out in each of these cabins. The only requirements I noticed were that:-

1. Shelter should be provided on the down platform at Wrafton.
2. No.4 semaphore signal at Pottington should be replaced by a ground disc.
3. The opening of the Swing Bridge should render it electrically impossible for the Pottington signalman to accept a train from Wrafton in the same way that he is now prevented from accepting one from Barnstaple Town.

Subject to these requirements of the fulfilment of which the Board of Trade should be informed, so that a re inspection may be ordered if considered necessary, I can recommend that sanction be given for the opening of the additional line of rails between Barnstaple Swing Bridge and Braunton.'

This double track section was opened to traffic on 4th August 1890, and work continued on the remainder until Maj.Gen. Hutchinson made his last inspection on

25th June 1891: '.....*I have inspected the widening of the line between Morthoe and Ilfracombe on the Barnstaple and Ilfracombe Branch of the London and South Western Railway.*

This additional line, which is about 3 miles 9 ch. in length, has been laid with the standard type of permanent way in use upon the London and South Western Railway. It is well ballasted and in good order. The curves and gradients are almost identical with those of the original single line, the sharpest curve having a radius of 14 chains, and the steepest gradient (2¼ miles in length) being 1 in 36.

The works consist of (1) a number of retaining walls, the highest being 20 ft. (2) the rebuilding of 3 under-bridges and 3 over-bridges, the former being all of small spans not exceeding 12½ft and the span of the largest of the latter being 27 ft; the abutments are all of masonry, as are also the tops, except in two of the under-bridges, where wro't iron troughs have been used; and (3) a tunnel in masonry, 70 yards long.

A general view of Ilfracombe station from the signal box in October 1907 showing, from left to right, five South Western horse boxes, a selection of coaches in the carriage sidings and platforms, the water tower, turntable and engine shed partially obscured by another horsebox, and some distinctive South Western wagons in the goods yard. The whole area is lit by gas lamps, the starting signals are mounted on a wooden post and dolls, and there is no release crossover from platform 2. Ilfracombe station stayed essentially in this form from doubling in 1891 to the re-building of the late 1920s. *Frank Box courtesy National Railway Museum*

Adams T1 class 0-4-4T No.363 prepares to depart from No.2 platform with a train described by the indicator - 'Through Carriages for London Waterloo'. In the carriage sidings, from left to right, are a four wheel luggage van, a six wheel saloon carriage built in 1885, and two coach set No.234. This was one of a number of sets rebuilt from 1890s 42ft and 45ft carriages with the two end passenger compartments converted to guard's brake compartments; official LSWR records show that this work was authorised in 1910, but Frank Box dated the photograph as October 1907, so there must be an error somewhere. The white posts carried flexible hoses which were used to re-charge the gas cylinders of the coaches of the period. *Frank Box courtesy National Railway Museum*

These works appear to have been all substantially constructed and to be standing well. There are no public road crossings. The fencing where new is of post and rail.

There are no stations between Morthoe and Ilfracombe - Morthoe was altered some time since to make it suitable for a double line; Ilfracombe Station does not at present require alteration, but in the new Signal Cabin and Signal arrangements, provision has been made for adding two more platform lines at some future period.

Morthoe Signal Cabin now contains 18 working levers and two spare ones. Ilfracombe new Signal Cabin contains 50 working levers and 10 spare ones.

The only requirements I noticed were that, at Ilfracombe, No. 7 signal should not come off without No.38 points, and that runaway points should be placed on the up line a full train's length on the down side of Morthoe up home signal.

No goods train should be allowed to draw out and stand at No.8 up advanced signal at Ilfracombe prior to starting, as this signal is on the gradient of 1 in 36.

Subject to these requirements and remarks, and to the points and signals at Morthoe and Ilfracombe being correctly coupled up to the levers which are to work them (which cannot be completely done until just before the new line is brought into use) I can recommend the Board of Trade to sanction the use of the additional line of rails between Morthoe and Ilfracombe. The line between Barnstaple and Ilfracombe is now double throughout with the exception of a short distance at Barnstaple.'

The double track was brought into use by the South Western on 1st July 1891.

A SILVER STRIKE?

In the 1970s after the line had closed the Area Manager at Barnstaple, Mr E.J. Maclaughan, received an elderly visitor, a man in his 80s who, like his father before him, had been the Crossing Keeper at one of the level crossings near Braunton. He asked to buy the large clock in the crossing box, which throughout his life had ruled his day. He then related the story that when a young man, his father had been a mason working on the doubling of the line. As part of his work each week he was required to send samples of excavated rock to Waterloo for analysis, and one day a concerned South Western official arrived to see him, to discover precisely where a particular sample of rock had come from. It transpired that the sample contained silver, possibly the end of the Coombe Martin silver lodes, and the last thing the South Western wanted on its line was a silver rush. The site was identified and sealed off with a thick wall of rock, and as a reward for his silence the mason was promised a job for life as a crossing keeper. Only at a very advanced age did he pass on the story to his son, who also kept the secret until after the line closed. Your author has been unable to check the authenticity of this account, or indeed whether the geology of the area supports it, but it is a good story.

ACCIDENT AT FOXHUNTERS INN

Meanwhile, going back a little, on 24th December 1889 there was an accident at *Foxhunters Inn*, between Morthoe and Braunton, when a train was derailed coming down the 1 in 40 gradient rounding the sharp 16 chain curve. Maj. F.A. Marindin conducted an enquiry for the Board of Trade and reported on 18th January 1890 in lengthy terms here summarised. The 3.54pm up train from Ilfracombe consisted of Ilfracombe Goods 0-6-0 No.394, meat van, LSW third class brake, GW composite and third class brake, all fitted with vacuum brake. About the middle of the curve the engine, followed by the train, jumped the rails and came to rest upright but nearly foul of the down line - the double track having opened the previous summer. One passenger was injured, there was minor damage to the derailed vehicles, but one rail and 125 chairs were broken. At this site the contractors, Lucas and Aird, had employed gangs of labourers to dig out gravel and rock from the lineside for use as ballast for the doubling works then in progress elsewhere on the line.

Maj. Marindin recorded a great deal of detailed evidence from a number of witnesses including Robert Whitehorn, locomotive inspector at Barnstaple, Arthur Docker and William Featherstone, the driver and fireman, William Lethaby and William Beer, the guard and assistant guard, James Lewis, William Gear, Albert Taylor, contractor's labourers, John Ross, contractor's ganger, William Skinner and William Smaldon, gangers, William Jones, platelayer, Frederick Meadway, Exeter locomotive foreman, and George Vallance, assistant traffic superintendent. From the evidence he concluded that there certainly was some small stone on the rail at the place of derailment, but not sufficient to cause the engine wheel to mount the rail unless the speed was higher than it should have been. South Western men put the speed at 20 to 25 mph, whilst bystanders put it at over 40 mph; the maximum line speed was 25 mph, but on examining signal box records he found that Morthoe to Braunton was often actually run in 9 minutes rather than the booked 15 minutes for this train, which was consistent with a speed of 40 mph. He found another contributory factor, in the combination of the long rigid wheelbase of the engine, 13ft 10in, and the tightness of the gauge on the sharp curve.

He expressed concern that the contractors' men were working on a line open to traffic without careful supervision by South Western staff. The curves and gradients, he found, were such that any high speed was certainly dangerous, and that steps should be taken to ensure that booked times were adhered to. He also stated that it would be safer if engines with a shorter fixed wheel base were made use of.

Just how the South Western responded to this report is not clear, but slight widening of the gauge on sharp curves and adherence to booked times would have been straightforward. By March 1893 only two Ilfracombe Goods were shedded at Barnstaple; a pair of O2 0-4-4Ts, which certainly had a shorter wheel base, were also there and may have taken over some duties on the branch. However, Ilfracombe Goods were still in evidence as late as 1907.

GENERAL PROGRESS

There were a number of other developments in the eventful years around 1890. On 2nd May 1890 Maj.Gen. Hutchinson reported to the Board of Trade on his inspection at Barnstaple as follows:- '.....*the siding connection which has been laid between Barnstaple Junction and Barnstaple Town Station on the Barnstaple and Ilfracombe Branch of the London and South Western Railway. The new connection is worked by a two lever ground frame, locked by the train staff in use on the section of the single line with the connection has been made. The arrangements being satisfactory...*' This was Shapland and Petters Siding.

In March 1891 the West Country was hit by a great blizzard which brought most transport to a halt. The last train from Barnstaple, a locomotive and three carriages, ran into a snowdrift on Monday 9th March, shortly after leaving Morthoe. The dozen passengers made their way back to the station where the ladies were accommodated by the station master Mr Lodder, and the gentlemen at the *Fortescue Arms*. On receipt of a telegraphed message a breakdown train with 20 men left Barnstaple at midnight, but it too became stuck in another snowdrift, this time a mile and a half to the Braunton side of Morthoe. The snow continued throughout Tuesday, but on Wednesday the Ilfracombe station master, Mr Dover, organised some 100 men, employed by both the South Western and

Lucas and Aird, who began to clear the line with the help of an improvised snowplough. The two trapped trains were released and normal traffic was resumed on Wednesday 11th when the 6.0pm train from Barnstaple reached Ilfracombe. A normal train service had operated between Barnstaple and Braunton, but the blizzard blocked many other routes.

A few months later, on 19th August 1891, the Barnstaple to Wrafton section was itself blocked when a sailing ship went aground on a falling tide, preventing the closure of the Pottington Swing Bridge. Shuttle train services were run on each side until the vessel was floated off on the next high tide.

Following the doubling of most of the line, the train service increased in the summer of 1891 to 12 down and 14 up services, and to 15 down and 16 up in the summer of 1898. The working timetable also stated 'Light engines may be expected to run between Barnstaple and Ilfracombe at times uncertain and without previous notice'.

THE LYNTON AND BARNSTAPLE RAILWAY

After a number of different schemes had been considered the Lynton and Barnstaple Railway Act was passed in 1895. This 1ft 11½in gauge line was to start at a new Barnstaple Town station and to run for 19¼ miles over Exmoor, reaching an altitude of 980ft before descending to the Lynton terminus at 700ft above sea level. On 26th October 1896 the Lynton and Barnstaple, South Western and Barnstaple Corporation came to an agreement on the new station arrangements; the South Western would surrender to the Corporation the site of the existing Barnstaple Town (formerly Quay) station, in exchange for land for the new station. This would be built by the South Western at a cost of some £6,000, to include narrow gauge accommodation for which the Lynton company would pay an annual rent of £150. It was also agreed that the South Western would stop all its passenger trains at the new station.

The Lynton and Barnstaple Railway opened to traffic on 16th May 1898, when the new Barnstaple Town station opened for the traffic of both companies. The old station closed the day before. Lt.Col. Yorke inspected the narrow gauge line on 4th May and the standard gauge on 5th, but curiously his report on the new standard gauge works was dated 19th May, three days after their opening to public traffic: '*I have inspected the new town station at Barnstaple on the London and South Western Railway. This has been built on an entirely new site about a quarter of a mile west of the old town station with the object of accommodating the traffic of the Lynton and Barnstaple narrow gauge railway which is about to be opened. The (London and South Western) line is single and is worked on the electric tablet system. Barnstaple station is single sided and is not to be used as a passing place for passenger trains although it is a tablet station. It would doubtless have been much better if this could have been made a proper pass-*

ing place with up and down platforms. But the situation of it with the river on one side and the town on the other renders such an arrangement practically impossible.

The station has plenty of platform space and excellent waiting accommodation including cloakrooms for both sexes. At the back of the western end of it there is a bay for the use of the Lynton and Barnstaple line and there are also two sidings one of the normal gauge and the other of the narrow gauge with a loading bank between them for the exchange of goods traffic.

A new signal box has been built at the station containing 14 levers all in use (No.8 being push and pull) and a gate wheel. The electric tablet instruments here are so interlocked that trains from opposite directions cannot be permitted to approach the station at the same time. The only requirement I noted was that No.5 lever should lock No.3.

Some alterations have been rendered necessary in the Pottington signal box which is the next box in the direction of Ilfracombe and where the single line terminates and the double line to Ilfracombe commences. This signal box controls the swing bridge over the river to which it is adjacent. The swing bridge remains unaltered and is electrically locked with the tablet instruments so that when a tablet is out for a train to pass in either direction between Barnstaple Town and Pottington the bridge cannot be opened. And vice versa when the bridge is released no tablet can be obtained at either end of the section.

The requirements noted by me at Pottington signal box are:-
1. The bridge releasing lever in the box should electrically lock signals Nos.5 and 6 in the Town signal box so that when the bridge is open these signals shall not be capable of being lowered.
2. A calling on arm to be placed below signals 5 and 6 of the Town box for the purpose of allowing a train after it has come to a dead stand to be drawn forward into the station when the bridge is open.
3. Nos.3 and 4 signals at Pottington box to be released by the issue of the up tablet.
4. Nos.3 and 4 signals to be locked by the issue of the down tablet.
5. A fastening to be fixed on the swing bridge in accordance with Board of Trade requirement No.69.

I also inspected a new ground frame between Pottington and the Town Station which contains 7 levers (2 of them being push and pull) which are correctly interlocked.

It would have been desirable to lock the tablet instruments at Barnstaple Junction with the Swing Bridge so that when a train was approaching the Town Station from the junction the bridge should be locked in its normal position, and vice versa, but this would entail, I am told, too great an interference with the traffic. But instructions should be issued that every train without exception must come to a stand in Barnstaple Town station.

Subject to compliance with this condition and the requirements named above I can recommend the Board of Trade to sanction the use of the new station to which this report refers.'

Ilfracombe station, from Cairn Top, during the later South Western period, at a busy time. The No.1 platform starting signal is 'off' and steam rises from the train engine and banker, both apparently T1 class 0-4-4Ts, as they seem to exchange a cock-a-doodle-loo of whistles before ascending the 1 in 36 bank with a train of 8 coaches. Another T1 heads coaches in No.2 platform and there is a variety of stock in the carriage sidings. *Paul Gower Collection*

He returned to check on his requirements, and on 17th September reported that they had been complied with. Built by Mr Gibson of Exeter, the new station at Barnstaple Town was well-received locally, and was the most attractive on the line. 114ft long and 21ft wide, it was built of local (Chestwood) stone with Bath stone dressings. One end was for the use of the Lynton company, with all necessary offices, together with a commodious general waiting room, booking and parcels offices, lavatories, etc. The single platform 330ft long was rendered more attractive by the ornamental iron and glass roof, supported on iron columns. The station master at Barnstaple Town was Mr E.C. Watkin, who for the previous eight years had been the clerk in charge

at the old station. How long this post lasted is not clear, for the station was normally supervised by the Barnstaple Junction station master. Apart from the South Western staff, who ran the station, the Lynton and Barnstaple employed a signalman for its own box and a man for transfer work at the interchange siding. The main L&B depot was just up the line at Pilton, where about 50 men were employed.

AN 1898 JOURNEY

In 1898 an early film was made, the cine camera being mounted on a truck propelled by a locomotive, the camera recording the part of the route through Barnstaple and the descent into Ilfracombe. The film commences at

Shapland and Petters siding, showing the ground frame, drop flap ground signals and gate closed across the siding, Westcott's vehicular crossing into the works, and then Westcott's pedestrian crossing, with the crossing keeper flagging the train on. There is a slow crossing of the viaduct over the Taw leading to a full passing view of the original Barnstaple Quay station, at this stage apparently intact but out of use. The original Barnstaple Quay signal box, similar in construction to Instow, is passed with the signalman flagging our progress and all its old signals, most mounted on tall wooden posts are still in situ. Passing over the two level crossings we arrive at the new Barnstaple Town station and signal box with a fleeting view of several railwaymen on the platform, but no train for Lynton. The new lattice post signals for Barnstaple Town are apparently in use, which suggests that the film was made within a few days of Col. Yorke's inspection of 19th May 1898.

In the loop siding a handful of surprised platelayers with their trolley observe our progress; the sight of a film crew on a wagon propelled by an engine was unusual, to say the least, a century ago. The exchange siding and ground frame are passed before crossing Pottington swing bridge, with the distinctive capstan set in its deck at the far end. The signalman on the steps of Pottington signal box ready to receive our single line tablet also seems surprised by our arrival but the road is set and the signals are off for our arrival on the double track section. Just before the end of this section of film we see Rolle's Quay siding coming in from the right.

The film resumes as the train passes under the last overbridge, No. 28, and covers the entire descent from here down the Slade Valley into Ilfracombe. As the line wends its way along the rocky hillside the wooden fencing and telegraph posts stand out. A check rail is fitted to the down track for some distance above and through the single bore of Slade tunnel. A signal wire connects the Ilfracombe distant signal to the box, and as we approach the terminus there is a profusion of five sets of wooden bracket signals, three in the down direction and two up, our signal being pulled off just as we approach. In the carriage sidings a tank engine shunts a variety of South Western and Great Western coaches, and slowing down to the buffer stops under the train shed the lack of any release crossover, which enforced the use of gravity shunting or a station pilot engine, is notable.

THE LATER SOUTH WESTERN PERIOD

At this time the Ilfracombe branch had reached almost the final stage in its development, save for the expansion of the terminus in the 1920s. This apart, the layouts and equipment installed in 1889-91 and 1898 lasted intact until the late 1960s, and have been fully described in Chapter One.

From 1887 onwards both the LSW and GW had competed for the summer

Photographed from Sticklepath Road bridge, the aftermath of the derailment at Barnstaple Junction West signal box on 26th June 1922. The train was the 11.42 goods to Ilfracombe - full details are in the text. *Paul Gower Collection*

The same accident photographed from the Barnstaple Junction footbridge, after partial clearance of the wreckage to allow an up train from Torrington, hauled by a 460 class 4-4-0 to proceed cautiously into the up platform. The goods train locomotive, T1 0-4-4T No.67, remains on the rails in light steam, but the wagons were not so fortunate. Also of interest is the signal box, built in 1912 to replace the original 1874 tall stone structure, and moved in 1924 to allow expansion of the station. *Paul Gower Collection*

at the Barnstaple end of the station instead of the Ilfracombe end, to ease some of the obstruction of the Caen Street crossing by trains. Initially, the receipts for platform tickets at Braunton fell sharply as a result, but remedial measures were taken. This was not the end of this story at Braunton because in 1948 there was a complaint from the footplatemen's union ASLEF that pedestrians often walked across the line in front of engines about to leave with down trains, with potential risk of injury, and the wicket gate lock was re-instated.

DERAILMENT AT BARNSTAPLE JUNCTION

On 26th June 1922 the 11.42am goods train from Barnstaple Junction to Ilfracombe, consisting of T1 0-4-4T No. 67, 22 wagons and a brake van, departed from Barnstaple Junction East along the up road, the down road being occupied. Through a signalman's error at Barnstaple Junction West the train was turned into the siding opposite the signal box and collided with the buffer stops. The engine kept to the rails but 5 wagons were derailed, the Ilfracombe branch being blocked until 3.50pm when the Exmouth Junction breakdown crane had cleared the wreckage from the line.

Since no passengers were involved the Board of Trade did not send an inspecting officer, so the subsequent enquiry was conducted by the South Western. The wagons damaged were LNW No.77314, GN No.36458, MR No. 42366, GC No.14479, NE box wagon No.16797, MR No.79070, GW No.25514, LNW No.9986, and LSW box wagon No.9446. Evidence was given by driver J. Gay, fireman J. Stone, guard Charles Duffin, signalmen Trickey and W. Blake, and station master F. Heath. Whilst the wreckage was being cleared a number of Ilfracombe branch trains were cancelled, some were worked by pilotmen, and there were numerous delays to other trains. The greatest delay was to the 12.40pm goods from Mortehoe, which was shunted into Rolles Quay Siding for 3hrs 45mins.

Signalman Blake admitted that he had, in error, pulled No.14 points after No.13 lever, thus causing the accident. The South Western management immediately suspended this 'wrong line' working at Barnstaple Junction, but this made for delays in goods train services. Two years later the problem was eliminated when the down loop platform was brought into use and such 'wrong line' working ended for good.

The end of the South Western came with the grouping at the end of 1922. For sixty years the South Western had been a good and consistent friend of those who had worked to bring the railway to Ilfracombe, and had provided first the financial incentives and then the capital to both build and later double the line.

season traffic to Ilfracombe. Initially the South Western held an advantage with a route of 226 miles from Waterloo with, from 1891, only 19 miles of single track - between Copplestone and Umberleigh. The Great Western route from Paddington via Bristol was 224¾ miles, with about 44 miles of single track between Norton Fitzwarren and Barnstaple Junction, including the reversal at Victoria Road. The 1905 opening of the Barnstaple East Curve and the 1906 Castle Cary cutoff reduced the Great Western route to 203¾ miles, giving a significant advantage, although the Devon and Somerset route was unsuited to express working. The South Western Act of 1906 included powers to double the Copplestone to Umberleigh section, but competition was getting too expensive. The Chairmen of the Great Western and South Western companies, Viscount Churchill and Sir Charles Scotter, opened negotiations in 1909, and on 13th May 1910 signed an agreement to pool all competitive traffic in the West Country. Receipts were to be shared between the two companies in proportion to traffic carried in 1908, less 25% working expenses on the distances saved.

There was a minor accident at Ilfracombe on 7th July 1910 when a locomotive ran into the rear wall of the engine shed, causing damage to a value of £40. Frequency of trains on the branch was still increasing, to 17 trains each way daily in the summer of 1909, plus a considerable number of light engine movements. The South Western ran summer dining car expresses to North Devon, and at Barnstaple Junction the Ilfracombe coaches were detached from the train, which ran through to Torrington. The Great Western ran through services from Paddington, and there were also through carriages from Liverpool, Manchester, Leeds and Brighton. These were usually

hauled on the branch by a South Western 0-4-4T, but a Great Western locomotive was recorded at the terminus during the 1914-18 period. On 8th August 1914 a Territorial Battery of the Devonshire Royal Garrison Artillery, consisting of 5 officers, 125 men, 36 horses and 4 guns left Ilfracombe at 6pm on a special train for Plymouth and the Great War. During the First World War the branch saw a reduction in services, and a number of local men left the area to serve in the armed forces; those who did not return are remembered on war memorials in every town and village.

In 1919 Braunton Parish Council and Mr Frank Chanter complained of the delays to pedestrians when a down train was at the station. Maj. Mount of the Board of Trade made an inspection in May 1920 to consider the circumstances in which the wicket gates could be unlocked by the signalman to enable pedestrians to safely cross the line, while a down train was in the platform. Eventually, in December 1922, it was decided to disconnect the locks on the wicket gates, with appropriate notices posted that 'persons will use the wicket gates at their sole risk'.

The Locomotive Engineer, Robert Urie, had been consulted and it appears that at this time the South Western paid the Braunton Electric Light Power Company £100 per year to pump all the water required at Braunton. There were small locomotive water tanks at both Barnstaple and Ilfracombe, though at Ilfracombe the price was prohibitive, so engines took water at Braunton whenever possible. If this practice were discontinued an extra 2,300,000 gallons of water per year would be needed at both Barnstaple and Ilfracombe, at a price of 8d and 1s 6d respectively per thousand gallons. It was decided to make changes, to allow assisting engines to be attached

An unusual scene at Braunton in Southern days - an N 2-6-0 on an up train of one coach, apparently carrying an Atlantic Coast Express destination board. This appears to be a one-off event, but no details have yet come to light. *Knights Photographers*

CHAPTER FIVE

THE SOUTHERN RAILWAY ERA 1923-47

THE GROUPING

The 1921 Railways Act organised the main line railways into four groups. The new Southern Railway comprised the London & South Western Railway, the London, Brighton and South Coast Railway and the South Eastern & Chatham Railways Managing Committee, together with a number of smaller companies. It also acquired the Lynton and Barnstaple Railway under special powers in the Southern Railway 1923 Act. As from 1st January 1923 the Southern owned all the railways in North Devon except for the Great Western's Barnstaple branch. However, the 1920s was a decade which would see even further developments on the railways of North Devon, some of which had been initiated in South Western days.

The South Western had found that the operation of Barnstaple Junction, with just one up and one down platform, was becoming more and more difficult during the busy summer period, even though both platforms were signalled for reversible working - an unusual feature in the Edwardian period. As we saw in Chapter Four, there was a derailment here in 1922. It was decided to put in a second down platform road, converting the existing down platform into an island, but this required the excavation of a large quantity of rock. The pointwork at the west end of the station was now very com-

plicated, with each of four tracks connected to the Torrington line and the three platform lines to the Ilfracombe line. The new layout was controlled by Barnstaple Junction West signal box, which had been opened in 1912 but in 1924 was moved sideways by a few feet. The new works were inspected and approved on 23rd July 1924 - surprisingly the newly installed signalling showed Torrington to be the main line and Ilfracombe the branch, although preparatory work was already in hand to reverse this arrangement the following year.

MAIN LINE STATUS

During 1924/25 the Southern Railway acquired a number of new N class 2-6-0s, built at Woolwich Arsenal to a South Eastern and Chatham design of Richard Maunsell, now its chief mechanical engineer. On 3rd and 4th March 1925 No. A837 with a seven coach train made a number of trial runs on the branch which proved satisfactory, the load being significantly greater than that managed by the M7 0-4-4Ts then in use. As from the start of the new summer timetable, on 12th July 1925, the principal passenger trains from Exeter to North Devon were hauled by Ns and ran through to Ilfracombe, with through carriages for Torrington detached at Barnstaple Junction. This was a reversal of the previous arrangements and

a response to the significantly higher level of passenger traffic on the Ilfracombe line. Through goods trains continued to run along the Torrington line, which had the heaviest freight traffic.

A prerequisite for the employment of these much larger locomotives was the provision of a longer turntable at the terminus. The *Southern Railway Magazine* of November 1925 carried the following report - '*The new turntable at Ilfracombe is one of four to be installed, the others being for Redhill, Ramsgate and Dover. Sixty five feet in diameter, it is capable of taking the largest and heaviest engines of the company, and is hand operated and fitted with ball bearings to ensure smooth and easy working. It replaces the old 42 feet diameter turntable near the engine shed at Ilfracombe, and is situated in a new position on the up line side. As will be seen from the photographs the work entailed a considerable amount of excavation, the height of the cutting in the hillside being some 35 feet.*' It would appear that this report was at least eight months old when published, as the March trials would not have taken place without the new turntable. However, a standard South Western fifty feet turntable would have sufficed for the Ns, as they did in many locations west of Exeter, and the cost of £9,000 would have been reduced significantly, with much less excavation. Its full length was not needed for another twenty years until the Bulleid Pacifics arrived, and if the larger Southern engines of the period such as the King Arthur 4-6-0s were to be employed then an expensive programme of strengthening the bridges all the way from Exeter would have been required. Perhaps the Southern got a bargain price for four identical turntables in 1925.

It was about this time that the Southern agreed to the regular employment of Great Western locomotives on some of that company's through trains to Ilfracombe. From now on GW 4-4-0s, 2-6-0s and 2-6-2Ts were to be seen, particularly during the summer season, and heavy GW trains over Mortehoe bank were sometimes assisted by Southern engines.

At Barnstaple Town there were a couple of developments involving the Lynton line. New narrow gauge rolling stock was delivered via the interchange siding, heavy items such as the new locomotive LEW requiring the services of the Exmouth Junction steam crane. As an

A second down platform road, connected to both the Torrington and Ilfracombe lines, was opened at Barnstaple Junction on 23rd June 1924. To make way for the necessary connections the Barnstaple Junction West signal box, opened in 1912, had to be moved several feet. Here we see the entire brick-built structure, complete with lever frame and connecting wires, being moved to its new site with the aid of baulks of timber and steel rails. *Paul Gower Collection*

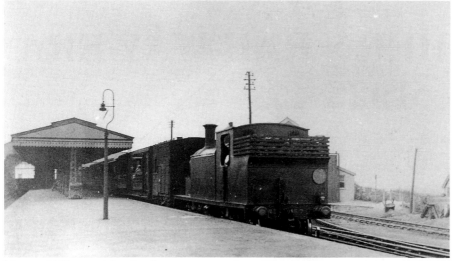

M7 0-4-4T No.57 with a local passenger train at Ilfracombe on 22nd July 1925. The Exeter and Waterloo services were entrusted to the new N class engines from the beginning of the new timetable on 12th July. The first vehicle is a South Western horsebox, and the others are a mixture of lengths and heights. The original locomotive shed and turntable are just visible. *H.C.Casserley*

On Friday 30th January 1926 South Western three coach set No.76 ran away during gravity shunting operations at Ilfracombe, coach No.2736 crashing through the buffer stops and wooden screen to come to rest as seen here. The Exmouth Junction steam crane was required to clear the wreckage. *North Devon Journal*

under gravity into No. 5 carriage siding where they were coupled to SR three coach set No. 76, which was to form the 6.10pm departure for Barnstaple. The locomotive now backed down into the carriage siding, was coupled up to the six SR coaches and drew them up the incline, still propelling the GW brake compo. When clear of the points the three coach set No. 76 was uncoupled from the other SR coaches, so that it could be run back by gravity under the control of a porter into Platform 2. Unfortunately the porter was elsewhere and set No. 76 ran down the gradient out of control, demolishing the stop blocks and wooden screen at the end of the platform. The leading coach, bogie third No. 2736, was forced over the embankment and bogie compo No. 4729 derailed and damaged. The Exmouth Junction steam crane was summoned to retrieve the coaches. Platform 2 was finally cleared at 1.35pm on Monday 1st February.

Evidence was given to the enquiry by Driver W. Stanbury, Guard Kemble, Porter-Guard S. Hatchley and Porter Paul. It was established that there had been a misunderstanding between Hatchley and Paul which had caused the accident. It was also found that the three coach set could have been shunted into the platform by the locomotive, and the Exeter Divisional Operating Superintendent D. S. McBright had instructed the Ilfracombe station master in October 1924 that gravitation should only be resorted to when absolutely necessary.

A second mishap occurred at Ilfracombe on 26th January 1931. The 6.40am freight train from Barnstaple Junction, behind N 2-6-0 No. A827, consisted of SR bogie corridor luggage van No. 2293 loaded with parcels and newspapers, GW vacuum box wagon No. 89748 loaded with flour, SR vacuum box wagon No. 45676 loaded with general goods, Parkend loaded coal wagon No. 163, GW

economy measure the Lynton and Barnstaple signal box was reduced to a ground frame, the single line tablet apparatus transferred to the South Western signal box, where three levers slotted the signals.

MISHAPS AT ILFRACOMBE

During the early Southern Railway period there were two shunting mishaps at Ilfracombe station. Like the Barnstaple Junction derailment of 1922, they did not involve passengers and were investigated internally. The first accident occurred on Friday 30th January 1926 after the 2.27pm passenger train from Exeter arrived at 4.23pm. The train, headed by N 2-6-0 No.A865, was made up of GW brake compo No. 6964, SR bogie third No. 657, SR brake compo No. 2537, and SR third brake No. 1412. At this time there was no run-round so gravity shunting was employed; on being cleared the locomotive propelled the whole train up the incline to halt outside the signal box. The three SR coaches were uncoupled, the locomotive and GW coach ran back down the line into the platform, and under the control of a porter the three SR coaches ran down

In January 1927 the Lynton and Barnstaple line's 2-4-2T LYN returned from Eastleigh works after a heavy overhaul, repainted in Southern livery. The locomotive was lifted off its well wagon at the Barnstaple Town interchange siding by the Exmouth Junction steam crane under the supervision of Barnstaple Permanent Way Inspector Pring, in the bowler hat, and the Pilton Yard Foreman, Mr Bale, (right). The crane has been shunted into the interchange siding with several wagons, whilst the well wagon straddles the crossover. *Knights Photographers*

The rebuilding of Ilfracombe station in the late 1920s included the lengthening of the platform using standard Exmouth Junction concrete components, raising the level of the old platform, extension of the awning, and replacement of the gas lamps with electric light. All these features can be seen in this 1968 photograph. *A.E.West*

The work involved was spread over a number of years; the new turntable was installed in 1925, as we have seen,, but in February 1929 the *Southern Railway Magazine* reported, with an odd exactitude, that the station alterations at Ilfracombe were '16% complete'. A later edition reported that the new signal box and connections were brought into use on Sunday April 7th, although official records give 10th. Col. A.C. Trench made his inspection and reported on 25th May 1929:-

'...I made an inspection on the 9th May of the new works at the Ilfracombe terminal station of the Southern Railway.

To accommodate the increasing holiday traffic at this point the general layout of siding accommodation has been altered and enlarged, the platform has been lengthened and the roofing extended; the station buildings are also being reconditioned and improved, a work which is still in hand. A new signal box and new turntable have been provided and an engine shed is also to be

Macaw No. 84827 loaded with round timber, two Lightmoor loaded coal wagons Nos. 388, 393 and SR goods brake van No. 55063. Following normal practice the train ran into No. 2 platform so that the parcels and newspapers could be unloaded from the luggage van. When this had been completed another N, No.A826, was attached to the rear of the train and drew it forward on to the up line on the 1 in 36 gradient beyond Nos. 14 and 17 points, so that the released A827 could pass to the shed. However, at this crucial point in the proceedings, 7.45am, the pin of the draw bar on the Lightmoor wagon No. 393 broke, with the result that the seven rear vehicles ran back down the 1 in 36 towards the station. The driver of engine A827, which had been moving up along platform 2, observed the breakaway and managed to stop and reverse before the runaway vehicles collided with the tender. One wagon was derailed and all the vehicles slightly damaged, the wreckage being cleared by 12.40pm with some delays to other trains.

Those giving evidence to the enquiry included Driver Stone (A826), Shunter Bowerman and Signalman Arscott. Mr McBright at Exeter subsequently gave instructions that the previous practice be discontinued, and that the freight train be admitted to the goods yard where the engine could be released without resort to the train being placed on the 1 in 36 gradient of the up line.

EXPANSION AT ILFRACOMBE

More powerful locomotives meant that longer trains carrying more passengers were now arriving at Ilfracombe, both on Southern and Great Western services. The trains were often too long for the platforms, so passengers in the rear coaches of non-corridor trains had to alight on to the ballast using wooden steps. Not only was this inconvenient for passengers, but it was also time-consuming to the extent that the next arrival was sometimes delayed. More carriage sidings were also needed to accommodate the extra rolling stock.

Probably during 1924, excavations began at Ilfracombe for the new engine shed, though only the turntable was put in at first. The considerable volume of spoil was used to extend the carriage sidings. It was hard work for the men employed cutting through the rock using pick, shovel and wheelbarrow. *Lens of Sutton*

Another feature of the rebuilding was the provision of a large new store for passenger luggage, constructed in concrete blocks and with corrugated asbestos roofing - seen here in 1968. *A.E.West*

Barnstaple Long Bridge, decorated for 'The Oldest Borough' celebrations in the mid-1920s. A double headed up train comes off the viaduct and is about to pass Westcott's foot crossing. M7 0-4-4T No.250, still in South Western livery, pilots an N class 2-6-0; such double heading was not required to assist the train engine on this level section, but was employed to return locomotives to Barnstaple shed. *Lens of Sutton*

constructed. The site is a difficult one for expansion; the ground falls steeply from the station and yard for most of their perimeter and rises in rock cutting on the remaining portion; the approach line from Barnstaple is on a falling gradient of 1 in 36 as far as the outer end of the platform easing to 1 in 71, and 1 in 353 as it approaches the buffer stops; this road and other platform road are substantially unaltered.

The level of the old platform is being raised to the standard level of the new portion and the whole is to be paved with tarmac when settlement is complete. Electric light is to be installed and the waiting rooms, conveniences, etc. are being considerably improved.

The permanent way alterations in the case of the running lines consist of 95 lb.B.S. material. These works were barely

completed and special attention is being paid to the new track until the ground and ballast is properly settled and consolidated.

The new signal box contains a new frame of 50 levers, of which 15 are spare. The locking is correct. A track circuit is provided from 250 yards in rear of the down outer home up to the down inner home signal which when occupied locks the down block commutator. The use of this commutator also requires the arm and lever of the down outer home to be normal and the levers of the inner homes and adjoining directing signals to be normal.

Owing no doubt to the new conditions of the frame, connections and permanent way, several of the levers were somewhat heavy to pull, though none was seriously difficult. I was assured by the Company's officers that this point would receive special attention and adjustment until the

track of the new siding connections etc. had thoroughly settled.

Special loading and braking instructions are in force (copy attached) to safeguard the working of trains over the steep gradients approaching Ilfracombe. The alterations now under report do not in substance affect the gradient and terminal conditions which have existed here for many years. I was informed that for some years past the platform lengths had been inadequate for certain trains and it had been necessary to detrain passengers in the rear vehicles by means of steps on to the ballast; also that the increase of length of platforms was intended to avoid this and did not mean that the length or weight of trains would be increased beyond what has been in force for several years past.

In view of the approach gradient and the drop immediately in rear of the buffer stops special precautions are certainly necessary and should it be desired to work increased loads into Ilfracombe the provision of a sand drag or other special terminal equipment will be for consideration by the Company.

Subject to attention to the point noted above re point lever operation, and the completion of the alterations to the station buildings, the works are in good order and the arrangements are satisfactory; I recommend approval be given thereto.' The new locomotive shed was opened subsequently without inspection.

DECLINE IN THE 1930s
The depression of the thirties badly affected traffic on the Ilfracombe line. The number of tickets issued declined from 213,763 in 1928 to 112,751 in 1936, and those collected from 407,137 to 236,611. The Southern fought back with a variety of measures, including many special excursion trains with cheap fares, a number for the National Sunday League. Some excursions were run to Ilfracombe over the weekend by both the Southern and the Great Western, whilst others originating there went to Bude, Plymouth, Exmouth and Bournemouth.

A sad victim of both the Slump and road improvements (designed in part, incidentally, to boost employment) was the Lynton and Barnstaple line which closed on 30th September 1935, after a life of only 37 years. Paradoxically, this brought extra traffic to Barnstaple Town during the summer of 1935 when a number of people came for a last journey on the line. During 1935-37 considerable amounts of scrap material, particularly rails, was forwarded from the interchange siding, the largest item being the 2-6-2T LEW, destined for a Brazilian coffee plantation. Following closure the large awning at Barnstaple Town was cut back as far as the station building and the interchange siding taken out, the points being retained as a safety trap to protect the swing bridge.

The up siding at the Ilfracombe end of Mortehoe station was removed in February 1933, but this caused some delays on busy summer Saturdays. The 2.21pm from Ilfracombe was often held up at Mortehoe by the detachment of the

In July 1931 an N Mogul with a local train of LSW three coach non-corridor set and bogie van runs down the Slade valley past the Ilfracombe fixed distant signal. *Frank Box courtesy R.E.Tustin*

In 1935 Driver W.H.Roulstone of Ilfracombe, who was already a Justice of the Peace, became Chairman of the Urban District Council. Here we see him wearing his civic chain of office in front of his locomotive, N class 2-6-0 No.1407. *Donovan Box courtesy M.S.King*

banking engine of the previous 2.5pm train, for the Ilfracombe signalman was unable to send the next train until Mortehoe station was clear. On 26th May 1936 new catch points were provided on the up line 655 yards on the Ilfracombe side of Mortehoe signal box, replacing those 482 yards away. This enabled an up train of two engines and 10 bogies to be brought to a stand at the up home signal, clear of the catch points. Subsequently on summer Saturdays the 'Section Clear but Station Blocked' signal was authorised on the up line from Ilfracombe to Mortehoe boxes, facilitating a departure from the terminus before station work had been completed at Mortehoe.

A different mode of transport appeared in 1934 when the North Devon Airport was opened at Chivenor, adjacent to the line near Wrafton station. The airport comprised a large grass field, a club-house and a workshop, and the Lundy and At-

lantic Coast Airline operated services to Lundy Island, Cardiff, Plymouth and the Channel Islands. Wrafton station carried a notice advertising the Lundy Island service, but the tiny aeroplanes of the period could carry only a handful of passengers. The RAF also used it occasionally for training pilots in the late 1930s, but on the outbreak of war all this changed.

WORLD WAR TWO

Although World War One had a minimal effect on the line the 1939-45 conflict was very different, with both the army and air force heavily involved. The RAF immediately requisitioned Chivenor, recognising its strategic importance for maritime operations in the South Western Approaches. Many truckloads of construction materials including cement, steel, bricks, timber and sheeting were forwarded to Wrafton, a volume of goods traffic far beyond the capacity of the short single siding there. However the Southern was able to accommodate the reduced traffic to North Devon on a single track between first Umberleigh and Chapelton, and then Umberleigh and Barnstaple Junction, so wagons were stored here on the up line and worked on to Wrafton when there was room for them in the yard. The same line, incidentally, proved useful for the storage of a large and varied assortment of carriages used to bring back troops from the channel ports following the 1940 Dunkirk evacuation. Eventually, a second siding was built at Wrafton, which eased the problem, and RAF Chivenor became an operational base in October 1940. There was considerable traffic at Wrafton thereafter, in RAF stores

On 12th September 1932 N 2-6-0 No.1829 arrives at Barnstaple Town with the up Atlantic Coast Express, formed of Maunsell corridor coaches carrying ACE destination boards. *Frank Box courtesy R.E.Tustin*

In September 1936 the only surviving Lynton and Barnstaple line locomotive, 2-6-2T LEW, only eleven years old, was dispatched from the Barnstaple Town interchange siding with the assistance of the Exmouth Junction steam crane. Rails and other scrap metal from the dismantled line was the last' traffic' to leave the interchange siding. LEW had been employed by the contractor dismantling the line, was subsequently overhauled and sent to Brazil to work on a coffee plantation. Rumours still occasionally emerge as to its survival in one form or another. *Knights Photographers*

With the opening of the new engine shed (again, constructed in concrete blocks) by the early 1930s, the general rebuilding was complete. An unidentified N class 2-6-0 departs from Ilfracombe with a train of South Western non-corridor coaches, a 48ft eight compartment third followed by a four coach set. The new bracket inner home signals, new signal box and extended carriage sidings can now be seen. *Frank Box courtesy National Railway Museum*

driver, Stanley Perkins, was killed; the crossing keeper had opened the gates to the road, unaware of the approaching train.

As the war developed it was realised that the very features which had made the area a possible invasion target were very appropriate for training Allied troops for the D-Day landings in Normandy. During 1943 and early 1944 large numbers of American troops arrived and training camps were established. One day a young porter, Norman Matanle, was in charge at Braunton when no less than six long trains of American troops arrived from Glasgow, where they had dis-embarked after sailing the Atlantic. It was more like a summer Saturday in traffic terms. Some 25,000 American troops trained at the Assault Training Centre at Woolacombe, with the bay often full of landing craft.

Their arrival brought a lively social change to the area - one day Guard William Hatchley was in charge of an up train from Ilfracombe when he noticed American soldiers moving along the train - using the footboards outside the carriages. Fortunately there was no accident before military police apprehended them on arrival at Braunton. The last down train from Barnstaple was nicknamed 'The Boozer' for obvious reasons, and saw a number of incidents. In May and June of 1944 they left by train for the south coast ports, for embarkation to Normandy and the Utah and Omaha beaches. Many fell in the heavy fighting, and they are now commemorated by a granite and bronze memorial overlooking Woolacombe beach.

In December 1943 the Commanding Officer of the U.S. Army Training Centre near Braunton expressed concern at delays to military goods traffic, due to the limited size of the goods yard, and requested additional siding accommodation. A scheme was prepared for an extra siding outside the up line, with a facing connection to the up line, on the Barnstaple side of Braunton Gates. It was to hold 36 wagons, but a cart road beyond the railway boundary would also be needed. The cost was given as £6,661 and the works would take two months, but apparently the scheme was not proceeded with.

The main local railway casualty of the war was the Barnstaple East Loop of the Great Western, which had been open

as well as servicemen. No.252 Squadron was the first to be based at Chivenor, being replaced by No.272 Squadron in April 1941 using Beauforts and Blenheims for the protection of convoys in the Atlantic and English Channel. A number of other squadrons served here, and in 1943 the runways were again extended, enabling No.59 Squadron to fly its huge B-57s. A wide variety of aircraft carrying important personnel also used Chivenor. German aircraft attacked the base several times during 1941 but it is not recorded if the line was hit. Following Dunkirk mili-

tary planners identified the flat sandy beaches of the Taw-Torridge estuaries and the open sea at Saunton and Woolacombe as a potential landing area for an enemy seaborne invasion force. Part of the defences in 1940-42 comprised an armoured train, carrying a crew of 31 soldiers, hauled by an ex-GER 2-4-2T No.7077, based at Barnstaple Junction. It patrolled the coastal lines between Barnstaple, Bideford and Braunton and even made one trip to Ilfracombe. Sadly it was involved in an accident with a lorry on Duckpool Crossing when the lorry

since 1925 for the summer season only and was closed on 4th September 1939 with the points clipped out of use, until 1960. During this period all through services from Taunton to Barnstaple Junction or Ilfracombe again had to reverse at Victoria Road.

THE POST-WAR PERIOD

After 1945 both passenger and freight traffic built up quickly. The Southern Railway in its last days made two innovations on the line. The new Bulleid West Country class mixed traffic Pacifics were introduced on principal Exeter to Ilfracombe services. Initially the only Southern turntable west of Exeter that could take a Bulleid Pacific was that at Ilfracombe, until in 1947 larger ones were installed at Okehampton and Padstow; the 50 ft. turntables at Barnstaple Junction and elsewhere could take nothing bigger than an N, and at Plymouth the 4-6-2s reversed on a triangular junction. In addition a Pullman car train, the 'Devon Belle', was inaugurated, on 20th June 1947. The main portion, including the observation car, ran from Waterloo to Ilfracombe, the final leg from Exeter on the first run being hauled by West Country No.21C117 ILFRACOMBE.

During the Christmas period, 1946, new West Country No.21C117 was named ILFRACOMBE during a ceremony at the station, by the Chairman of the Urban District Council, Mr Carruthers Bell, seen here on the left of the footplate wearing his chain of office and the fireman's cap. The fireman, Mr Bill Muskett, is on the right. *Bill Muskett collection*

The N class took over all principal passenger services from the start of the summer 1925 timetable. Here we see No.A858 on a down train of South Western vehicles headed by a three coach non-corridor set passing under bridge No.6, near Heanton Court, on a down local service about 1930. *A.Halls courtesy R.J.Sellick*

Above. In 1958 N class 2-6-0 No.31840 shunts a rake of Bulleid coaches in Ilfracombe carriage sidings. *B.P.Hoper Collection*
Below. On Saturday 27th July 1963 2-6-0s Nos. 31856 and 6327 descend the 1 in 40 bank towards Heddon Mill with the 6.37pm train from Ilfracombe to Taunton. *Peter W. Gray*

CHAPTER SIX

THE BRITISH RAILWAYS ERA 1948-1975

NATIONALISATION 1948

Under the terms of the 1947 Transport Act the new British Railways came into existence on 1st January 1948, with high hopes for a new era. All the Southern lines west of Exeter became part of the Southern Region but this was not to last for long; in April 1950 they all were transferred to the Western Region but day to day operation remained in the hands of the Southern management at Exeter Central. In February 1958, with the exception of lines in the Plymouth area, they all returned to the Southern - until January 1963 when the Western Region gained complete control of all Southern lines west of Wilton. In 1964 the Western initiated the first of a number of major changes to all these lines.

Both the Southern Railway and the Great Western had their own considerable establishments at Barnstaple, and the new British Railways management soon set about rationalisation. Firstly, full load freight traffic was concentrated at Barnstaple Junction and sundries and general merchandise at Victoria Road, and in 1952 the GW engine shed was closed, its engines and men transferring to Barnstaple Junction. On 12th June 1960 Victoria Road station was closed to

passenger traffic, all Taunton trains then running direct to Barnstaple Junction via the reopened East Curve. It seems very strange that, from 1945-60 when passenger traffic was very heavy indeed, particularly on summer Saturdays, all through trains to Ilfracombe had been obliged to reverse at Victoria Road. The track and signal boxes were there, so the heavy summer holiday trains could have been run without this unnecessary delay.

POST-WAR RECOVERY

After the Depression of the 1930s, six years of war, and then rationing which lasted several years more, the British public was ready for some well-earned relaxation. This manifested itself in the family holiday of a week or two at the seaside; the line was to play a major part in this and passenger traffic reached its highest ever levels. Holidays were taken in hotels, boarding houses, holiday camps, chalets, residential caravans and camping sites, and the railway also made its own contribution with camping coaches. Holidays were usually taken on a Saturday to Saturday basis, and it was not just the better off; many more families than ever before were acquiring the 'holiday habit'.

Although convenient for those who provided the holiday accommodation, the concentration of travel on summer Saturdays brought problems to the railway; until the mid-1960s the Ilfracombe line dealt with as many as 10,000 passengers on a summer Saturday, far more than weekdays. Numerous full length express trains ran from Ilfracombe to Waterloo, with one notable train advertised as starting from Mortehoe and Woolacombe. Others ran from Ilfracombe over the Taunton route to Paddington, Manchester Exchange, Wolverhampton Low Level and Cardiff General. Despite the long single line sections from Barnstaple, and reversal at Victoria Road, the heavy traffic was handled expeditiously, which is more than can be said for Torbay and Cornwall on the Great Western, where long delays became endemic. Parcels traffic, particularly passenger luggage in advance, was heavy and freight reached very healthy levels.

Many readers will have happy memories of their seaside holidays in the area, with heavy trains of Southern green or British Railways maroon coaches hauled up Mortehoe bank by a West Country or 43XX, an N or M7 banking at the rear. The locomotive water supply at

Early in British Railways days, on 21st January 1949, West Country No.S21C109 LYME REGIS, still in Southern Railway livery, prepares to leave platform 1 at Ilfracombe with the 12.15pm train for Waterloo. *R.K.Blencowe collection*

On Saturday 25th July 1964, during the last summer season in the heyday of the station, there is a variety of rolling stock on view at Ilfracombe including two diesels new to the line. In platform 2 is a NBL Type 2 on an Exeter line train, in platform 1 is an ex-GWR 43XX class 2-6-0 on a Taunton line train, and a diesel multiple unit is berthed in the goods reception road. There is only one wagon visible in the goods yard, barely a month before the goods services were completely withdrawn. *Peter Swift*

Ilfracombe was augmented with the provision of a second tank at the engine shed.

RAILWAY REPORTS

Spectacular as all this traffic might be, British Railways could only move it by maintaining a large number of locomotives and carriages which earned their keep only for six or eight days of the year, which was proving to be uneconomic. Deregulation of transport in the 1950s brought more lorries on to the roads, and they began to erode freight traffic, particularly after the 1955 ASLEF strike.

More and more families could afford their own car, so railway passenger journeys made right through the year began to decline. The government appointed Dr Richard Beeching from ICI as the new Chairman of British Railways, and in March 1963 he published his recommendations in *The Reshaping of British Railways*, popularly known as the Beeching Report. This recommended the development of freight and fast passenger services on the main lines, concentrating on the profitable bulk flows of traffic, and the elimination of large numbers of un-

profitable stations and branch lines. A series of maps illustrated the situation, showing the minimal level of passenger and freight traffic at less than 5,000 passengers and 5,000 tons of freight per week, although these average figures were greatly exceeded by the summer passenger traffic. Passenger receipts at Wrafton were less than £5,000 per year, and at Braunton, Mortehoe and Woolacombe, and Ilfracombe between £5,000 and £25,000 a year. The picture at Barnstaple was unclear. However, as we saw in the traffic figures in Chapter One, many more tickets were collected at these stations than issued, so sales of return tickets to stations on the line were counted in receipts for other stations all over the country. In common with many other lines in the West Country the report proposed the complete withdrawal of all services.

Later in 1963, the *North Devon Railway Report*, written by David St John Thomas and sponsored by the Dartington Hall Trustees, was published. It accepted that receipts for passenger and goods traffic covered less than half the costs of the railway system in North Devon, with many stations and trains covering less than a fifth of their costs, and carried the results of an extensive traffic survey carried out on 7th May 1963. This showed the line to have some of the busiest stations in North Devon, with only the Exeter line having a greater number of passengers per train. The difficulty was that about 75% of the annual passenger traffic was carried in just three summer months. The Exeter to Ilfracombe passenger service earned £150,000 but cost £485,000 annually. Closure of the line would have a very serious effect on the economy of Ilfracombe, which was heavily dependent on the holiday trade, a quarter of all visitors arriving by train. The

One of the last steam trains to visit Ilfracombe was the 'Exmoor Ranger' organised by the RCTS and Plymouth Railway Circle on 27th March 1965. In platform 1 we see ex-GWR Collett goods 0-6-0 No.3205 with the four coach train, to be banked to Mortehoe by Ivatt 2-6-2Ts Nos.41206 and 41291, which had brought the train into the terminus. GWR 0-6-0s did work on the line, but not often. Note that the tracks in the goods yard, closed six months previously, have already been lifted. *Peter W.Gray*

On 28th May 1968 at Braunton the crossover on the Ilfracombe side of the station had been clipped and padlocked to enable the single track to connect to the down line, with a 15mph speed restriction. The building on the left of the track was the powerhouse of the Braunton Electric Light Power Company which pumped water from the river Caen to the adjacent water tower for locomotive and other non-drinking purposes. Again, some signalling was retained to protect the level crossing. *A.E.West*

On Saturday 31st August 1968 Warship D820 GRENVILLE departs from Braunton with the 7.30am Paignton to Ilfracombe train, passing a foot crossing and the signal protecting Georgeham Crossing. After running round at the terminus this formed an express from Ilfracombe to Paddington. *M.Squire*

run. Soon local footplatemen were being trained to drive diesel multiple units, North British Type 2 locomotives of the D6300 series and Hymek D7000s. The heavy summer trains of the 1964 season were shared between steam and diesel to Ilfracombe, but this was the last summer to see such heavy traffic.

On Sunday 5th September 1964 the last Atlantic Coast Express from Waterloo arrived at Ilfracombe. The next day the Western Region management brought in a completely new service, with dmus running between Exeter St Davids and Ilfracombe in connection with express trains from Paddington. A downgraded semi-fast service was provided from Waterloo to Exeter St Davids, but through journeys on to Ilfracombe were positively discouraged by very poor connections. The first Beeching recommendation to be implemented was the complete withdrawal of all goods services, on 7th September 1964, not just on the Ilfracombe line but on many of the former Southern lines west of Exeter. Full loads were now dealt with at Barnstaple Junction with the sundries and collection and delivery lorry service at Victoria Road. The main goods traffic to remain on the railway was military stores for RAF Chivenor, delivered by road from Barnstaple. Complete closure of the Barnstaple - Taunton line came on 1st October 1966, with the exception of the Barnstaple Junction to Victoria Road goods branch; this now made little difference to the Ilfracombe line, there having been no through summer Saturday Ilfracombe - Taunton services since 1965.

Although it was never spelled out publicly at the time, the policy of the government and the Western Region was to maintain a limited passenger service as economi-

report recommended that the train service be reduced to four or five diesel multiple unit trains daily, that the line to be singled with passing loops at Braunton and Mortehoe and Woolacombe, automatic lifting barriers to be installed at level crossings. Barnstaple Town should be reduced to a halt and Wrafton closed.

DIESELISATION AND DECLINE

It was not until June 1963 that the first diesel was seen on the Ilfracombe line, when a cross country unit made a trial

On 3rd October 1965 the last steam-hauled train ever to visit the line was the 'Exeter Flyer'. Double-headed from Exeter to Barnstaple Junction by BR Standard 2-6-4Ts Nos.80039 and 80043, the train split into two parts, which then visited Torrington and Ilfracombe. Here we see No.80039 at Ilfracombe's platform 2, the whole goods yard having already been lifted. *Lens of Sutton*

By 28th April 1970 Ilfracombe station had been reduced to its final simple form, with platform 2 and a run round loop in the middle of a site cleared ready for future re-development. *S.C.Nash*

Ilfracombe. Surprisingly, Barnstaple Town signal box was retained as a block post, but Pottington signal box was reduced to a ground frame, Wrafton and Braunton reduced to level crossing ground frames, Mortehoe and Woolacombe signal box closed, and at Ilfracombe the signal box closed, replaced by two new ground frames which controlled the points for the run round. The Barnstaple Junction 'B' to Barnstaple Town block section was operated by Western Region Electric Train Token, and Barnstaple Town to Ilfracombe worked under the 'One Engine in Steam' regulations using a red round wooden train staff, with attached Annetts key used to unlock the ground frames at Ilfracombe. Each level crossing retained distant and home signals in both directions. Control of Pottington Swing Bridge was now from Barnstaple Town signal box, although the bridge was swung only two or three times a year, for maintenance purposes. When this took place station staff at Braunton were instructed to hold an up train until the bridge was closed. Although the singling did save the cost of a number of signalmen, more crossing keepers were required, and it is questionable if the efforts of the signalling and civil engineers might have been better employed elsewhere than on a line destined to close within three years.

Station staff numbers were reduced gradually, starting in 1964 on the withdrawal of goods yards, some goods staff moving to similar employment at Barnstaple whilst others were made redundant. Next came signalling redundancies in 1967, and then on Monday 30th September 1968 the Western Region brought in a Conductor/Guard scheme on

cally as possible until buses and coaches could take over. The 1968 *West of England Divisional Plan* had a target of 'closure or operation under grant'. Sadly, the issue was settled by the legacy of the 1874 light railway construction - in only 14 miles there were 11 level crossings, all of which had to be manned. Only some of these were suitable for conversion to automatic operation. In comparison, the 39 miles between Exeter and Barnstaple had only four such crossings by 1980, two operated by signal box at Crediton and Eggesford, and two by automatic open crossings, at Salmon Pool and Umberleigh Gates.

SINGLING THE LINE 1967
Although the line was doomed, a number of economy measures were introduced, the most obvious being singling. This was effected from 17th December 1967, the official documentation giving a wealth of detail. The single line was formed from the existing up line from Pottington to Braunton, thence via the spiked and clipped crossover on the Ilfracombe side to the down line, and by a slew at Mortehoe to the up line, terminating at Ilfracombe No.2 platform. All points were taken out of use pending recovery, except those for a run round loop and siding at

On the last day, 3rd October 1970, a path was found for a special train, the 'Exmoor Belle', run by the Locomotive Club of Great Britain, Railway Correspondence and Travel Society and Plymouth Railway Circle. Here we see the special, a diesel multiple unit, descending the 1 in 36 down the Slade valley into Ilfracombe. *M.Squire*

Again on the last day, 3rd October 1970, we see a service train passing over the River Taw at Barnstaple at high tide. Commercial Road level crossing box can be seen to the left of this fine last view. *M.Squire*

the surviving passenger lines west of Exeter, to Okehampton and Ilfracombe. All booking offices were closed, with the sole exception of Barnstaple Junction, and passengers now purchased their tickets from the Guard. Parcels traffic was dispatched and received at Braunton and Ilfracombe, and received at Barnstaple Town; most remaining station staff were made redundant. George Facey was the station foreman at Ilfracombe until closure; it was a demoralising and difficult time, particularly on a summer Saturday when he had to turn away passengers from the only remaining through train to Paddington if they had not obtained their compulsory seat reservation in advance.

CLOSURE 1970
The Ministry of Transport announced the closure of the line on 31st December 1969. The figures given were revenue of £13,300 against expenses of £93,300. This figure comprised track and signalling £56,400, terminals £23,400 and movement £13,500. The first item covered the level crossings and signal boxes, but just how the unstaffed halts and run round loop at Ilfracombe cost £23,400 annually is difficult to see. However it is of interest to note that the revenue earned was covering movement costs. It was certainly a fact at this time that no railway closure went ahead without considerable dispute about the figures given by British Railways. The line closed on Monday 5th October 1970, the last train on Saturday 3rd being the 7.55pm departure, an eight car diesel multiple unit carrying about 500 passengers.

A PRESERVATION ATTEMPT 1971-74
Usually, complete closure of the railway was followed fairly quickly by track lifting and the sale of stations but not in this case. No doubt inspired by successful railway preservation schemes elsewhere, the North Devon Railway Preservation Society was formed by businessmen and enthusiasts in 1971 to preserve the whole line, and on 19th February 1973 the North Devon Railway Company was incorporated. On 31st December agreement was reached with British Railways for the purchase of the entire line and its equipment for £410,000, and on 20th July 1974, the line's centenary, the share issue was launched for a capital of £1,000,000 in 10p shares. At the same time there was an appeal to raise funds for the preservation of Standard Class 4 2-6-4T No.80136, then at Barry scrapyard. The acting chairman of the company died on 2nd December, and in February 1975 it was disclosed that the share issue had raised only about £20,000, and that many subscribers had not received their share certificates. There was a subsequent enquiry by officers of the Board of Trade but the company went into liquidation, the funds raised having been used to pay expenses. An unfortunate legacy of this unsuccessful venture was the disillusionment of local investors, who subsequently were less inclined to back other railway preservation schemes which were less ambitious and had a better chance of success.

British Railways had left all the track and equipment in situ whilst the company sought to raise its capital. On Wednesday 26th February 1975 a class 25 diesel carrying headcode 1Z01 hauled

an inspection coach carrying a party of engineers on a survey of the line and buildings. At every level crossing the train had to stop to allow the crew to open and shut the gates. At Ilfracombe the special was met by a party of enthusiasts, local press and television reporters, but this was to be the very last train.

THE END OF THE LINE
In October 1975 a firm of contractors from Scunthorpe moved on to the line to remove the track, using a tractor to haul lengths of lifted rail, which were then removed by lorry. By now the line had been in decline for a decade and many parts of it had been vandalised, so the remaining station areas and Barnstaple bridge were an eyesore, the latter until its removal in the summer of 1977. The site of Ilfracombe station was quickly sold and the company Pall Europe built a factory for the production of high grade medical filters. Braunton station site was redeveloped and Wrafton station sold for private occupation. After lying derelict for some years Mortehoe and Woolacombe was developed as a tourist attraction with two coaches on short lengths of track between the platforms. Barnstaple Town station building, including the awning, has been redeveloped as a restaurant with new buildings on the trackbed, whilst the signal box has been retained as a museum for the Lynton and Barnstaple Railway Preservation Society. A number of the level crossing keepers cottages have been adapted as private houses. Parts of the trackbed in the Barnstaple and Braunton areas have been converted to footpaths, whilst the rest has reverted to nature.

On 25th July 1931 N class 2-6-0 No.A857 arrives at Barnstaple Town with the down Atlantic Coast Express. The front coach is an 'Ironclad' corridor third, followed by Maunsell corridor coaches including the restaurant car, which ran right through from Waterloo to Ilfracombe daily. Departure from Waterloo was 10.40am with an Ilfracombe arrival at 3.57pm. There are no wagons at the interchange siding but a there are a number in the loop, probably destined for Rolles Quay. *Frank Box courtesy R.E.Tustin*

An N Mogul calls at Barnstaple Town in 1932 with a long train of six Southern and two Great Western bogies. There are several narrow gauge wagons visible in the interchange siding. The photograph is taken across the Taw from the site of Westcotts shipyard. *Frank Box courtesy R.E.Tustin*

CHAPTER SEVEN

TRAFFIC AND TRAIN SERVICES

A SURVEY OF PASSENGER TRAIN TRAFFIC

Ilfracombe was one of the Southern's best patronised lines in the west country, with two very well situated stations at Barnstaple Town and Braunton, popular holiday resorts and good local and long-distance services, particularly during the summer season. The line developed a healthy regular traffic with local people travelling daily to Barnstaple Town for jobs, school and college, for shopping (particularly on Fridays at the Pannier Market) and entertainment at the theatre, cinema, and Barnstaple Fair in September. For local passengers from other routes, including the Exeter line, Barnstaple Town was a far more convenient station than the Junction. For the Pannier Market a number of farmers' wives travelled here by train every week carrying baskets loaded with eggs, cheese, butter, rabbits, poultry, fruit and vegetables for sale to their many regular local customers.

The normal long-distance passenger traffic was augmented by servicemen reporting for duty at RAF Chivenor and was greatly increased by visitors to the resorts during the summer season. During its lifetime passengers and parcels for the Lynton line transferred across the platform at Barnstaple Town. The core of the long-distance services was provided by through coaches to Waterloo, expanded to through trains in the season, when Taunton services were extended to Paddington, the Midlands the North, and South Wales.

Table 1 shows the Southern Railway traffic returns for a typical year, 1930, showing all returns for the line with the exception of tickets issued by the Great Western's Ilfracombe Town Office. Of the total of 561,005 tickets issued and received twice as many were collected than issued,

TABLE 1 SOUTHERN RAILWAY STATISTICS 1930		
	Tickets Issued	Tickets Collected
Barnstaple Town	71,711	141,819
Wrafton	3,129	4,313
Braunton	45,096	59,224
Mortehoe	17,798	43,440
Ilfracombe	46,245	125,717
Ilfracombe Town Office	2,513	
Total	186,492	374,513
For comparison		
Barnstaple Jcn	52,743	103,289
Torrington line (4 stations)	109,037	170,857

for many passengers bought return tickets from their home station. With about 600 passengers using its single platform every day, Barnstaple Town was the busiest station west of Exeter, with the exception of the Plymouth area, but the numbers fell in 1935 with the closure of the Lynton line. Almost as many tickets were issued at Braunton as at Ilfracombe, many for local trips to Barnstaple. The large numbers of tickets collected at Mortehoe and Ilfracombe reflected the seasonal holiday traffic. Table 2 shows the results of the passenger traffic census carried out by the North Devon Railway Action Committee on Tuesday 7th May 1963, a fairly typical quiet day with no holiday or market traffic. Barnstaple Town came second to the Junction which had now inherited all the Taunton line traffic after the closure of Victoria Road to passengers but, as in 1930, the Ilfracombe line proved far busier than the Torrington line, with an average of 12.69 passengers between stops. But averages can be misleading; the Atlantic Coast Express carried more passengers to Ilfracombe than the preceding five trains put together. About this time on a peak summer Saturday some 10,000 passengers used the line, 5,470 arriving at Ilfracombe alone on 27th July 1957.

TABLE 2 NORTH DEVON RAILWAY CENSUS 7th May 1963 Passengers Joining and Leaving Trains (Child = 0.5) n.a - not available		
	Joining	Leaving
Barnstaple Town	144	127.5
Wrafton	n.a.	n.a.
Braunton	71	78
Mortehoe	41.5	42.5
Ilfracombe	89.5	93
Total	346	341
for comparison		
Barnstaple Jcn	330.5	287.5
Torrington line (4 stations)	140	115

Battle of Britain No.34072 257 SQUADRON awaits the road at Ilfracombe No.1 platform with the 10.0am Ilfracombe to Waterloo train on 15th September 1963. In the early 1990s this locomotive was restored and was at work on the Swanage Railway. *J.Scrace*

A six coach Southern train ascends the bank near *Hunters Inn* behind an N 2-6-0 piloted by an Adams Jubilee 0-4-2 No.632. The formation consists of Maunsell corridor coaches: brake compo, third, three compos and a dining car. The six coaches are well within the 180 tons limit for an N so the A12 is not, strictly speaking, required. *A.Halls courtesy R.J.Sellick*

Passenger train traffic also included luggage in advance, parcels, newspapers, mailbags, milk churns, hampers of rabbits, and the large variety of other items carried in the luggage compartments and vans. For many years the first down and last up trains carried the mails,

TABLE 3 PASSENGER TRAIN SERVICES		
Number of passenger trains arriving daily at Ilfracombe (Sundays excepted)		
August 1874	5	
Summer 1887	7	
Winter 1890	7	
Summer 1891	8	
Summer 1898	12	
October 1898	8	
Summer 1909	17	
Summer 1925	14	weekdays
	19	Saturdays
Summer 1932	16	weekdays
	24	Saturdays
Summer 1958	10	weekdays
	25	Saturdays
Summer 1964	11	weekdays
	18	Saturdays
Winter 1968-9	5	

making connections at Exeter with a number of long distance mail and Travelling Post Office services. In the early evening, Post Office staff brought their mailbags to the stations at Ilfracombe, Braunton and Barnstaple Town (where Lynton mailbags were transferred), and collected those arriving early in the morning. The first down train normally brought the newspapers both direct from London, leaving Waterloo about 1.15am, and from Plymouth which were transferred at Yeoford. This van carried *NEWSPAPER TRAFFIC WATERLOO ILFRACOMBE* roofboards.

The area had several horticultural businesses which forwarded mushrooms, flowers and other produce, particularly from Braunton where up to half a dozen vans were despatched all over the country. Each station booking office handled a large number of parcels of all descriptions for both local businesses and individual

customers. Passenger luggage in advance was very substantial during the season, extra staff coming in for the purpose. Other seasonal traffic at Ilfracombe also included scenery and costumes for visiting theatrical companies, and a circus which had its own train.

PASSENGER TRAIN SERVICES

Table 3 shows the number of passenger trains arriving daily at Ilfracombe from Barnstaple Junction or beyond during the lifetime of the line. Normal weekday services built up slowly from the original five, the opening of the Barnstaple Junction Railway having little immediate effect because Great Western through carriages were attached to existing South Western services. The doubling of 1889-91 brought only a moderate immediate increase, but by the opening of the Lynton line in 1898 there was an improved service, with the difference between winter and summer levels of service becoming apparent. The summer of 1909 saw a maximum weekday service of 17 arrivals. Sunday services on the line began with the June 1890 timetable, with one train each way. The

installation of the new 65ft turntable at Ilfracombe brought about several changes, with the summer 1925 timetable including through train working from Exeter, Ilfracombe becoming the main line from Barnstaple and Torrington the branch. Many through trains from the Great Western now normally ran separately, some worked by Southern and others by Great Western locomotives, although there were still some occasions when Great Western coaches were attached to Southern trains. For the next 40 years, with a wartime lull, the pattern of a basic weekday service, greatly augmented on summer Saturdays evolved, some of the extra trains being excursions with cheaper tickets. Efficient work by Ilfracombe station staff was essential to clear arriving trains of both passengers and luggage so that the coaching stock could be shunted away to clear the platform for the next arrival. By 1968-69 the service had shrunk to a minimal level.

Most passenger trains ran the full length of the line and called at all stations, but there were a few exceptions. Wrafton provided little passenger traffic and from the opening of the line several trains, usually the principal ones to and from Waterloo, passed it without stopping. The summer 1932 service included a Saturday 10.15am from Ilfracombe to Waterloo which called at Mortehoe, Braunton and then ran non-stop to Exeter St David's whilst the 10.30am had an unadvertised stop at Mortehoe and then ran non-stop to Barnstaple Town. The 11.35am ran non-stop from Mortehoe to Barnstaple Junction. The absence of the Barnstaple Town stop on two of these services was in contravention of the 1896 agreement with Barnstaple Corporation and of the 1898 Inspecting Officer's instructions. On summer Saturdays from 1949 to 1964 the up Atlantic Coast Express ran non-stop from Barnstaple Town to Yeoford, omitting the Barnstaple Junction stop. In 1874 trains were allowed between 53 and 55 minutes between Barnstaple Junction and Ilfracombe, which had been reduced to 36 - 44 minutes by 1913, and to 35 minutes mini-

West Country 4-6-2 No.34026, then unnamed but later YES TOR, prepares to leave Ilfracombe with an up train on 13th June 1952. The carriage sidings are unusually empty for a summer day. *R.E.Tustin*

mum in 1932. Time eased further in the 1950s, when trains were often heavier.

There were occasional 'short' workings such as in the summer 1914 timetable - a 2.30pm Ilfracombe to Mortehoe and 6.0pm return (by summer 1925 the return was at 5.10pm). The 'Boozer' service on weekend evenings towards the end of the Second World War ran from Barnstaple Junction to Braunton, Braunton to Barnstaple Town, Barnstaple Town to Braunton, and Braunton to Barnstaple Junction, the M7 running round its four coaches at each station. Between 1946 (it was 10.4am that year) and 1964 there was a summer Saturday 10.0am express from Mortehoe to Waterloo, worked up from Ilfracombe as empty stock. In the opposite direction the 8am summer Saturdays from Barnstaple Junction terminated at Morthoe, and then ran to the terminus as a van train, not requiring platform accommodation.

THROUGH SOUTHERN TRAIN SERVICES

During the Victorian period many railway timetables were published giving departure times from Ilfracombe and arrivals at Waterloo, but the requirement to change trains once or twice en route was not well publicised. Evidence of through trains or carriages comes from explicit statements in public timetables and *Bradshaw*, but until British Railways days even these were occasionally unreliable. The most reliable evidence comes from carriage working diagrams and from working timetables. Table 4 lists the known departures from each end of the line. No evidence has yet come to light of through services when the line opened in

A typical long distance train on the line for many years included through corridor coaches from both Waterloo and Paddington. In 1932 an N class Mogul coasts down the 1 in 36 bank under Cairn Top and over bridge No.32 with a Great Western toplight brake composite and three Southern Maunsell corridor coaches, two thirds and a brake composite. Some Great Western coaches also provided through services from the Midlands and North. *Frank Box courtesy National Railway Museum*

TABLE 5 (OTHER THROUGH) SOUTHERN PASSENGER TRAIN SERVICES		
	From Ilfracombe	To Ilfracombe
Summer 1889	Bradford(MR) via Templecombe,	from Bradford(MR) via Bath Bath, Templecombe
July 1922	10.5am to Brighton via Salisbury	from Brighton via Salisbury arr.7.48pm
Summer 1932	4.45pm to Eastleigh	Yeovil Town arr.10.50am
Summer 1958		Yeovil Town arr.10.58am
Saturdays		Yeovil Town arr.12.9pm
		Portsmouth arr.6.15pm

1874, but Waterloo Instructions of 1876 show through workings on the 9am and 10.45am departures, in each case a third, a composite and a van for Ilfracombe. Until 1925 the Ilfracombe Branch working timetable was self-contained, but it subsequently became incorporated in the North Devon Line timetable which gave arrivals and departures at both Exeter and Waterloo. As can be seen from the table the core of the service this century were Waterloo departures on or about 1am, 9am, 11am, 1pm and 3pm, with five Ilfracombe departures spread over the morning and early afternoon, at about 8.10am, 10.30am, 12.20pm, 2.20pm and 3pm. For much of the year two or three through carriages sufficed for each departure but during the summer

season in South Western days there were a couple of North Devon and Ilfracombe expresses. The whole train ran between Waterloo and Barnstaple where the Ilfracombe coaches were detached, the dining car running right through to Torrington. Stops were usually made at principal stations but in the summer of 1905, when competition with the Great Western was at its height, the 10.40am express from Waterloo ran without a booked stop from Sidmouth Junction to Barnstaple Junction. By the summer of 1909 the 11.10am North Devon and Ilfracombe Express from Waterloo called only at Salisbury, Exeter Queen Street, and Exeter St David's before Barnstaple Junction, although the 12.0 noon express made extra stops at Axminster, Seaton Junction and Sidmouth Junction. The fastest journey times from Waterloo to Ilfracombe were 6hr 32min in 1887, 5hr 12min in 1905 and in 1932, 5hr 2min in 1958, and 4hr 51min in summer 1964.

As business built up there were more through services and at peak periods whole trains ran either to North Devon, or exclusively to Ilfracombe. The summer Saturday timetable for 1932 shows nine through services in each direction, several with dining cars right through. In 1958 there were eleven down and nine up. For the Southern (Western Section) the Ilfracombe line became one

TABLE 4 THROUGH PASSENGER TRAIN SERVICES TO WATERLOO		
	Waterloo dep.	Ilfracombe dep.
1878	9.0, 10.45am	n.a.
July 1891	9.5, 11.0am	10.25am, 3.25pm
Summer 1905	10.40, 11.10am 1.0, 3.30pm	8.20, 10.15am 12noon, 1.38pm
Summer 1913	9.0, 11.10am 12.50, 3.30pm	9.40, 10.45, 11.45am 1.37pm
July 1922	9.0, 11.0am 1.0, 3.0pm	8.0, 10.5am 12.5, 3.0pm
Summer 1925	12.15SO, 8.50,10.40 11.0am,1.0,3.0pm	10.25, 10.45am, 12.23 1.35,3.50pm
Winter 1925-6	8.45, 11.0am, 1.0, 3.0pm	8.25, 10.22am, 12.15, 1.35, 2.50pm
Summer 1932	12.30SO,8.40,8.44SO 10.35, 11.45amSO 12noonFO, 2.0SO, 3.0, 3.15pmSO	8.15, 10.15SO,10.30, 11.0SO,11.35amSO 12.20NS, 1.0SO, 2.5FSO 2.20, 2.56pm
Winter 1938-9	9.0, 11.0am, 1.0 3.0pm	8.15, 10.30am, 12.20, 2.8, 3.10pm
Summer 1939 (Weekdays)	1.30, 10.35am, 1.0, 3.0, 6.0pm FO	8.15, 10.30am, 12.30, 2.10, 3.10pm
Summer 1939 (Saturdays)	1.30, 8.45, 10.24, 10.35am, 1.0, 2.0, 3.0pm	8.15, 9.0, 10.10, 10.30, 11.35am, 12.45, 2.5, 2.25, 3.0pm
Summer 1958 (Weekdays)	1.15, 9.0, 11.0, 11.5am, 1.0, 3.0pm	8.10, 9.0am,12.20, 2.20, 3.0pm
Summer 1958 (Saturdays)	7.38, 8.22, 8.35 8.57, 10.15, 11.0am 12.5, 1.0, 3.0pm	8.10, 8.50, 10.0, 10.30, 11.30am, 12noon, 1.45, 2.10, 2.55pm
Summer 1964 (Weekdays)	1.15, 11.0am	8.20,10.30am
Summer 1964 (Saturdays)	12.45, 8.35, 10.15 11.0, 11.45am, 1.0, 3.0pm	8.10, 10.0(Mortehoe), 10.30am, 12 noon, 2.10, 2.55pm

An N class 2-6-0 enters Barnstaple Town on 3rd July 1934 with the up Atlantic Coast Express, the 10.30am from Ilfracombe due at Waterloo at 4.14pm. This year there was no weekday restaurant car from Ilfracombe, it ran only on Saturdays. Up to 1935 Atlantic Coast Express passengers had connections across the platform here for the Lynton line. There are several standard gauge wagons in the interchange siding. *Frank Box courtesy R.E.Tustin*

No.34070 MANSTON departs from Mortehoe on 9th September 1963 with the up Atlantic Coast Express, the 10.30am from Ilfracombe to Waterloo. The first coach is a Maunsell open third (by then second), for Exeter, and the other three are Bulleids, for Waterloo. *J.Scrace*

On 29th July 1951 Battle of Britain No.34059 SIR ARCHIBALD SINCLAIR departs from Mortehoe with the down Devon Belle, the 12 noon from Waterloo due at Ilfracombe 5.27pm. *R.J.Sellick*

of its most important summer holiday destinations, second only to the Bournemouth and Portsmouth lines. The 1.10am service from Waterloo was provided by attaching a carriage to the overnight newspaper train and featured in local advertisements for a cheap day out in London, passengers travelling up the previous day. But the summer of 1964 saw the end of through Waterloo trains, with two weekday services in each direction, together with six up and seven down on Saturdays. Not every service followed the patterns described so far: the Great Western will be covered later, but Table 5 details some services from Ilfracombe which originated or terminated elsewhere. During the pre-grouping period the Midland Railway sought to extend its services to the south west via Bath, the Somerset and Dorset line and Templecombe, where through coaches were attached to South Western trains to complete their journeys. The July 1922 through service to Brighton was a carriage attached to the 10.5am Waterloo train as far as Salisbury, where it was transferred to a Cardiff to Brighton train. This subsequently also acquired a through portion from Bournemouth, arriving in Brighton at 5.42pm. In the return direction the service left Brighton at 11.20am, arriving at Ilfracombe at 7.48pm in similar fashion. The up service was attached to the Atlantic Coast Express for several years, until its withdrawal in 1930.

For some years the train arriving at Ilfracombe at about 10.50am was a through service from Yeovil Town, as, in the 1950s, was the one about 12 noon. On summer Saturdays between 1950 and 1963 there was a through train from Portsmouth; in 1958 for example, it left at 12.15pm to arrive at Ilfracombe at 6.15pm, although there was no corresponding up working. The train was notable in that it brought a Nine Elms Pacific to the line. In summer 1925 there were 1.59pm and 7.56pm arrivals from Salisbury and a 4.35pm departure for Eastleigh. The first, about 2pm, was running in the late 1940s, but in 1932 it had started from Exeter. In summer 1932 the 4.45pm departure ran through to Eastleigh and eventually reached Waterloo.

There were a couple of services which terminated along the North Devon line. In the late 1940s and from 1957 to 1964 the first up service from Ilfracombe at 6.50am worked as far as Kings Nympton, from where it returned to Barnstaple Junction as a commuter train. In the summer of 1964 the 4.50pm from Ilfracombe ran as far as Yeoford, returning at 7.14pm to arrive back at 8.53pm, making connections with Plymouth trains in both directions at Yeoford.

THE ATLANTIC COAST EXPRESS

As long ago as 1876 the 10.45am train from Waterloo conveyed through carriages to Devonport, Ilfracombe and Torrington. Later this departed at 11.0am and by early this century Plymouth, Bude, Padstow, Exmouth and Sidmouth were added. During the summer it was expanded to two or three trains. In 1913 the

Near *Hunters Inn* (Heddon Mill up distant in far background) and two Southern M7 class 0-4-4Ts haul a six coach rake of modern Great Western coaches up the bank. No.378 is the train engine. The working is just over the limit for a single M7, which was 44 wheels, or 140 tons. *A.Halls courtesy R.J.Sellick*

11.10am from Waterloo comprised four corridor coaches, including dining car, for Torrington and five for Ilfracombe, calling at Salisbury and Exeter Queen Street (where locos were changed), Exeter St David's, and Barnstaple Junction, where the branch engine was attached to the Ilfracombe coaches. These arrived at the terminus at 4.10pm. The up train left Ilfracombe at 9.40am and arrived at Waterloo at 3.0pm. This long established service continued into the Southern Railway period, when a new policy of naming both locomotives and principal trains was brought in.

The Southern's manager, Sir Herbert Walker, held a competition in

ployed east of Exeter, and N 2-6-0s thence to Ilfracombe. The up working left Ilfracombe at 10.22am, with restaurant car and the through coach to Brighton, and arrived at Waterloo at 3.39pm. In each direction calls were made at Salisbury, Exeter Queen Street, Exeter St David's, Portsmouth Arms (on request) and all stations from Barnstaple Junction to Ilfracombe, with a Yeoford stop in the up direction only.

The pattern of Atlantic Coast Express services became, essentially, one train in the winter season, two in the summer, and up to six at peak periods, not all to Ilfracombe. The Southern encouraged seat reservations, enabling it to run suf-

Atlantic Coast Express stopped between Exeter and Barnstaple at Eggesford in both directions, and Yeoford in the up. In the post-war years the Atlantic Coast Express from Ilfracombe settled down to one train each way Mondays to Saturdays. On summer Saturdays this was independent of the Torrington train. Accelerations on the main line brought the arrival time of the down service to 3.55pm at Ilfracombe in the early 1960s, and then 3.51pm in the last two years until the train ceased to run on 5th September 1964, the four minute improvement coming from an acceleration between Braunton and Mortehoe.

THE DEVON BELLE

The Southern Railway had but a few months left when, on 20th June 1947, it introduced the Devon Belle for the summer season. At this time the Southern was experiencing a shortage of coaching stock, and the Pullman company had a number of coaches in storage, two of which were converted to observation cars. Running over the weekend, on Fridays, Saturdays, Sundays and Mondays only, the down service left Waterloo at 12 noon, with booked stops at Sidmouth Junction, Exeter Central (where a Plymouth portion was detached), Exeter St David's, Barnstaple Junction, Barnstaple Town, Braunton, Mortehoe, to arrive at Ilfracombe at 5.32pm. An unadvertised stop was made at Wilton where the Merchant Navy locomotives were changed, whilst the light Pacific from Exeter required a banker up to Mortehoe with its heavy load of eight, later increased to ten, Pullmans, including the observation car, which was turned on the Ilfracombe 'table. The up service also departed from Ilfracombe at 12 noon, arriving at Waterloo at 5.20pm. The normal single fare from Waterloo to Ilfracombe was £2 18s 11d first class and £1 15s 4d third, which attracted a Pullman supplement of 8s 4d first class and 4s 6d third. The 1947 season service continued until 27th October. An important feature was the facility to reserve a seat and avoid the overcrowding which was common at the time on other services. But seat reservations were re-introduced in 1948 for weekday services and in 1949 for weekends, which reduced the attraction of the Devon Belle. The 1948 season ran from 14th May to 26th October with the addition of a down train on Thursdays and an up train on Tuesdays; Wednesday became the only day of the week without a Devon Belle. The 1949, 1950 and 1951 seasons were similar, but due to limited patronage the Plymouth portion was withdrawn for 1950 and for subsequent seasons. In March 1952 the Exeter *Express and Echo* carried an obituary mourning the demise of the Devon Belle due to lack of patronage, but this proved premature. The Devon Belle continued to run during the summer of 1952 but was cut back to a down train on Fridays, both ways Saturdays and Sundays and up on Mondays. The same pattern operated during the summers of 1953 and 1954, except that in 1954 the down Friday train departed Waterloo at

TABLE 6 (THROUGH PADDINGTON) PASSENGER TRAIN SERVICES		
	from Paddington	from Ilfracombe
July 1891	9.10am	10.25am
Summer 1905	10.51, 11.35am, 3.3pm	8.0am, 12.17, 3.5pm
Summer 1925	9.0am, 12.5, 3.30pm	9.55am,12noon,2.50pm
Summer 1932	12.20SO, 9.0am, 12FO	9.55, 10.40FSO, 11.50am
	12.5pmSO, 3.30	2.55, 3.40pm
Summer 1937	12.20SO,9.35SO,	9.50SX, 11.0amSO,
	10.0SX 12.5FSO,2.15	12noon
	2.15SO, 3.30pm	
Summer 1957SO	11.30am	12.25pm
Summer 1965SO	arr.1.16, 3.20,4.40pm	8.15,10.45am,2.45
Summer 1970SO	8.10am	1.55pm
1970	Paddington services ran via Exeter St David's	

1925, inviting employees to suggest a name for the train. The winner was Guard Frank Rowland of Waterloo, with the *Atlantic Coast Express*. Subsequently Guard Rowland moved to Torrington, where he became a Town Councillor, but sadly died in 1932 as a result of injuries received in a shunting accident at Marland Clay Works. The first two trains to carry the title ran on 19th July 1926. The main portion (the train also conveyed through coaches for Plymouth and Torrington) of the 11.0am from Waterloo, including the restaurant car, arrived at Ilfracombe at 4.24pm. King Arthur 4-6-0s were em-

ficient reliefs, all under the Atlantic Coast Express description. For a time the Wrafton stop was omitted, mandatory Portsmouth Arms and Umberleigh stops introduced, and the Brighton coach withdrawn. Departure times from Ilfracombe varied, but settled down to 10.30am in the 1930s. For much of the year a single N 2-6-0 sufficed, but with heavy peak period trains a second and sometimes even third locomotive was required over Mortehoe bank. The title was dropped during the war, but unofficially reappeared in 1946, sometimes on the wrong train, and officially in 1947. In the 1950s the

Barnstaple bus station during the Southern Railway period, with a nostalgic collection of road vehicles. Just behind the buses can be seen Commercial Road level crossing box, built on the site of the 1874 Barnstaple Quay signal box, the view made possible by the demolition of the 1874 Barnstaple Quay station. The down outer home signal is mounted on a tall lattice post, later replaced by a short rail-built post. Bus services radiating from here served many rural communities, providing the onward services connecting with the trains. *Medeva Gallery*

4.40pm, made extra stops at Salisbury (where the engine took water to work right through to Exeter) and Axminster, arriving at Ilfracombe at 9.48pm. This was the pattern until its last journeys, down on Saturday 18th September 1954 and up the next day.

Conceived as a short term solution to a post-war stock shortage, the Devon Belle ran for but eight summer seasons; not only was it expensive to operate with its poor utilisation of vehicles and staff, but was often poorly patronised. In contrast the Bournemouth Belle ran daily between Waterloo and Bournemouth, one Pullman set providing both down and up services from 1946 to 1967. One more Pullman train did in fact visit Ilfracombe, on 19th October 1963, hauled from Paddington to Taunton by FLYING SCOTSMAN, to Ilfracombe by 2-6-0s Nos.7317 and 7332 and returning via Exeter Central where the LNER Pacific relieved the 2-6-0s. On summer Saturdays from 1955 a 12 noon (later 12.5pm and 11.45am) from Waterloo and 12 noon from Ilfracombe ran to similar timings to the Devon Belle.

GREAT WESTERN SERVICES
As we have seen, the Devon and Somerset Railway and its successor the Great Western, operated a coach service from its Ilfracombe office to its Barnstaple station from 1874, in competition with South Western trains. This lasted until June 1887 when the Barnstaple Junction Railway opened and its through service reached Ilfracombe. On arrival of Great Western trains from Taunton at Barnstaple Victoria Road, the through carriages were detached and taken to Barnstaple Junction, where they were attached to the rear of South Western trains to Ilfracombe. A similar procedure was followed in the up direction. Initially, the Great Western restricted these carriages to passengers for the Ilfracombe branch only. Apparently the first Great Western through service between London and Ilfracombe ran from 1 July 1889. In March 1891 three trains daily each way were advertised with through coaches between Ilfracombe and Taunton, and in July there were five such services, one of which conveyed through carriages each way between Ilfracombe and Paddington. These basic arrangements continued until 1925, with principal Ilfracombe trains carrying through coaches for both Waterloo and Paddington. Table 6 gives some details of the through services to Paddington. The Great Western's London service suffered several handicaps in the Victo-

rian era which made it inferior to its rival, the LSWR. The GW route to Ilfracombe ran via Bristol, and although practically the same length as the LSW, incorporated a slow single-track country branch line between Taunton and Barnstaple. At Barnstaple through carriages had to be worked back out of the terminus across to the Junction, where there was often a delay before the departure of the next South Western service to Ilfracombe, often one which had departed later from London. The first decade of this century saw a number of improvements, including the opening on 1st July 1905 of the Barnstaple East Curve, enabling through running between Taunton and Barnstaple Junction, by-passing the Victoria Road terminus. That summer there were three through services each way between Paddington and Ilfracombe. On 2nd July 1906 the Castle Cary main line to the south west opened, the two measures together reducing the journey by some 22¾ miles. Increasing traffic in the summer season enabled the Great Western to run through expresses which split at Taunton into Minehead and Ilfracombe sections. The Torbay Express slipped a four coach portion for Ilfracombe, including a dining car. However, by the summer of 1913 the Barnstaple East Curve was seeing only modest use; it was not opened until July that year, for only six down (but no up) trains. All other services reversed at Victoria Road. The Barnstaple East Curve was closed every year outside the summer season. However, as shown in Table 7, the through Great Western services were not restricted to Paddington, or for that matter to its own system. For the 1912 summer season the Great Western ran a through coach which left Manchester London Road at 8.20am and travelled via Sheffield Victoria, Nottingham Victoria, Loughborough, Banbury, Swindon and Bristol to arrive at Ilfracombe at 6.51pm, the return service leaving Ilfracombe at 12.17pm to arrive at Manchester at 10.22pm.

Moving on to July 1922 the 9.30am departure from Ilfracombe appears to

Excursion traffic was encouraged to and from Ilfracombe, particularly by the Southern Railway, to combat the decline in all traffic during the Slump of the 1930s. N class 2-6-0 No.1406 is about to depart from platform 1 with a Southern Railway Sightseeing Excursion. *Donavan Box courtesy M.S.King*

	TABLE 7 (OTHER THROUGH GREAT WESTERN)	
	PASSENGER TRAIN SERVICES	
	from Ilfracombe	**to Ilfracombe (arrival times)**
July 1922	9.30am to Manchester	
August 1925		5.50pm from W'hampton
Summer 1932	2.55pm to Birmingham	7.40am from North
FO or SO	8.25pm to Manchester	8.35am from Midlands,LNER
	10.40pm to Midlands	5.23pm from W'hampton
Summer 1957 SO	8.25am to Manchester	6.35pm from W'hampton
	9.25am to Cardiff	
	10.55am to W'hampton	
Summer 1965 SO	10.20am to Cardiff	3.38pm from W'hampton
	11.10am to W'hampton	4.20 Carmarthen

TABLE 8
SOUTHERN SUNDAY EXCURSIONS   SUMMER 1932

Timing No.

297	10.0am to Bournemouth via Templecombe and SDJR.Return12.28 (17th July, 14th August, 11th September only)
307	10.0 from Salisbury. Arr.2.20pm. Dep.7.20pm (31st July, 28th August, 25th September only)
309	10.42 from Exmouth. Arr.1.17pm, Dep 8.15pm (24th July, 21st August, 18th September only)
310	10.0 from Plymouth via Yeoford (rev). Arr.1.36pm, Dep.7.20pm (17th July, 14th August, 11th September only)
313	10.0 to Plymouth via Yeoford (rev). Return 11.5pm (24th July, 21st August, 18th September only)
314	10.0 to Bude via Torrington, and Bristol. Return 11.12pm (31st July, 28th August, 25th September only)
315	10.0 to Paignton and Exeter. Return 10.30pm (7th August, 4th September only)
318	10.0 from Bude via Torrington. Arr.1.36pm, Dep. 7.30pm (7th August, 4th September only)
320	11.0 from Torrington. Arr. 12.20pm, Dep.9.10pm (31st July, 28th August, 25th September only)

EXCURSION TRAINS

During the 1920s and 1930s all the railway companies sought to protect their revenues in difficult times by running cheap excursion trains, which were well patronised. Table 8 gives details of the variety of excursion trains using the line in the summer of 1932. Both the Southern and Great Western ran long distance excursions leaving on Friday nights and arriving Saturday mornings. Sunday excursions, including those in conjunction with the National Sunday League, were for the day only. There was a wide variety of origins and destinations, with each service typically operating two or three Sundays over the summer. Trains came from Salisbury, Exmouth, Plymouth, Bude and Torrington, with excursions from Ilfracombe to Bournemouth, Plymouth, Bude, Bristol, Paignton and Exeter, leaving at 10am. There were a number of interesting features to such workings. The Bournemouth excursion travelled up the main line to Templecombe where, after reversal, it travelled down the Somerset and Dorset. Excursions to and from Plymouth travelled to Yeoford where they reversed, but in the absence of a turntable there a long length of tender first running was required. The Bude excursions involved reversal at Barnstaple Junction and Halwill Junction. The Torrington to Halwill Junction line was specially opened for the purpose, for light engine movements to position the E1R locomotive working the line were necessary. Whether the revenue earned justified this expense is debatable.

THE FINAL YEARS

From 7th September 1964 the new Western Region timetable was introduced, a service of diesel multiple units together with a few locomotive hauled trains. The January-June 1965 timetable included ten down trains, originating from Barnstaple, Exeter Central (4), Exmouth, Salisbury, Sidmouth, Honiton, and Exeter

have been a 'Great Western only' train which split on arrival at Taunton at 12.35pm. Some coaches went forward at 12.43pm as part of the 'Ilfracombe, Minehead, Bristol and Bath Tea Car Express' to Paddington, arriving at 4.5pm. Other through coaches departed at 1.6pm on the Plymouth to Liverpool 'Luncheon and Tea Car Express', travelling via the Severn Tunnel, Hereford, Shrewsbury and Crewe, where they were detached to arrive at Manchester London Road at 7.30pm. Another Paddington service left Ilfracombe at 11.45am, and there were two down services, but there was no advertised through coach from Manchester.

The installation of the 65ft turntable at Ilfracombe in time for the summer 1925 timetable not only enabled the Southern to introduce its N class 2-6-0s but it also facilitated more through working of Great Western locomotives, several trains being booked for working by GWR engine and guard, particularly at weekends, although other Great Western trains were still worked by the Southern. Great Western trains now ran independently and this speeded up the service between Taunton and Ilfracombe. The pattern was similar in summer 1932, except that there were a couple of times when Great Western through coaches for Ilfracombe were again attached to Southern trains at Barnstaple Junction. The Barnstaple East Loop was now used more extensively, with as many as nine down passenger trains and three up, although it was closed out of season. Through services were operating between Ilfracombe, Paddington, Wolverhampton, the Midlands and the North via the Severn Tunnel. Often through trains for Ilfracombe included several coaches, particularly dining cars, which were destined for Victoria Road; trains using the East Curve detached these at Barnstaple South Junction and they were worked into the terminus by a shunting engine, with a corresponding manoeuvre at Barnstaple East Junction in the up direction.

Summer Saturdays in 1939 saw a very full service including 9.35am, 12.6pm and 2.15pm Paddington to Ilfracombe and Minehead expresses, an 8.10am Birming-

ham to Paignton and Ilfracombe, a 10.40am Wolverhampton to Ilfracombe and Minehead, both travelling via Stratford-upon-Avon and Cheltenham Malvern Road, an 9.15am Ilfracombe to Bristol, and a 9.50am Ilfracombe to Manchester via the LMS. Other GWR trains ran between Taunton and Ilfracombe. The outbreak of war curtailed these services and Taunton trains ventured no farther than Barnstaple Junction after reversal at Victoria Road, the East Curve being shut for the duration.

Through weekday services between Ilfracombe and Taunton ceased completely after 1939 but after the hostilities summer Saturday long distance services built up again. In 1951 there were services to Cardiff and Birmingham Snow Hill and by the late 1950s to Paddington, Wolverhampton Low Level, Manchester Exchange and Cardiff. These then declined until their last summer, 1965, when there were just the Wolverhampton and Cardiff trains left (the latter originating at Carmarthen).

On 31st August 1968 Warship No.818 GLORY rounds the curve into Barnstaple Junction with a four coach Ilfracombe to Paddington service, which will be combined with another train at Exeter St David's. There is a good view of the Devon Concrete works and the new buildings of Barnstaple in the background.

TABLE 9 SOUTHERN RAILWAY FREIGHT TRAFFIC STATISTICS 1930			
	Loaded wagons forwarded	Loaded wagons received	Total loaded wagons
Barnstaple Town	-	-	-
Wrafton	53	642	695
Braunton	317	2157	2474
Mortehoe	112	795	907
Ilfracombe	2226	4429	6655
Total	2708	8023	10731
for comparison			
Barnstaple Junction			23684
Torrington line (4 stations)			28348

St David's, with nine up trains for Exeter Central (5), Kingswear, Honiton, Barnstaple and Exmouth. Connections were made with expresses to Paddington, the Midlands and the North at Exeter St David's but they were not always good, and passengers were discouraged from using the Waterloo route. From 24th May there was also an 11am from Ilfracombe to Paddington which ran seven days a week and combined with an up Falmouth train at Exeter St David's. A corresponding down train left Paddington at 11.30am and arrived at 4pm - the fastest ever London service. Until 23rd May the three Sunday services were provided by bus from Barnstaple, but after this there were five down and four up services, including the Paddington service.

The 1965 summer Saturday timetable showed 17 down trains including six on the Devon and Somerset route, three from Paddington and one each from Taunton, Wolverhampton and Carmarthen, and 18 up including the return workings plus two more for Taunton. The 11.05am from Paddington and 10.45am return both ran along the Great Western route to Castle Cary, then via Yeovil Pen Mill to pick up the South Western route. But this was the last season that through services for Ilfracombe used the Devon and Somerset route. During the last five summer seasons the few remaining Paddington trains ran via Exeter St David's. The summer 1966 service of 9 down and 8 up trains was reduced to 5 each way from the introduction of the new timetable on 2nd October 1966, with no departures from Ilfracombe between 11.30am and 3.18pm. This minimal service, operated by only one train on the line at any time, led to the singling of the route from 17th December 1967. In the summer of 1968 the service was five trains each way daily to Exeter St David's, augmented by two Paddington expresses on Saturdays. The pattern was similar in 1969 and 1970 except that there was just one Paddington express - in 1970 this was the 8.10am from Paddington, arriving at Ilfracombe at 1.10pm and returning at 1.55pm. Compulsory seat reservations were required to board the Paddington expresses at Ilfracombe and there were often far more passengers than available seats, which created great difficulties for the few remaining station staff.

CONNECTING BUS SERVICES
With the exception of Wrafton every station on the line boasted one or more bus services to get passengers to their final destinations. Barnstaple Town was situated close to the town bus station from where a number of services ran to the suburbs and to outlying villages, too many to mention here. From Braunton station a bus service ran to Saunton Sands, Croyde and Georgeham. From Mortehoe station buses ran to Woolacombe, and from Ilfracombe station they ran to the town, Combe Martin and Lynton. In Victorian days horse-drawn coaches were employed, followed by motor buses for most of this century. The Southern National Omnibus Company was established for these services by the Southern Railway.

NEWSPAPER AND MAIL TRAFFIC
The overnight trains bringing newspapers and mail in time for morning doorstep delivery were distinctive features of the service to Ilfracombe. Back in South Western days there was a goods and mail train which left Exeter Queen Street at or about 2.35am for Torrington, connecting with a mail and goods from Barnstaple Junction which arrived at Ilfracombe around 7.05am. By 1932 it left Exeter for Torrington at 2.10am, but there was also a portion of the 1.30am newspaper train from Waterloo, which reached Ilfracombe at 7.35am. This was also advertised as a passenger service from Salisbury, but from Barnstaple Junction was described as a mixed train.

Both these services were still running in the mid-1950s. The 1.15am from Waterloo (1.10am in public timetables) included two passenger coaches for Ilfracombe. It went forward from Exeter Central at 5.6am and ran non-stop to Barnstaple Junction, arriving at Ilfracombe at 6.50am. There was also a News Van B which was attached to the 5.21am passenger from Exeter Central to Ilfracombe, arriving at 7.41am. This van carried not only the London newspapers but also the Plymouth paper, the *Western Morning News*, which was loaded at Yeoford off the 1.25am from Plymouth Friary.

The 2.6am Mail and Freight from Exeter Central made a lengthy call at Exeter St David's to collect mail from the Paddington to Penzance Postal train, and detached another Van B at Barnstaple Junction to be attached to the 5.21am from Exeter Central, which thus arrived at Ilfracombe at 7.41am conveying both the newspapers and mail. The News Van B returned to Waterloo on the 3.0pm passenger from Ilfracombe, while the mail Van B went on the 7.42pm which was allowed 11 minutes at Exeter St David's to unload mail for the Penzance to Paddington Postal.

A SURVEY OF FREIGHT TRAFFIC
During this century Ilfracombe became more important than the Torrington line for passenger traffic, it was always less important for freight. Table 9 shows the Southern Railway statistics for 1930, showing the Ilfracombe line to have only half the loaded wagon traffic of Barnstaple Junction alone, and only about a third of the traffic on the Torrington line. These figures are slightly misleading, because under the Southern's accountancy system Barnstaple Junction included the returns for Shapland and Petters Siding and Rolles Quay Siding, so the figures given apply to Wrafton downwards. Of these loaded wagons Braunton accounted for about a quarter and Ilfracombe about two-thirds. On the Torrington line there was heavy traffic forwarded in clay and coal, and on the Exeter line in livestock, but there was no such predominant feature on the Ilfracombe line. Indeed, about three quarters of loaded wagons carried traffic received at stations on the line, and only a quarter traffic forwarded, so many wagons left the line empty. Much of the inward traffic was coal, some direct from collieries and some imported from South Wales at Fremington on the Torrington line. Coal and oil for Ilfracombe engine shed was among this. Other mineral traffic received included basic slag used by local farmers and stone used for road building and repair. Under the heading of general merchandise came a wide variety of goods including fertilisers and animal feedstuffs, corn, flour and seeds. Building materials came under this heading, stone, bricks, sand, cement, timber, steel, tiles, pipes and sanitary fittings. The distinctive white bricks seen in a number of buildings in the area came from the Marland brickworks via Torrington.

Many smaller consignments arrived in goods vans running on regular schedules, as we have seen in Chapter One. At Wrafton and Mortehoe traffic was insufficient to justify a large conventional goods shed so a small building was provided on the down platform and consignments unloaded from 'road vans' in South Western days. These were goods guards vans with special compartments; at each stop the guard unloaded the small consignments into the goods shed or on to the platform. From later South Western times onward, these road vans were replaced by 'road boxes', standard box vans usually ventilated for perishables, and sometimes equipped with vacuum brake that they might run at least part of their journey in a passenger train. In later years the Ilfracombe line had daily road box services from Nine Elms goods station in London, Exeter Queen Street and Plymouth Friary. Many of the goods sold in local shops arrived in this way, with priority given to the distribution of perishable items such as meat, fish, fruit and vegetables. Other regular consignments included clothing, bedding, glass pottery and china, ironmongery and stationery.

There was a small amount of livestock, and beasts arriving at Ilfracombe

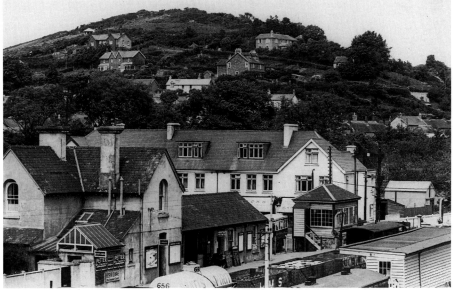

An up goods train at Braunton with five wagons between two brake vans - an arrangement often employed to keep the unfitted train under control descending Mortehoe bank. The Pratts Spirit tank wagon will be returning empty from the oil depot at Mortehoe or Ilfracombe, and the Stoneycombe open wagon to the quarry near Dainton. The distant arm is now painted in the later style of yellow with a black chevron. *Knights Photographers*

On 13th September 1963 N 2-6-0 No.31838 climbs up the 1 in 36 bank past the Ilfracombe outer home signal, with a freight for Barnstaple. Several of the wagons will be road vans lightly loaded on their return journeys together with empty coal wagons. *John Scrace*

TABLE 10 FREIGHT TRAIN SERVICES

	Barnstaple Jcn.dep.	Ilfracombe dep.
1874	mixed passenger and freight trains	
October 1887	10.10am, 1.0pm	11.40am, 4.35, 6.10pm
May 1891	5.15, 10.10am,12.55pm	11.30am, 3.0, 6.0pm
June 1898	5.25, 10.10am,12.35pm	11.20am, 8.10pm
	Pottington freight when required	
Summer 1907	5.10, 10.16am	11.30am to Mortehoe
	12.10pm ex Mortehoe Q	1.35pm
	4.0pm to Pottington	4.35pm ex Pottington
Summer 1913	5.10, 10.40am	1.50pm
	12.55pm ex Braunton	12noon to Braunton
	4.2pm to Pottington	4.35pm ex Pottington
Summer 1925	10.2, 11.45am	11.35am, 1.55pm
	4.5pm to Pottington	5.50pm ex Pottington
Summer 1932	6.0, 10.15am	11.15am, 3.26pm
	11.22am to Pottington	11.52am ex Pottington
	3.54pm to Pottington	4.49pm ex Pottington
Summer 1958	6.38, 10.45am	3.14pm, 7.0pm Q
Weekdays	4.25pm to Pottington	5.28pm ex Pottington
		6.50pm ex PottingtonQ

were often destined for the slaughterhouse adjacent to the station. Some general merchandise and agricultural produce, particularly sugar beet in season, was forwarded from each yard. At Barnstaple, high quality furniture and panelling was forwarded from Shapland and Petters Siding and corn, flour, and animal feedstuffs from Rolles Quay Siding.

FREIGHT TRAIN SERVICES

Table 10 illustrates the development of freight on the line from opening in 1874 until withdrawal of all such facilities, on 7th September 1964. In view of the rather limited amounts involved, the freight train services might at first sight seem somewhat generous, but the steep gradients up to Mortehoe limited goods to 11 loaded vehicles including a brake van for an M7, or 15 for an N, and as we have seen, most freight ran through to Ilfracombe. With the one exception of the Ilfracombe - Mortehoe - Ilfracombe goods early this century all goods trains on the line ran to or from Barnstaple Junction, but not beyond. Here wagons were shunted to or from the principal freight services running between Torrington and Exeter or Torrington and Nine Elms (Feltham in Southern days). When the line opened there was no specific goods train in the working timetable and, as revealed in the 1880 derailment, trains were mixed. Specified goods trains were certainly running by 1887. A feature during most of the South Western period was the Mail and Goods which left Barnstaple about 5.15am, connecting with the 2.35am Goods and Mail from Exeter to Torrington, conveying wagons for Ilfracombe with road van traffic only for other stations. Apart from this, there were usually two goods trains each way between Barnstaple and Ilfracombe, and one or two between Barnstaple and Pottington. In LSW days, including 1907 and 1913, there was one goods train up from Ilfracombe to Braunton or Mortehoe; wagons could be left here to be collected later by the 1.35pm (later 1.50pm) goods which could cope with the heavier load after the ascent to Mortehoe. There were stringent regulations as to any shunting movements at Mortehoe, to ensure that there were no runaways in either direction. None are recorded but there was a breakaway from a goods train ascending the bank, the wagons being derailed at the catch points above Heddon Mill signal box.

With its single crossover, Wrafton could be shunted only by up trains, so wagons for this siding had to be worked down to Braunton and return to Wrafton for shunting into the yard. Down trains could shunt Rolles Quay Siding and usually one morning down freight was allowed a few minutes to do so, but most of the work was carried out by the afternoon Pottington freight train which had time to shunt, clear the outgoing wagons, and place incoming wagons in the right order for the various customers. This train also shunted the Barnstaple Town interchange siding and Shapland and Petters Siding, and in earlier years there was also a morning freight to Pottington.

Ilfracombe Goods 0-6-0 No.0394 inside Barnstaple Junction shed in October 1907. This was one of the last of the class, delivered by Beyer Peacock in 1880, and differed slightly from the first 1874 examples which, for example, acquired Adams boilers and chimneys. No.0394 was the locomotive derailed on Christmas Eve 1889 at *Foxhunters Inn* whilst travelling faster than the 25 mph speed limit on the line. By 1907 only a couple of Ilfracombe Goods remained at Barnstaple, most duties being covered by more modern engines. Withdrawn by the South Western in 1913 No.0394 was acquired by Col. Stephens to work on the East Kent Railway until 1930. *Frank Box*

Adams 460 class 4-4-0 No.0475 outside Barnstaple Junction shed on 21st July 1925. These engines worked from Barnstaple to Exeter and Torrington for many years and during the mid-1920s also worked summer Sunday trains to Ilfracombe. *H.C.Casserley*

CHAPTER EIGHT

LOCOMOTIVES AND ROLLING STOCK

Adams T1 class 0-4-4T No.69 in October 1907, outside Barnstaple Junction shed. It was one of seven of the class working the Ilfracombe line at this time. When they arrived is not clear, but sister locomotive No.68 was derailed here heading a goods to Ilfracombe in 1922. *Frank Box*

CONTRACTOR'S LOCOMOTIVES

James Taylor, the contractor, is known to have employed three locomotives during the construction of the line; the first reports of their use occur in January 1874 so it seems likely that at least one had arrived during 1873. They included a ballast engine, 'Whitmore', and a four coupled tank engine 'Gnat'. When Lucas and Aird carried out the doubling of the line in 1889-91 there is no record of their own locomotives so it would appear that the South Western supplied engines as required.

BEATTIE LOCOMOTIVES THE ILFRACOMBE GOODS

The Ilfracombe Goods 0-6-0 locomotives, of which eight were built, lasted for up to 30 years on the line and afterwards six of them had a further lease of life on several light railways managed by Col. Stephens, achieving a working life of some 60 years. As we have seen, one of the original 1870 directors of the Barnstaple and Ilfracombe Railway was Joseph Beattie, the highly respected Mechanical Engineer of the South Western since 1850. On his death in 1871 he was succeeded by his son, William George, whose achievements

failed to impress and was required to resign in 1877.

The South Western's Locomotive Committee discussed the motive power requirements of the line in 1871-72 but were not satisfied with William Beattie's proposals. They approached the Manchester firm of Beyer Peacock, who had already supplied a number of locomotives to Joseph Beattie's designs, with a specification of their requirements. Beyer Peacock suggested a light 0-6-0, similar to ten supplied to Sweden in 1866 which had proved completely satisfactory in service. The Locomotive Committee decided to order three for immediate delivery in 1873, Nos.282, 283, 284, two more in 1874, Nos.300, 301, and subsequently No.324 in 1875 and Nos.393, 394 in 1880. Although ordered during William Beattie's tenure of office the Ilfracombe Goods was essentially a standard Beyer Peacock design used for mixed traffic purposes.

Nos.282 and 283 hauled the special train on 30th June 1874, and No.284 another on 16th July. No. 282 was derailed maliciously at Pottington in 1880, and No.394 was derailed at

TABLE 1 ENGINE WORKING DIAGRAMS 1919		
arr.	ILFRACOMBE DUTY 891	dep.
	Ilfracombe	9.10am
9.53am	Barnstaple	10.25
11.11	Ilfracombe	11.40
12.26pm	Barnstaple	3.45pm
4.35	Ilfracombe	6.8
6.48	Barnstaple	7.32
8.17	Ilfracombe	
	ILFRACOMBE DUTY 896	
	Ilfracombe	1.20pm
2.5pm	Barnstaple	2.20
3.5	Ilfracombe	4.35
5.19	Barnstaple	6.14
6.58	Ilfracombe	
	BARNSTAPLE DUTY 890	
	Barnstaple Jcn.	
	Shunt	8.55am
9.0am	Barnstaple GW.	9.20
9.25	Barnstaple Jct.	
	Shunt	1.7pm
1.51pm	Ilfracombe	3.0
3.43	Barnstaple Jcn	4.25
5.14	Ilfracombe	7.23
8.4	Barnstaple Jcn	
	BARNSTAPLE DUTY 892	
	Barnstaple Jcn	8.18am
9.8am	Ilfracombe	9.40
10.23	Barnstaple Jcn	11.25
1.1pm	Ilfracombe	1.50pm
3.21	Barnstaple Jcn	
	Rolles Quay Goods	

On 8th November 1907 an unidentified Adams A12 class 0-4-2 and group of railwaymen pose for the camera at Ilfracombe No.2 platform. **This was one of the largest tender locomotives that could be turned on the 42ft turntable available between 1895 and 1925, but this is the only record of one of the class at the terminus.** *Phillipse - Paul Gower Collection*

Foxhunters Inn in 1889. Initially two of the class were allocated to Barnstaple, with one shedded overnight at Ilfracombe, to operate the five daily trains, with a reserve engine at Exeter. As the train service gradually increased, three engines were shedded at Barnstaple. Other members of this useful and versatile class were employed on the Sidmouth branch and the Exeter area. In March 1878 Nos.300 and 301 were allocated to Barnstaple and in March 1881 Nos.283, 393 and 394. In June 1881 Nos.300 (away at Nine Elms under repair), 393 and 394 formed the Barnstaple complement, with Nos.282 and 283 at Ilfracombe; by March 1892 the engines were Nos.301, 324 and 394. Following upgrading of the track completed in 1887, doubling the line in 1889-91, and Maj. Marindin's Accident Report of 1890, the monopoly of the Ilfracombe Goods came to an end, though they continued on some services. In March 1893 the Barnstaple allocation was down to two, Nos.283, 394; by mid-1907 Nos.324 and 394, and by the end of 1908 No.300 only. Two were withdrawn in 1905, but the other six were acquired by Col. Stephens over the period 1910-1918 to work on the Kent and East Sussex, Shrop-shire and Montgomeryshire and East Kent Railways, where they lasted until the 1930s.

ADAMS LOCOMOTIVES

William Adams succeeded William Beattie in 1878, and was an outstanding locomotive engineer, producing elegant, efficient and powerful locomotives for the South Western. Following Major Marindin's report he was responsible for implementing the changes recommended, but unfortunately little detailed evidence is available for the Ilfracombe line until 1907, leaving a gap of some 17 years. Don Bradley, the South Western locomotive historian, states that the earlier Adams 4-4-0s were employed, and 380 class Nos.384, 391 were at Barnstaple shed in March 1892, as were O2 class 0-4-4Ts Nos.190, 197 and A12 class 0-4-2 No.547. All three classes had the shorter fixed wheelbase recommended by Marindin. The original 40ft Ilfracombe turntable, large enough for an Ilfracombe Goods but not much else, was replaced in 1895 by a 42ft version which could just take a 380 or an A12, but none of the other Adams 4-4-0s of which the 460, T3 and X6 classes certainly worked on the Exeter - Barnstaple - Torrington line. If they did work to Ilfracombe then some tender-first running was involved. Bradley records that 380 class 4-4-0s Nos.381, 383 and 384 were based at Exmouth Junction in 1905 and their duties included work on the Ilfracombe line. With their 5ft 7in driving wheels the mixed traffic 380 class would have been more suited to Mortehoe bank than the express 4-4-0s with 6ft 7in drivers. In the autumn of 1907, however, some considerable evidence at last comes to light. In October Frank Box recorded that the line was operated principally by

N class 2-6-0 No.31835 shunts stock at Ilfracombe in August 1956. *Photograph P.W.Gray.*

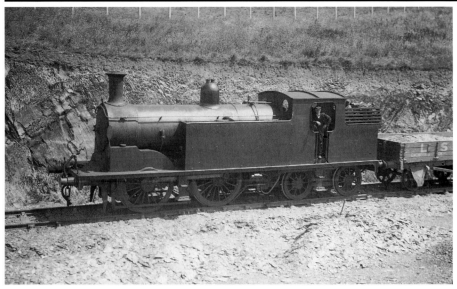

Displaced from their London suburban work by the gradual electrification of the system, the Drummond M7 tanks first arrived on the line about the end of the First World War. This is No.57, still in South Western livery, on 22nd July 1925 on an Engineers train, clearing spoil from the site of the new Ilfracombe engine shed. *H.C.Casserley*

Adams T1 0-4-4Ts, Nos.1, 2, 4, 69, 361, 363 and 367; he photographed several of these together with Ilfracombe Goods No.394 at Barnstaple shed and an unidentified O2 on a train on Barnstaple bridge. There is also a Phillipse photograph dated 8th November of an unidentified A12 0-4-2 at Ilfracombe. The allocation of Barnstaple shed in March 1922 was comprised entirely of Adams locomotives, many of which could have worked to Ilfracombe: T1 0-4-4Ts Nos.68 and 80, O2 0-4-4Ts Nos.177 and 216, A12 0-4-2s Nos. 612, 616 and 633, 460 class 4-4-0s Nos.460, 472 and 526, and three other 4-4-0s - Nos.586, 559 and 658 of classes X2, T3 and X6 respectively. On June 26th 1922 T1 No.67 was derailed at Barnstaple Junction whilst working the 11.42am goods to Ilfracombe.

Later evidence of Adams locomotives comes from undated photograph, probably about 1930, of A12 No.632 piloting an N Mogul up Mortehoe bank. Bradley also records that during the 1925-28 period 460 class 4-4-0s Nos.460, 462, 468, 470, 473, 475 and 476 were shedded at Barnstaple for the services to Exeter, Torrington and Halwill, and on summer Sundays worked to Ilfracombe. The 65ft. turntable was now in place at Ilfracombe so they could be turned there.

DRUMMOND LOCOMOTIVES

Dugald Drummond was Mechanical Engineer from 1895 until 1912, a worthy successor to Joseph Beattie and William Adams. He took very seriously his responsibility for locomotives throughout the South Western system, and to facilitate this the Directors allowed him to build a small locomotive with a short saloon attached behind the cab. This 4-2-4T, No.733, was officially known as 'Mr Drummond's Car', and unofficially as 'the Bug'. A shortcoming in its design was that the brakes acted only on the single pair of driving wheels and on a visit to Ilfracombe 'the Bug' slipped on wet rails and crashed into the buffer stops. On the next visit a

vacuum braked coach was attached to provide extra braking, but the locomotive almost stalled on the ascent of Mortehoe bank.

In *The Railway Magazine* in 1919 Frank Box stated that Drummond tanks were now working the line, mentioning No.25 in particular. This is the first mention of the M7 class 0-4-4Ts which worked on the line for almost half a century. No.22 was photographed in late South Western days at Ilfracombe. Although none was recorded in March 1922, Nos.36, 242, 250, 256, 377 and 668 were allocated to Barnstaple in 1933. Nos.23, 36, 42, 44, 247, 250, 321 and 670 were there in 1947 and Nos.30247, 30251, 30253, 30254, 30255, 30256, 30670 in 1959. By 1962 only two, 30251 and 30670, remained. Unlike many other areas where push-pull trains operated, Barnstaple had no requirement for motor fitted M7s, but the class had a number of duties on the line, including local passenger and goods trains, yard shunting at Barnstaple, and Ilfracombe on summer Saturdays, and banking or piloting heavy trains up both banks to Mortehoe. In BR days M7s were normally seen on the Ilfracombe line only on summer Saturdays. They also had a number of duties on the Torrington line and were the most long-serving locomotive class in North Devon.

Other Drummond classes occasionally appeared, but such visits appear to have been rare. In September 1932 Frank Box recorded 700 class 0-6-0 No.690 hauling an up train of three Great Western bogies from Ilfracombe and one Saturday afternoon in the 1950s No.30691 was observed shunting at Rolles Quay; such Exeter based goods engines regularly brought freight trains to Barnstaple and Torrington however. In the March 1937 issue of *The Railway Observer* it was reported that K10 and L11 class 4-4-0s had replaced M7s on the line; those noted included K10 No.389 and L11s Nos.134, 159 and 170. Subsequently it was reported that 'since 5th March' the

M7s had taken over again, and that the M7s had taken over the 4-4-0 duties on the Torrington line owing to the Torrington turntable being under repair. Since the Torrington turntable had been taken out completely several years previously there must be some other explanation. However, it was certainly the case that K10s, L11s, and in earlier days S11s, worked into North Devon from Exeter. Drummond's most famous class, the Greyhound express T9 4-4-0s, occasionally reached North Devon, and in the summer of 1952 No.30717 was allocated to Barnstaple. Whether it worked the line is not known, but on 21st April 1953 No.30715 hauled a special inspection train to Ilfracombe, conveying senior Southern Region and Western Region officers. It may be mentioned here that none of the Drummond or Urie 4-6-0s, or indeed any Southern 4-6-0s, ever worked into North Devon, being too heavy for the bridges.

MAUNSELL LOCOMOTIVES

Just like the Ilfracombe Goods before them, the N class 2-6-0 also came to Ilfracombe almost brand new, many of them built at Woolwich Arsenal to the SECR design of Richard Maunsell, who had become the Chief Mechanical Engineer of the Southern Railway. The Ns arrived on the line in 1925 and were employed mainly on the principal Exeter - Ilfracombe services inaugurated with the summer timetable. No.A837 was the first to arrive, making trial runs in March 1925, and soon Nos.A839, A841, A849 and A857 were allocated to Barnstaple shed, with numerous others at Exmouth Junction as soon as the new locomotives had been run in. No.A865 was involved in the mishap at Ilfracombe in 1926, and Nos.A826 and A827 in 1931. When the last Ns were completed at Ashford Works in 1933-34 Exmouth Junction initially employed Nos.1406, 1407, 1408, 1409 on the Ilfracombe trains, but the individual locomotives varied over the years. Main line status, incidentally, initiated in 1925, had another effect on the motive power on the line, because a number of the locomotives duties were now the responsibility of Exmouth Junction. The shed could send to Ilfracombe any locomotive appropriate for the purpose, and a far greater number were available, compared to Barnstaple. Occasionally, locomotives from further afield, including Yeovil and even Nine Elms, visited Ilfracombe on excursion or summer Saturday trains. Some Barnstaple to Ilfracombe trains remained in the hands of M7s, while Barnstaple shed usually had several Ns (Nos.1830, 1833, 1835, 1840 and 1848 in 1939; 31842 and 31843 in June 1959). Apart from passenger services the Ns also served on freight and banking duties, particularly after the West Country Pacifics had taken over the principal passenger trains in the mid 1940s. They were still at work almost up to the end of regular steam on the line in 1964.

In the late 1930s up to ten U1 class 2-6-0s were shedded at Exmouth Junction and may have visited the line then,

Table 2 ENGINE WORKINGS SUMMER 1957 Weekdays

Exmouth Junction Duty 527 7P5F (WC Class)

	Ex Jc Loco	1.53am		
1.57	Exeter Central	2.6	F	
4.55	Barnstaple Jcn	6.38	F	
7.22	Ilfracombe			
	F shunting	7.25-7.40		
		7.40		
7.45	Ilfracombe Loco yd	7.55		
8.0	Ilfracombe	8.10	P	
10.11	Exeter Central	10.20		
10.24	Ex Jc Loco	12.41pm		
12.45	Exeter Central	1.28	P	(9.0 Waterloo)
3.42	Ilfracombe			
	Ilfracombe Loco yd	4.25		
4.30	Ilfracombe	4.48	P	
7.3	Exeter Central	7.11		
7.14	Ex Jc Loco			

Exmouth Junction Duty 531 4P5F (N class)

	Ex Jc Loco	3.15am		
3.18	Ex Jc yard	3.30	F	
4.37	Yeoford			
	F shunting	4.45-6.55		
		7.9	F	(6.0 Ex Jc)
8.35	Barnstaple Jc			
	Barnstaple Loco	10.25		
	Barnstaple Jc	10.45	F	
12.36pm	Ilfracombe			
	F shunting	12.40-12.55		
	C shunting	1.50-2.20		
	Ilfracombe Loco yd	3.0pm		
	Ilfracombe	3.14	F	
4.38	Barnstaple Jc	4.48		
4.53	Barnstaple Loco	5.0		
5.5	Barnstaple Jc	5.15	P	
5.56	Ilfracombe			
	C shunting	6.0-6.20 and 6.40-6.55		
	Ilfracombe	7.0	P	
7.34	Barnstaple Loco			
	Stable for Duty 573 next day			

Exmouth Junction Duty 526 7P5F (WC Class)

	Ex Jc Loco	4.35am		
4.39am	Exeter Central	5.6	P	(1.15 Waterloo)
6.50	Ilfracombe			
	C shunting	7.0-7.25		
	7.45-8.30 & 8.50-9.15	9.15		
9.20	Ilfracombe Loco yd	10.0		
10.5	Ilfracombe	10.30	P	
12.24pm	Exeter Central	1.10pm	P	
2.46	Yeovil Jcn			
	returning to Ex Jc Loco	8.52		

Exmouth Junction Duty 528 7P5F (WC Class)

	Ex Jc Loco	4.35am		
4.39am	Exeter Central	5.21	P	
7.41	Ilfracombe	7.51		
7.56	Ilfracombe Loco yd	8.40		
8.45	Ilfracombe	8.55	P	
11.4	Exeter Central	11.12	P	
12.42pm	Yeovil Jcn			
	returning to Ex Jc Loco	7.45		

Exmouth Junction Duty 523 7P5F (WC Class)

	Ex Jc Loco	1.1am		
1.4am	Ex Jc Yd 1.20	F	(4.30 Wadebridge)	
	to Yeovil Jcn & Tn	6.25	P	
8.8	Exeter Central	8.31	P	
10.52	Ilfracombe			
	C shunting	11.0-11.20		
11.25	Ilfracombe Loco	12.0noon		
12.5pm	Ilfracombe	12.20pm	P	
2.23	Exeter Central	2.25		
2.28	Ex Jc Loco	4.25		
4.29	Exeter Central	5.5	P	(1.0 Waterloo)
7.17	Ilfracombe	7.37		

7.42	Ilfracombe Loco	8.10	
8.15	Ilfracombe	8.30	P
9.9	Barnstaple Jc	9.30	
9.35	Barnstaple Loco		
Stable for Duty 572 (FX) 529 (FO)			

Exmouth Junction Duty 524 7P5F (WC class)

	Yeovil Loco	5.15am		
5.20am	Yeovil Town			
	C shunting	5.20-7.20	7.50	P
9.29	Exeter Central	9.40	P	
12noon	Ilfracombe	12.10pm		
12.15pm	Ilfracombe Loco	2.5		
2.10	Ilfracombe	2.20	P	
4.24	Exeter Central	4.26		
4.29	Ex Jc Loco			

Wadebridge Duty 603 7P5F (WC class)

	Padstow	8.30am	P	
11.58	Exeter Central	12.0noon		
12.4pm	Ex Jcn Loco	1.49pm		
1.53	Exeter Central	2.21	P	(11.0 Waterloo)
4.11	Ilfracombe			
	Ilfracombe Loco	5.30		
	Ilfracombe	5.50	P	
6.28	Barnstaple Jc	6.41	F	(5.25 Torrington)
9.33	Ex Jc yard	9.53		
9.56	Ex Jc Loco			

Exmouth Junction Duty 525 7P5F (WC class)

	Ex Jc Loco	6.25am		
	to Axminster and return			
9.0am	Ex Jc Loco	11.3		
11.7	Exeter Central	11.27	P	(8.12 Salisbury)
1.48pm	Ilfracombe	1.58pm		
2.3	Ilfracombe Loco	2.45		
2.50	Ilfracombe	3.0	P	
5.24	Exeter Central	5.26		
5.29	Ex Jc Loco	6.6		
6.10	Exeter Central	6.52	P	(3.0 Waterloo)
9.6	Ilfracombe			
	C shunting	9.10-9.25	9.25	
9.30	Ilfracombe Loco			
	Stable for Duty 529 FX 572 FO			

Exmouth Junction Duty 529 7P5F (WC class)

	Ilfracombe Loco	6.20am		
	Ilfracombe	6.50	P	
7.52am	Kings Nympton	8.30	P	
8.52	Barnstaple Jc			
	Barnstaple Loco	11.0		
	Barnstaple Jc	11.23	P	(tender first)
11.58	Torrington	12.45pm	F	
2.29	Barnstaple Jc	2.40		
2.45	Barnstaple Loco	4.50		
	Barnstaple Jc	5.8	F	(4.15 Bideford)
7.4	Exeter Central Gds	7.11		
7.14	Ex Jc Loco			

Barnstaple Junction Duty 572 7P5F (WC class)

	Barnstaple Loco	7.30am		
7.35am	Barnstaple Jc	7.39	P	(7.5 Torrington)
8.58	Exeter Central	9.38	P	
11.8	Yeovil Jc	11.10		
11.15	Yeovil Loco	1.31pm		
1.36	Yeovil Jc (turn)	2.20	P	(12.46 Salisbury)
3.35	Exeter Central	4.21	P	
5.46	Barnstaple Jc	5.55	P	
6.37	Ilfracombe	6.52		
6.57	Ilfracombe Loco	7.25		
7.30	Ilfracombe	7.42	P	
10.7	Exeter Central	10.36		
10.40	Ex Jc Loco			

F Freight
P Passenger
All other workings are Light Engine

---

tle of Britain classes. A number were named locally, including No.21C105 BARNSTAPLE, 21C117 ILFRACOMBE, 21C143 COMBE MARTIN, 21C144 WOOLACOMBE, 21C146 BRAUNTON, 34093 SAUNTON and 34094 MORTEHOE, the last two being completed in British Railways days. In some places, including Barnstaple and Ilfracombe, a civic ceremony was held when the Mayor or Chairman of the Council named the locomotive at the station. When the Devon Belle was inaugurated in summer 1947 No.21C117 ILFRACOMBE hauled the Pullman cars to and from Exeter. The Pacifics were allocated to Exmouth Junction but worked diagrams requiring them to be shedded overnight at Ilfracombe or Barnstaple. Others, allocated to Salisbury and even Nine Elms, had duties which brought them to Ilfracombe, usually on summer Saturdays. A number of the class were rebuilt to a more conventional design at the cost of an increase in weight which prohibited their use in North Devon, but this was not an operational disadvantage. The class took over most passenger services on the line, assisted by Ns on the goods, until the end of steam traction in 1964.

GREAT WESTERN LOCOMOTIVES
A variety of Great Western locomotives hauled their trains into Barnstaple Junction from 1887, but there handed them over to the South Western for onward haulage to Ilfracombe. Just when the first Great Western locomotive reached Ilfracombe is not known, but a 4-4-0 was recorded there during the First World War. It would appear that the Southern and Great Western reached agreement just after the grouping for Great Western locomotives and guards to work some of their trains to Ilfracombe, although others continued to be worked by the Southern. The installation of the 65ft turntable at Ilfracombe in 1925 facilitated the use not just of the Southern Ns but also Great Western locomotives off the Taunton to Barnstaple line. The summer 1924 timetable included the footnote 'Worked by G.W.Co's engine and guard', particularly for excursion trains.

Arthur Halls photographed Bulldog class 4-4-0 No.3348 LAUNCESTON in fine form ascending Mortehoe bank on a heavy train, before losing its name/ number plate in November 1930. 4-4-0s Nos.3348, 3361, 3444 and 3453 were recorded on the GW Barnstaple line in the 1920s and 1930s and all may well have reached Ilfracombe. About 1925 a number of 43XX class 2-6-0s began to appear, joined later by 63XX and 73XX versions. These became the mainstay of Ilfracombe - Taunton trains up to the end of steam in 1964. The 43XX class were assisted by 2-6-2Ts of the 45XX and 55XX classes over much of the 1925 to 1960 period. During the early 1960s the 2-6-0s in use included Nos.5336, 6326, 6327, 6345, 7303, 7320, 7326 and 7337. The Southern's 1934 and 1960 Working Timetable Appendixes also provided for the use of Great Western 0-6-0 goods locomotives but only a few records of their use have

---

although no evidence has come to light. In the summer of 1961 U1s Nos.31901-31904 were again at Exmouth Junction and some were seen on the Ilfracombe line. In 1943 Exmouth Junction received a number of U class 2-6-0s in exchange for Ns and they too were seen on the line. During the mid 1950s Yeovil-based U class 2-6-0s regularly visited Ilfracombe with Sunday excursion trains.

A number of Maunsell rebuilds of the ex LBSCR E1s, the E1R class 0-6-2Ts, were sent to Barnstaple in the late 1920s to replace ageing Adams 460 class 4-4-0s on both the Torrington to Halwill and Torrington to Barnstaple lines. Occasionally they found their way to Ilfracombe. R.W. Kidner photographed No.2697 on a passenger train at Braunton, and Frank

Box recorded No.2696 banking up to Mortehoe in 1932-33. Some were employed for many years banking heavy trains up the 1 in 37 from Exeter St David's to Central but during the E1Rs' time in North Devon, up to the mid-1950s, Ns and M7s were the preferred bankers up to Mortehoe

BULLEID LOCOMOTIVES
Twenty years after the Ns, the unusual and revolutionary West Country 4-6-2s arrived on the line, as the Second World War ended. In August 1945 Nos.21C101 EXETER, 21C102 SALISBURY and 21C103 PLYMOUTH started work on the principal trains between Exeter and Ilfracombe, and were soon joined by many others of both the West Country and Bat-

From the mid-1920s to the mid-1940s the Southern Railway employed M7 0-4-4Ts and Ns on almost all its Ilfracombe line trains, although other classes made occasional appearances. At Ilfracombe on 5th August 1933 we see one of each class, together with a wide variety of Southern and Great Western coaching stock. In the goods yard is a Parkend coal wagon, both a horse-drawn delivery wagon and a lorry loading at the goods shed, and a number of taxis awaiting custom in the station approach. *Frank Box courtesy R.E.Tustin*

steam locomotive duties on the Ilfracombe line. On at least one occasion a train left Ilfracombe double headed by steam and diesel locomotives. From 6th September 1964 most of the new Exeter - Ilfracombe service was provided by three coach diesel multiple units, with some locomotive hauled trains. These were mainly diesel hauled but steam engines were seen from time to time during the autumn. Diesels were required for the summer Saturday Paddington to Ilfracombe expresses and these often brought Warship (class 42 and 43) diesels to the resort, working the whole journey; sometimes Hymeks also appeared on these trains but they were beyond the powers of the North British type 2s. Locomotives recorded on the line include North British type 2 No.6344, Hymeks Nos.7011, 7097, 7098, 7100, and Warships Nos.803, 818, 820, 821, 844. The final train, the inspection saloon on 26th February 1975, was hauled by a class 25 diesel.

come to light, including No.3205 on a special on 27th March 1965. All Great Western locomotives working to Ilfracombe had their steps cut back to 8ft 4ins to negotiate Barnstaple bridge, and in the 1930s a number were fitted with automatic token exchangers to speed progress along the single track Devon and Somerset route. In the 1930s Great Western locomotives running direct from Taunton to Ilfracombe via the Barnstaple East Curve arrived carrying a white disc with a large letter B above the centre of the buffer beam. The purpose was to assist the Norton Fitzwarren signalman, Minehead trains carrying an M.

IVATT LOCOMOTIVES
Starting with No.41298 in July 1953 a number of Ivatt LMR 2-6-2Ts arrived at Barnstaple shed to take over the duties, first of the E1R 0-6-2Ts and then the M7 0-4-4Ts. They first made their impact on the Barnstaple - Torrington - Halwill section but later appeared on the Ilfracombe line, particularly on banking duties, No.41314 being photographed in 1957. The following saw service in North Devon over the period 1953-1964: Nos.41208, 41210, 41213, 41214, 41216, 41223, 41224, 41230, 41245, 41248, 41249, 41276, 41283, 41290, 41294, 41295, 41296, 41297, 41298, 41308, 41310, 41312, 41313 and 41314.

BRITISH RAILWAYS LOCOMOTIVES
In the mid-1960s, in the dying days of steam traction in North Devon, Exmouth Junction shed began to use BR standard locomotive classes occasionally in North Devon. During the 1963-64 period 4MT 2-6-4Ts covered some N class diagrams. The 'last' steam train to Ilfracombe, on 3rd October 1965, 'The Exeter Flyer', was hauled by Nos.80039 and 80043, the train splitting at Barnstaple Junction into two parts, each of which visited both

Torrington and Ilfracombe. Steam returned on 1st May 1994, when Nos.80079 and 80080 worked a steam special to Barnstaple as part of the Exeter 150 celebrations. At the true end of steam, in 1964, Exmouth Junction 4MT 4-6-0s of the 75XXX series occasionally worked through to Ilfracombe, No.75025 being recorded on Barnstaple bridge.

DIESELS
In May and June of 1963 the monopoly of steam traction in North Devon ended when a North British type 2 and a cross-country diesel multiple unit arrived for clearance tests. Barnstaple footplatemen went to Plymouth for a fortnight's course in driving these types, together with the Hymeks, and during the summer of 1964 the type 2s and Hymeks began to work

SOUTH WESTERN ROLLING STOCK
The first carriages used on the line were 4-wheelers, about 20-25ft in length with four or five compartments, for first, second and third class passengers. There were brakes only on the engine and tender, and when braking the train the driver

Table 3 (SOUTH WESTERN RAILWAY) FORMATION OF TRAINS 1878		
Down Trains from Waterloo		
9.0am	Devonport Engine 1 van 1 third 2 composites 1 third 1 van	
	Ilfracombe 1 third 1 composite 1 van	
10.45am	Devonport Engine 1 van 1 third 2 composites 2 thirds 1 van	
	Barnstaple and Ilfracombe 1 third 1 composite 1 van	
	Torrington 1 composite 1 third 1 van	

blew the whistle to alert the guard to screw down his brake in the brake or 'break' van. Normally there were two brake vans, one at each end of the train,

From the mid-1920s to the mid-1960s the Great Western and Western Region employed 43XX 2-6-0s on services between Taunton and Ilfracombe - this is No.6327, coming off Ilfracombe shed on 3rd August 1963 ready for its next turn. N 2-6-0 No.31843 is inside the shed. *S.C.Nash*

Table 4 WATERLOO CARRIAGE WORKINGS Summer 1913
July 18th to September 20th

8.50am
1 corr. third brake Plymouth
1 corr. third
1 corr. compo
1 corr. third brake

1 corr. brake compo Ilfracombe
1 corr. third brake

1 dining saloon Exeter
1 corr. brake compo
1 corr. third brake
1 compo (3.3) ThO

11.10am
1 corr. third brake Torrington
1 corr. tricompo
1 dining saloon
1 corr. brake compo

1 corr. brake compo Ilfracombe
1 corr. third brake
1 corr. compo
1 corr. third
1 corr. third brake

12.50pm
1 corr. third brake Torrington
1 corr. tricompo
1 dining saloon
1 corr. tricompo
1 corr. brake compo

1 corr. brake compo Ilfracombe
1 corr. third brake
1 corr. tricompo
1 corr. third brake

1 corr. brake compo Exmouth
via Budleigh Salterton

1 corr. compo Sidmouth
1 corr. third brake

1.0pm
1 corr. third brake Plymouth
1 corr. third
1 corr. compo
1 corr. third brake

1 corr. brake compo Padstow

1 corr. brake compo Bude

1 dining saloon Exeter

1 corr. brake compo Ilfracombe

1 corr. tricompo Seaton
1 corr. third brake

1 corr. tricompo Lyme Regis
1 corr. third brake

1 tricompo SO Salisbury

3.30pm
1 corr. third brake Plymouth
1 corr. third
1 corr. compo
1 corr. third brake

1 dining saloon Exeter

1 corr. brake compo Torrington
1 corr. third brake

1 corr. brake compo Ilfracombe

1 corr. brake compo Templecombe thence
1 corr. third brake 5.55pm to Exeter

1 corr. brake compo Salisbury thence
1 corr. third brake 5.18pm to Yeovil

Table 5 ILFRACOMBE CARRIAGE WORKINGS Summer 1955 Weekdays

Train	Destination	Formation	Previous Service Time	From	Due
6.50am	Barnstaple Jn	2-set (63-75) 3 WR set MX	MO	Berth	
8.10R	Exeter Ctl	1 third MO (until 18/7) 1 bke compo (new) MX 2 thirds MFO (com 22/7)			
	Waterloo	3-set (770)		Berth	
8.55	Salisbury	3-set (770)		Berth	
10.30 R	Exeter Ctl Waterloo	1 third 1 third MFO (also TWT 26/7 to 25/8) 2-set(63-75) 8.0am	8.0am	Berth Barnstaple Berth	8.46MO MX
12.20pm R	Exeter Ctl FO (com 19/8) Waterloo	1 bke compo 1 third 1 third 1 bke cpo (new)	1.15am "	8.0am Ba'ple Jcn Berth Waterloo "	8.46 6.50 "
2.20 R	Exeter Ctl Waterloo (until 19/8)	3-set 1 third 1 third 2-set(63-75)	MO 6.25am M X	Berth Yeovil Town F.P. Berth	10.52
3.0 R	Waterloo	1 news van B 1 third MFO 1 bke cpo (new) MFX 1 bke cpo FO (until 12/8) 1 bke cpo (new)	5.21am 8.0am 5.21am	Exeter Ctl Berth Barnstaple Jn Exeter Ctl	7.42 8.46 7.42
4.48	Waterloo Exeter Ctl	1 PMV (4) 1 third 3-set	8.8am 6.25am	Berth Salisbury Yeovil Town	1.48 10.52
5.45	Barnstaple Jn	3 W.R.set	9.0am	Waterloo F.P.	3.40
7.42	Exeter Ctl	2-set(63-75) FO 3-set(770) FX com 19/8 1 van B	9.0am 8.8am 5.21am	Waterloo Salisbury Exeter Ctl	3.40 1.48 7.42
8.30	Barnstaple Jn	1 third FX 1 third 1 bke cpo(new) 2 thirds FO 1 bke cpo(new)FO	11.0am 5.55pm " 11.0/11.5am	Waterloo Barnstaple Jn Waterloo	4.11 6.37 4.11
	Berth	3-set (770)	7.50am	Yeovil Town	12.0
FX	Berth	2-set (63-75)	9.0am	Waterloo R.P.	3.40
	Berth	1 third FX 1 third MFO (also TWT 26/7 to 25/8) 1 bke cpo (new)FX	11.0am	Waterloo	4.11
FO 15/7 to 26/8	Berth	1 kitchen Buff car (3) 1 refreshment saloon	11.5am	Waterloo	4.11
FX	Berth	3 W.R.set	5.15pm	Barnstaple Jn	5.56
FO	Berth	4 L.M. corrs	5.15pm	Barnstaple Jn	5.56
FO	Berth	3 L.M.corrs	5.55pm	BarnstapleJn FP	6.37
	Berth	3-set (770)	1.0pm	Waterloo	7.17
	Berth	1third 1 rest car (30) FO 1 open third FO 2-set (63-75)	3.0pm	Waterloo	9.4

---

if not all vehicles being four wheelers. Although soon replaced on more important services, four wheelers soldiered on in local services for some years, Frank Box photographing such a train on Barnstaple bridge in October 1907. The South Western started building longer six wheelers in the late 1870s, vehicles of about 28-34ft with up to six compartments, and these more modern vehicles were soon employed on the prestigious through services from Waterloo, where there was competition from the Great Western. About this time the distinctive South Western salmon pink and umber dark brown carriage livery was introduced. These six-wheelers can be seen in a number of Victorian and Edwardian photographs and lasted on the line until about the grouping.

The South Western started building bogie carriages in the early 1880s. The first were 42 to 46ft long, with arc roofs and up to seven compartments, whilst in the 1890s 48ft vehicles were introduced, some of which boasted the luxury of lavatories adjacent to some compartments. During a six hour journey between Waterloo and Ilfracombe lengthy stops at Salisbury, Exeter and Barnstaple were necessary for the passengers to use the station toilets. At this stage there appeared the 'brake tricomposite' coach which boasted first, second and third class compartments, together with a brake and luggage compartment. This was an ideal vehicle for through traffic between Waterloo and the West Country branches including Ilfracombe during the quiet traffic periods, and this type was extensively used by many railway companies for cross country services. In the 1900s some 56ft versions were also built, and tricomposite brake No.847 has been restored at the

National Railway Museum at York, a unique preserved South Western carriage. In the late 1940s the 6.50am from Ilfracombe to South Molton Road comprised a locomotive hauling a single ex-railmotor brake composite with its distinctive gates. Non-corridor bogie stock, sometimes re-built, could still be seen in traffic as late as the 1950s, the last being withdrawn in 1959. Corridor stock arrived in the mid-1900s with several trains built specifically for the West of England expresses. The coaches were 52, 54 and 56ft long with side corridors and compartments, except for the dining cars which

---

both with a guard or brakesman, and despite the steep gradients no mishap has come to light. Goods wagons were sometimes included in trains of the early period. In 1881 the South Western commenced fitting all its carriages with automatic vacuum brakes and over the period 1884-87 Adams fitted the Ilfracombe Goods engines with steam brakes for the engine and vacuum ejectors for the train brakes. Table 3 gives extracts from the Waterloo Formation of Trains 1878, most

Table 6	DEVON BELLE PULLMAN CAR FORMATIONS		
Ilfracombe Portions Summer 1947			
Train1	Train 2	Type	Seats
Minerva	Princess Elizabeth	1st Parlour	24
Cynthia	Rosamund	1st Kitchen	22
Fingall	Geraldine	1st Kitchen	22
35	34	3rd Parlour	42
169	249	3rd Kitchen	30
60	32	3rd Kitchen	36
65	27	3rd Brake	30
14	13	Observation	27
At peak periods two extra cars were added to the formations.			

were saloons with distinct clerestory roofs. Out of season the Ilfracombe portion of Waterloo expresses was a corridor tricomposite either by itself or paired with a corridor third brake, the dining car running only as far as Exeter. However, in the summer season whole North Devon corridor expresses were run, with four or five coaches for Ilfracombe, although the dining car ran to Torrington. Waterloo Carriage Workings 1913 in Table 4 gives the details. Second class disappeared during the Great War but both the earlier wooden-panelled and later Ironclad corridor stock made appearances on the line for most of the Southern Railway period.

The small number of summer Saturday through trains from and to Paddington were powered by more powerful locomotives, such as the Hymeks. No.7011 is seen here passing Bridge No.6 near Heanton Court in 1969. *M.Squire*

One of the last recorded workings of South Western corridor stock to Ilfracombe was on summer Saturdays in 1945, when the arrival from Salisbury at about 2pm comprised a three coach set.

SOUTHERN COACHES
The Atlantic Coast Express included a restaurant car daily between Ilfracombe and Waterloo from its inauguration in 1926 until 1933 when it was transferred to Padstow, but the Saturday service always had a restaurant car right through, with two services in 1938 and 1939. As new Maunsell corridor stock became available it replaced the older South Western corridors on the principal expresses. The olive green coaches were 59ft long and comprised the full range of first, third, composite, brake and restaurant coaches, the brake composites being used for less well patronised through services.

After the Second World War Bullied corridor coaches in the familiar Southern green livery appeared. The body length was 64ft 6in and there was again

a full variety of types. Following South Western and Southern practice there were a number of 2, 3, 4 and 5 coach sets in addition to the individual vehicles such as the ubiquitous brake composite. The 63-75 2 coach sets comprised a brake composite and a semi-open brake third. The 770 three coach sets comprised a semi-open brake third, a corridor composite, and another semi-open brake third, whilst the 830 five coach sets comprised semi-open brake third, corridor third, corridor composite, corridor third, semi-open brake third, all these types of set working regularly to Ilfracombe in the 1950s. Table 5 gives details of the weekday Ilfracombe Carriage Workings in the summer of 1955, whilst the summer Saturday workings are shown in Chapter Ten. Coaches in use at the end of steam in 1963 and 1964 were a mixture of Bulleid and BR Mark 1. The formation of Pullman cars in the first season, 1947, of the two Devon Belle sets is given in Table 6.

BRITISH RAILWAYS COACHES
British Railways Mark 1 coaches began to arrive in the mid-1950s, and included three coach sets of the 770 type and four coach sets. There was also a triple restaurant car set of First class Diner No.S9, Kitchen Car No.S80009, and Third class Diner No.S1006, which regularly worked to Ilfracombe on summer Saturdays in 1955, as part of the 12noon express from Waterloo, returning on Sundays. British Railways Mark 1 coaches were in almost universal use for the limited number of locomotive hauled trains in the late 1960s. Rakes of 4, 8 and 9 in the corporate blue and white livery were observed on trains linking Ilfracombe with Paignton and Paddington on summer Saturdays, multiple units dealing with all other traffic.

GREAT WESTERN COACHES
Great Western trains from Taunton usually comprised some local coaches, for many years a B set which comprised a pair of non-corridor brake composites, together with any through coaches from Paddington or other routes either slipped or detached from expresses at Taunton. By the 1930s the more generous Great Western loading gauge, a legacy of the broad gauge, enabled it to run coaches as long as 70ft but these could not negotiate the tightly curved Barnstaple bridge, so 60ft vehicles were diagrammed for the Ilfracombe services. Dining cars were usually detached at Barnstaple Victoria Road, but occasionally reached Ilfracombe. Full details of the Great Western Coach Workings for 1938-9 are given in Table 7.

Table 7 GREAT WESTERN COACH WORKINGS   1938-9
Ilfracombe through coaches only

September 26th 1938 - July 2nd 1939
Down trains from Paddington Weekdays
9.0am Paignton SO from 27th May
    60ft Third
    60ft Bk Compo

10.30am Penzance
    60ft Slip

1.40pm Penzance
    60ft Bk Compo

Up trains to Paddington from Ilfracombe
9.50am   60ft Slip
    60ft Bk Compo

11.0am SO 60ft Van Third from
24th June 60ft Third
    60ft Compo
    60ft Van Third

Summer 1939 Weekdays
Down Trains from Paddington
12.20am Kingswear
    Van Third
    60ft Third
    60ft Van Third

9.0am Paignton
    60ft Van Third
    60ft Compo
    60ft Van Third

9.35am Minehead SO
    60ft Bk Compo
    60ft Dining Car
    three 60ft Thirds
    60ft Bk Compo

12.6pm Ilfracombe SO
    three 60ft Thirds
    60ft Van Third
    60ft Compo
    60ft Van Third

1.40pm Penzance SX
    60ft Bk Compo

2.15pm Minehead SO
    two Thirds
    Bk Compo

3.30pm Penzance
    60ft Bk Compo

Up trains from Ilfracombe to Paddington
12.15pm Minehead SO
    Bk Compo
    60ft Third
    60ft Van Third
    60ft Compo
    60ft Third
    60ft Van Third

9.50am Ilfracombe SX
    60ft Van Third
    60ft Compo
    60ft Third
    60ft Van Third

12.0 noon Ilfracombe
    60ft Bk Compo MO
    60ft Van Third
    60ft Compo
    60ft Van Third

1.30pm Penzance
    60ft Bk Compo

GENERAL THROUGH TRAINS
8.10am Birmingham to Paignton SO
    two Thirds   Birmingham to Ilfracombe
    Bk Compo

10.40am Wolverhampton to Ilfracombe SO
    Bk Compo
    three Thirds
    Compo
    Van Third

10.0am Paignton to Bristol SO (9.15am ex Ilfracombe)
    two Thirds
    Compo
    Van Third

Cross Country Trains to and from LMS Line
9.50am Ilfracombe to Manchester SO
    Van Third
    four Thirds
    Compo
    Van Third

Near *Hunters Inn* with Heddon Mill up distant signal in the background Great Western Bulldog 4-4-0 No.3348 LAUNCESTON hauls six Great Western bogies up the 1 in 40 bank assisted by a Southern M7 0-4-4T banker. The photograph was taken before November 1930, when the combined name/number plate on the cabside was replaced. The Bulldog class was allowed an unassisted load of 145 tons, or 6 coaches of 24 tons each up the bank, but often assisting engines were provided even if not strictly required. *A.Halls courtesy National Railway Museum*

Passing Heddon Mill up distant signal N class 2-6-0 No.839 hauls an eight coach train up the 1 in 40 , banked by an unidentified M7 class 0-4-4T. The formation includes a variety of South Western and Maunsell stock, some carrying Atlantic Coast Express boards, so it would appear that this is a relief to the main Atlantic Coast Express, probably about 1930. *Photograph R.C.Riley Collection.*

CHAPTER NINE

WORKING OVER MORTEHOE BANK

THE TWO BANKS

In the down direction trains leaving Braunton station, 27ft above sea level, ascended for some six miles to arrive at Mortehoe, 624 ft above sea level. Initial gradients of 1 in 74 and 1 in 96 soon stiffened to more than three miles at 1 in 41 and 1 in 40, including a sharp 16 chain radius curve through 120 degrees at *Foxhunters Inn* which increased the rolling resistance of a long train. Down trains leaving Braunton were able to take a run at the bank, speeds up to 40mph (the maximum on the Braunton - Mortehoe section in both directions) being reached at Heddon Mill, just before the 1 in 40 commenced. A mile later, the lowest speed of the ascent was reached as the train slowed for the long *Foxhunters Inn* curve, and then speed recovered on the straighter sections until slowing for Mortehoe station. The layouts at Braunton and Mortehoe facilitated the attachment of assisting engines either as pilot in front of the train engine or as banker at the rear.

Even with a fairly light train, drivers and firemen had to work together skilfully on the banks. An example of the difficulties encountered came during the Second World War when a young inexperienced crew on M7 No.247 took the 5.15pm from Barnstaple Junction, four GWR bogies well loaded with school children returning home. The fireman had built up a very full fire in the firebox by arrival at Braunton and then sat back to enjoy the view all the way up to Mortehoe. But just after leaving Mortehoe the train brakes came on, and on inspection very little fire was found remaining in the firebox. An embarrassed crew had to build up the fire again for some time until the vacuum pressure reached the 25psi necessary to release the GWR brakes - the M7 at 21psi had not been affected.

In the up direction the buffer stops at Ilfracombe were 257ft above sea level but with only three miles available to reach Mortehoe the climb was even steeper, 1 in 363 and 1 in 71 along the platform, then 1 in 36 from the platform end for more than two miles, curving up the side of the Slade valley before the gradients eased approaching Mortehoe. Speeds up the 1 in 36 were usually no more than 15-25 mph, the fastest speeds of the ascent being reached on the easier grades just before slowing down for Mortehoe. It was easy enough to attach a pilot engine at the terminus, but when a banking engine was required it had to shunt to the buffer stops before the carriages arrived in the platform, propelled by either the train engine or station pilot. Normal practice was for assisting engines to be detached at Mortehoe and then to work back to where they had come from for their next banking turn, although at the beginning and end of the day they worked from or to Barnstaple shed. A number of photographs record the double-heading of trains which did not require a second engine; this practice was preferred to light engine movements which occupied an extra path on a very busy line. Normally engines worked chimney first up the bank to maintain the maximum

N class 2-6-0 No.31818 assists Battle of Britain 4-6-2 No.34072 with the up ACE in August 1962. *Photograph Peter Gray*

The Commission's engine must not pass the siding gate at which point vehicles must be exchanged.

Before allowing the train to leave on the return journey the guard or shunter in charge must, after satisfying himself that the driver is in possession of the electric token, obtain permission by telephone from the signalman at Barnstaple Junction " B " for the train to proceed to Barnstaple Junction " B " home signal. Should the telephone fail the guard or shunter in charge must so advise the driver and instruct him to proceed cautiously and to be prepared to stop at Barnstaple Junction " B " home signal.

VEHICLE RESTRICTION.—Bogie stock with step boards between the bogies fitted at a height of less than two feet from rail level to the underside of the brackets supporting such step boards, other than S.R. bogie guards vans Nos. 201 to 280 inclusive and 350 to 399 inclusive, must not pass over the bridge between Barnstaple Junction and Barnstaple Town.

This restriction does not apply to vehicles with short step boards attached only to the bogies.

BARNSTAPLE TOWN.

ROLLES QUAY SIDING.—This siding is on the up side between Wrafton and Barnstaple Town with access by a trailing connection in the down line. The points are operated from Pottington signal box.

Guards will be assisted when shunting this siding by a porter from Barnstaple Junction who must pin down sufficient wagon brakes to act as a buffer stop for vehicles shunted into the siding.

Drivers must give a series of engine pop whistles when vehicles are being propelled to the end of the siding.

BRAUNTON—ILFRACOMBE.

PASSENGER TRAINS.—All trains between Braunton and Ilfracombe must have vehicles with a brake compartment as follows :—

Not exceeding 180 tons.—1 bogie vehicle with a brake compartment. This vehicle to be included in the total tonnage and, in the case of vehicles conveying passengers from Braunton to Mortehoe & Woolacombe or Ilfracombe to Mortehoe & Woolacombe, it must be attached at the rear of such vehicles except when an assisting locomotive is provided in the rear.

Exceeding 180 tons.—2 bogie vehicles with brake compartments, 1 of these vehicles must be marshalled at the rear. These vehicles to be included in the total tonnage and the guard must travel in the rear brake vehicle.

Two horse boxes, cattle vans, carriage trucks, vans or similar vehicles fitted with the continuous brake complete and provided with a hand brake may be attached outside the rear vehicle with a brake compartment, but this number must not be exceeded.

Should the continuous brake become inoperative, the load must be reduced so that the train may be safely controlled on any part of the inclines with the hand brake power available.

ASSISTANCE ARRANGEMENTS.—The undermentioned instructions regarding the assistance of trains from Braunton to Mortehoe & Woolacombe and from Ilfracombe to Morthoe & Woolacombe are supplementary to those appearing in Table " J ". When the loads are within those specified for the class of locomotive concerned it may be necessary in certain conditions for an assisting engine to be provided and such assistance must be arranged at the request of the driver.

The maximum loads for passenger and coaching stock trains worked by one locomotive are as follows :—

Class	Tons
Braunton to Mortehoe & Woolacombe	
West Country & Battle of Britain	240
N.	180
U.	150
M.7	140
T.9	100
L.M. 2 (2-6-2T)	140
W.R. 63 XX	190
W.R. 45 XX	150
W.R. 22 XX	120
Ilfracombe to Mortehoe & Woolacombe	
West Country & Battle of Britain	205
N.	180
U.	150
M.7	140
T.9	100
L.M.2 (2-6-2T)	140
W.R. 63 XX	180
W.R. 45 XX	140
W.R. 22 XX	110

Trains exceeding the weights shown must have an assisting engine which may be attached at the front provided the load does not exceed 280 tons. When this tonnage is exceeded the assisting engine must be attached at the rear. Trains must not consist of more than 88 wheels.

When a freight train requires assistance, the assisting engine must be attached in rear.

FREIGHT TRAINS—MORTEHOE & WOOLACOMBE TO BRAUNTON OR ILFRACOMBE.—Trains must not exceed a load equal to 25 loaded wagons inclusive of brake van.

A train worked by one locomotive only must have brake vans attached, with a man in each, as follows :—

Load inclusive of brake van.	Brake van to be provided.
Not exceeding equal to 15 loaded wagons	1 heavy van.
Above 15 and not exceeding 25 loaded wagons	2 heavy vans.

When two brake vans are attached, one van must be placed at the rear of the train and the other behind the eleventh vehicle of the train.

A train worked by two locomotives must have both locomotives at the front and in such cases one brake van only need be provided.

The driver and guard will be held responsible for communicating with one another and observing the requirements of Rule 131 (ii) when circumstances indicate that the state of the rail would be unfavourable for the prompt stoppage of trains.

Should any fitted vehicles be attached, they must, as far as practicable, be marshalled next to the locomotive and the brake pipes connected, in which case they need not be included when calculating the number of brake vans required.

FITTED STONE TRAINS.—Stone trains, fitted with the continuous brake throughout, must be operated in accordance with the instructions applicable to passenger trains, except that the load must not exceed six loaded bogie hopper wagons and two fitted brake vans.

MORTEHOE & WOOLACOMBE.

FREIGHT TRAINS.—Before shunting operations with an up train are commenced, the rear portion of the train must be propelled to the down line over the crossover at the Braunton end of the station and made secure in accordance with the relevant rules.

When a down train is required to shunt, the rear portion must be set back into the down sidings.

ILFRACOMBE.

SHUNTING.—Freight vehicles must not be hauled up the incline during shunting operations except in unavoidable cases when a brake van, in which the shunter must ride, must be attached at the station end.

BARNSTAPLE JUNCTION "A" TO SWIMBRIDGE.
BARNSTAPLE JUNCTION "A".

An Auxiliary Electric Key Token Instrument has been provided for the Barnstaple Junction "A" to Swimbridge Section and is situated at the Exeter end of the down platform.

WORKING OF AUXILIARY KEY TOKEN INSTRUMENT.

Prior to the departure of an up train or light engine for Swimbridge, the station foreman must obtain permission by telephone from the signalman at Barnstaple Junction "A" signal box for a key token to be withdrawn and give the description of the train for which the release is required. The key token must be lifted from a column of the magazine, the key end of the token engaged on the centre pin of the instrument and given a half turn to the left (anti-clockwise). Upon the indicator changing from "Locked" to "Free" the station foreman must give the key token a further half turn to the left, withdraw it from the instrument and advise the signalman by telephone that this has been done. The key must be placed in a pouch with the name of the section showing and delivered to the driver.

In the event of an up train or light engine for which a key token has been drawn not proceeding, arrangements must be made between the signalman and the station foreman for the key token to either be replaced in the instrument in the manner described in the following paragraph or be taken to Barnstaple Junction "A" signal box.

Upon the arrival of a down train or light engine from Swimbridge at Barnstaple Junction station, the station foreman must obtain the key token from the driver and engage the key end of the token on the centre pin of the instrument, give it two half turns to the right (clockwise), withdraw it from the centre pin and lower it into a column of the magazine. The station foreman must then advise the signalman by telephone that the key token has been placed in the instrument. The station foreman must remain at the telephone until advised by the signalman that all is in order.

---

level of water over the crown of the fire-box, but sometimes they worked tender first.

Extracts from the Southern Railway Working Timetable Appendix of 1960 are included, but several general features should be mentioned here. In 1934 the same regulations applied to both banks, Braunton to Mortehoe and Ilfracombe to Mortehoe, but in 1960 the maximum loads for each class of engine were lower for Ilfracombe to Mortehoe. In both years

the absolute maximum length for passenger trains was 88 wheels, eleven bogies corresponding to the length of Ilfracombe No.2 platform. Again in both years, when the weight of the train exceeded the limit for the train engine an assisting engine was required. If the load did not exceed 280 tons the assisting engine could be attached at the front of the train, but for trains heavier than 280 tons the assisting engine had to be attached at the rear of the train. There are many recorded cases of heavy passenger trains being hauled by two or three locomotives on the banks, but to date

only one example has come to light of a freight train receiving assistance; although appropriate regulations were in force freight trains were usually relatively light.

The regulations for freight trains were drawn up with different considerations, particularly the safe descent of the banks. The 1934 maximums were 11 loaded wagons including a brake van for an M7 or 15 for an N - trains which could be hauled up the banks without undue difficulty. Unlike passenger trains, with their continuous vacuum brakes, freight trains could be stopped only by the engine brake and the brake van, so at least one 20 ton brake van was included. If any vacuum braked vehicles were included in

---

TABLE 1 DOWN TRAINS BRAUNTON TO MORTEHOE
Two or Three Engines
SOUTHERN RAILWAY PERIOD 1920s and 1930s

M7 No.322	M7 No.378	A12 No.632	Bulldog No.3348
N	6 GW bogies	N	6 GW bogies
11 SR bogies	M7	6 SR bogies	M7
M7	photo	photo	photo
photo			
M7 No.34	N No.1836	N No.1409	M7 No.356
M7	M7 No.250	N No.1828	M7 No.377
144 tons	138 tons	192 tons	206 tons
log	log	log	log
N No.1832	N No.1841	M7 No.376	N No.1831
M7 No.242	M7 No.250	N No.1840	E1R No.2696
M7 No.34	M7 No.256	M7 No.669	M7 No.376
11 SR bogies	11 SR bogies	11 SR bogies	10 SR bogies
(360 tons)	(354 tons)	(355 tons)	(325 tons)
log	log	log	log

For trains in Frank Box's logs there was no record of whether the assisting engines were piloting or banking

---

TABLE 2 UP TRAINS ILFRACOMBE TO MORTEHOE 2 or 3
Engines SOUTHERN RAILWAY PERIOD 1920s and 1930s

N No.1840	N No.1408	N No.1832	M7 No.256
N No.1853	M7 No.376	M7 No.36	M7 No.375
109 tons	91 tons	6 SR bogies	169 tons
log	log	(192 tons)	log
		log	
N No.1843	N No.1854	N No.1846	GWR 2-6-2T No.5569
N No.1406	N No.1407	M7 No.242	M7 No.256
11 SR bogies	272 tons	258 tons	N No.1838
(258 tons)	log	log	9 GW bogies
log			(254 tons)
			log
M7 No.375			
M7			
train			
photo			

the train they were to be marshalled next to the engine, if practicable, and the vacuum brake connected up. As we have seen in Chapter One a broken coupling on a down goods led to the derailment of several runaway wagons, on catch points at Heddon Mill.

THE SOUTH WESTERN PERIOD

The Ilfracombe Goods 0-6-0s were restricted to six coaches including a manned brake van at each end, with the first recorded double headed trains of 8, 12 and 13 four wheel coaches on 30th June and 20th July 1874. For goods trains the limit was eight wagons and a brake van. During the later South Western period Adams T1 class 0-4-4Ts were allowed to take 44 wheels unaided over the banks, while the Drummond M7s were allowed 48 wheels. As we have seen from the 1913 carriage workings, there were normally up to five through carriages, of 40 wheels, which were within these limits. The banking and pilot engine sidings at Braunton and Mortehoe were certainly in situ at the time but the first record of regular double heading appears in 1919, when complaints were made about delays to pedestrians at Braunton level crossing.

THE SOUTHERN PERIOD

The summer 1925 timetable appears to have heralded the era of heavy summer trains double or triple headed over the banks. Tables 1 and 2 include evidence from photographs taken by Frank Box and Arthur Halls and also train logs recorded by Frank Box, who recorded some 40 trips from Braunton to Mortehoe, and 64 from Ilfracombe to Mortehoe. It is unfortunate that no record has yet come to light of the train engine, pilot engine and banking engine(s), but for Southern trains it seems safe to suggest that if an N 2-6-0 was

On Saturday 1st September 1962 the 12.25pm train from Ilfracombe to Taunton ascends the 1 in 36 bank towards Mortehoe station hauled by ex-GWR 2-6-0 No.7337, piloted by M7 class 0-4-4T No.30667. *Photograph Peter W. Gray*

involved it was the train engine, working right through to Exeter. For the Great Western 9 coach train it would appear that the 55XX 2-6-2T was the train engine, working right through to Taunton; whether both the M7 and N were banking is not clear.

TABLE 3 DOWN TRAINS BRAUNTON TO MORTEHOE Two Engines BRITISH RAILWAYS PERIOD 1950s and 1960s

43XX No.6346	LMR No.41298	M7 No.30667	WC No.34067
5 GW bogies	43XX No.7337	43XX No.7337	5 SR bogies
LMR No.41298	4 GW bogies	4 GW bogies	N No.31856

BB
7 SR bogies
M7 No.30254
All information from photographs

Description of Block Signalling on Main Lines Absolute Block unless otherwise shown (Dots indicate BlockPosts)	Stations and Signal Boxes	Distance between signal boxes		Additional running lines		Loops and Refuge Sidings		Permanent speed restrictions miles per hour		Catch points, spring or unworked trailing points	Gradient (Rising unless otherwise shown) 1 in	Engine Whistles L—long S—short C—crow				
												Down		Up		For
		M	Yds	Up	Down	Description	Standage Wagons E. & V.	Down	Up	Position		Main or Fast	Slow or Goods	Main or Fast	Slow or Goods	
	COLEFORD JUNCTION TO ILFRACOMBE—contd.															
	Barnstaple Junction "A"	4	434													
	"B" (See page 66 for Torrington line)	0	359					15	15	Between Barnstaple Junction and Pottington signal box						
	Barnstaple Town Station	0	957													
	Pottington	0	642					40	40	Between Pottington signal box and 213 m.p.						
	Wrafton Station	4	89													
	Braunton Station	0	1623									1L		1L		When approaching Caen Street crossing (Down stopping trains when leaving platform)
												1L		1L		When approaching Church crossing
	Heddon Mill Crossing	2	394							C. Down, 345 yards before reaching home signal	83	Willingcott Crossing—continuously from whistle board to crossing				
	Mortehoe and Woolacombe Station	3	1058							C. Down, 410 yards before reaching home signal	40					
	Ilfracombe Station	2	1604							C. Up, 410 yards before reaching home signal.	76					

On Saturday 27th July 1963 the 8.0am train from Wolverhampton Low Level to Ilfracombe ascends the 1 in 40 near Willingcott, hauled by ex-GWR 2-6-0 No.6346 and banked by Ivatt 2-6-2T No.41298. *Photograph Peter W.Gray*

THE BRITISH RAILWAYS PERIOD

By this time Bulleid Pacifics were rostered for many duties and they were considerably more powerful than the locomotives previously used. But they did have a reputation for slipping due to oil leaks, insensitive regulators and springing which transferred the locomotive weight from the driving wheels to the bogie and pony truck, although the last feature was common to all Pacifics. Drivers of heavy trains starting from Ilfracombe became very skilled at getting the best out of these engines which once on the move benefited from the free steaming boiler. They were allowed 240 tons unaided up from Braunton to Mortehoe and 205 tons from Ilfracombe to Mortehoe and these sections required more frequent relaying than others, due to the hard working of the locomotives. No record has yet come to light of three locomotives working a train during this period. Two light Pacifics or one with an N could cope with the maximum 11 Southern bogies, and a 43XX and an N with the maximum 9 Great Western bogies allowed over the Barnstaple to Taunton route. Details of double headed trains photographed during this period are given in Tables 3 and 4. Apart from the Devon Belle the working of heavy trains during this period was almost completely restricted to summer Saturdays, so there was no need for double heading on weekdays. This train was a West Country duty from Exeter, but passengers in the observation car at the rear had an excellent view of the front end of the N or M7 banking the heavy train up to Mortehoe.

A pair of bunker-first M7s, No.375 leading, prepares to depart from platform 1 at Ilfracombe with a passenger train, about 1930. The leading vehicle is a brake third or composite of unknown pre-grouping origin but apparently now in Great Western livery, so this would appear to be a through service to the North, Midlands or South Wales via Taunton. *Frank Box courtesy National Railway Museum*

TABLE 4 UP TRAINS ILFRACOMBE TO MORTEHOE Two Engines BRITISH RAILWAYS PERIOD 1950s and 1960s			
BB No.34079 43XX No.6346 5 GW bogies	BB No.34072 SR bogies N No.31818	BB No.34075 BB No.34069 SR bogies	N No.31856 43XX No.6327 4 GW bogies
M7 No.30254 43XX No.7304 GW bogies	N No.31834 43xx No.7303 6 GW bogies	N No.31834 43XX No.7320 GW bogies	N No.31843 43XX No.5336 GW bogies
BB No.34065 BB No.34075 SR bogies	BB No.34079 Hymek No.7098 SR bogies	BB 55XX 4 GW bogies	55XX No.5503 4 GW bogies M7
Hymek No.7100 9 SR bogies Hymek No.7097	N 14 wagons N		

On 4th August 1951 a four coach train of Western Region stock destined for Taunton ascends the 1 in 36 up the Slade valley from Ilfracombe, the 55XX class 2-6-2T assisted by a Bulleid Pacific. The load is well within the abilities of the 55XX, which was allowed 110 tons, but such double-heading, though not strictly required, was often seen on summer Saturdays. *R.J.Sellick*

A unique photograph of a goods train climbing the 1 in 36 up the Slade valley with two N class locomotives working hard. The lengths of rail in the foreground suggest that parts of the down line are being re-laid, so the wagons may well be loaded with either new or spent ballast for the civil engineers. *Paul Gower Collection*

On 14th June 1958 No.31834 takes water at the Braunton up platform, while M7 0-4-4T No.30250 waits in the holding sidings for the next banking turn. No.31834 will shunt across to these sidings when the tender is replenished. *R.E.Tustin*

Pacifics No. 34107 'Blandford Forum' and No. 34072 257 SQUADRON bring the up Atlantic Coast Express past Mortehoe up distant signal and fogman's hut on 27th July 1963, the locomotives and ten coaches all being Bulleid designs. *Peter W. Gray*

On Saturday 27th July 1963 the 12.25pm train from Ilfracombe to Taunton ascends the 1 in 36 past the Slade reservoirs, headed by 2-6-0s 6346 and 31838. *Peter W. Gray*

On 1st September 1962 the 8.50am train from Taunton to Ilfracombe runs down past the Slade reservoirs behind M7 0-4-4T No.30667 and ex-GWR 2-6-0 No.7337. *Peter W.Gray*

Saturday 29th August 1964, and an empty stock train from Ilfracombe hauled by N class 2-6-0 No.31846 passes Mortehoe up distant signal. *S.C.Nash*

On Saturday 1st September 1962 the 10.30am Atlantic Coast Express from Ilfracombe to Waterloo, hauled by Battle of Britain class 4-6-2 34072 257 SQUADRON and banked by N class 2-6-0 No.31818, slowly ascends the 1 in 36 bank past Slade reservoirs. For such a heavy train, which often comprised eleven coaches, the assisting engine had to be attached to the rear of the train rather than the front. *Peter W.Gray*

CHAPTER TEN

SUMMER SATURDAYS

SETTING THE SCENE

Following the wholesale rationing and restrictions of wartime, family holidays at the seaside quickly became very popular in the late 1940s, and the south west of England was the principal holiday area, a trend encouraged by Great Western and Southern advertising. The railways catered for a very high proportion of holiday travel, almost invariably from Saturday to Saturday, and coped with a volume of traffic not seen before or since. It reached a peak about 1957 and then slowly declined with the advent of both the family car and cheap package holidays to Spain and other countries, where hot dry weather was almost guaranteed. Even after the Beeching axe, the Ilfracombe line was kept open, until 1970, to avoid damaging the tourist trade. This chapter deals with the period from about 1948 to 1964, when the services were rationalised.

The whole railway system, and the lines to Ilfracombe in particular, were well prepared to meet the challenge of this volume of traffic. There were plenty of paths for extra trains along the double track and plenty of berthing sidings at the terminus. The short single line section at Barnstaple did not cause any significant problems. On weekdays there were usually two freight trains from Barnstaple Junction to Ilfracombe and a third to Pottington Signal Box, but on Saturdays these were reduced to one, retimed, and light enough to be hauled by an M7, thus making more resources available for passenger work. At Barnstaple and Exeter there were sufficient suitable locomotives to cope with the traffic. But even more important were the human resources, the men who were well prepared to move up a gear from the weekday to the Saturday traffic needs. At Heddon Mill the crossing keeper was a passed signalman, so on Saturdays this opened up as a signal box to provide an extra block section. On the footplate passed cleaners moved up a grade to become firemen, taking the places of passed firemen who became drivers. Boiler washouts and other maintenance was scheduled during the week so that the maximum number of locomotives and crews were available for the holiday trains. For Waterloo services, a large number of West Countries and Ns were available, with 43XX Moguls for the Taunton route. All three types, together with M7s and Ivatt tanks, also assisted with the banking. Extra men were drafted in to help the locals, for whom a summer Saturday day off was unthinkable. Railwaymen from afar would qualify for a lodging allowance, but at the height of the season rooms were both scarce and expensive, so many slept in a quiet station office or in an empty coach.

On the Ilfracombe line a critical factor was the two platforms at the terminus. If No. 1 platform was occupied by a departure and there was a delay in clearing an arrival at No. 2, then the next had to wait outside the station. There were other constraints further afield, on the two single track routes into North Devon. On the Southern there was a 19 mile stretch from Copplestone to Umberleigh with five passing loops, several of which were too short to cross two full length trains. When this was necessary at stations such as Kings Nympton, one train had to reverse into a siding, the points locked by a porter with a block of wood in the absence of a facing point lock. In theory, trains with no booked stop had to slow down at each of the 7 intermediate stations, to exchange tablets, but in practice it didn't always happen that way. On the Great Western there was a single track route of some 38 miles from Barnstaple Junction to Milverton, involving a reversal at Victoria Road up to 1960, but crossing loops were longer and laid out to permit trains from both directions to enter simultaneously. Automatic token exchangers speeded up the service. These constraints

Ex-GWR 2-6-0 No.7326 approaches Mortehoe on Saturday 27th July 1963 with the four coach Ilfracombe to Cardiff General train. *Peter W. Gray*

On 18th August 1962 a Taunton train is about to depart from Ilfracombe platform 2, with M7 No.30254, bunker-first, piloting 43XX Mogul No.7304. This may well be the 10.55am departure for Wolverhampton which in the late 1950s loaded to six coaches, with the M7 working right through to Barnstaple. *N.D.Mundy*

certainly did cause some problems, but these were minor in comparison to the chaos on the Great Western main line between Taunton and Paignton, where delays of several hours became commonplace.

In practice, for most of our 1948-64 era the 'weekend' ran from Friday to Monday inclusive. The passenger luggage in advance arrived on scheduled services, including extra vehicles at peak periods, at Braunton, Mortehoe and Ilfracombe, where as far as possible the collection and delivery vehicles would clear the traffic by Friday evening. Even the large luggage store at Ilfracombe had insufficient space for all that arrived for the weekend, particularly because it was also needed for luggage collected from hotels and guest houses for guests returning home. Extra road vehicles, drivers and porters had to be brought in to assist the local men in this work. Apart from the Devon Belle and, in 1948, the 8.10am from Ilfracombe and 2.50pm from Waterloo, there were no postwar restaurant car services on weekdays. On Fridays, however, a number of cater-

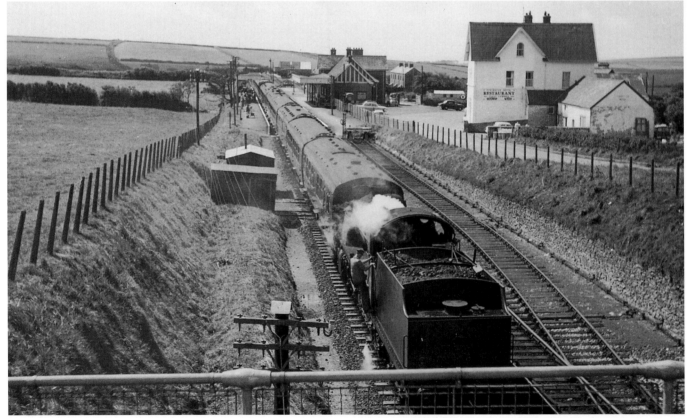

On 8th August 1964 a long express for Waterloo has just arrived at Mortehoe, banked up from Ilfracombe by this N 2-6-0. The fireman is climbing down to uncouple the engine from the rear coach, so that after the train has departed the N can run forward and then reverse over the crossover (at present occupied by the rear coaches) and return to Ilfracombe for its next turn. *P.Swift*

TABLE 1 EXTRACT FROM WORKING TIMETABLE
SATURDAYS ONLY 14th June - 13th September 1958 formations taken from 1957 Locomotive Duties (Table 2) and 1955 Carriage Workings (Table 3). Details shown apply in full only from 12th July to 9th August.

DOWN TRAINS

	12.25 Wloo	1.15 Wloo	2 L.E.s	5.26 Ex.C	L.E.	5.20 Tn	
Barnstaple Jn a.	5.23	6.4		6.51		7.16	
d.	5.29	6.8	6.35	6.57	7.15	7.29	8.0
Barnstaple Town	5a33	6a12	6.38	7a1	7.18	7a33	8a4
Pottington SB	5.34	6.13	6.39	7.2	7.19	7.34	8.5
Wrafton	5a41	6a20		7a9		7a41	8a12
Braunton	5g47	6j27	6.47	7e14	7.27	7g47	8g18
Mortehoe	6c 6	6a45	7.5	7e34	7.44	8c6	8.35
Ilfracombe a.	6.14	6.53	7.14	7.42	7.52	8.14	
Formation	N 3 (M7) Note 1	WC 7 (M7)	N 3	WC 3 (M7)	N	N 43xx 6 Note 2	WC 2

	6.20 Tn	7.0 Tn	6.25 Yeovil	8.30 Tn	7.45 Yeovil	Fgt	
Barnstaple Jn a.	8.10	9.10	10.3	10.35	11.17		
d.	8.15	9.13	10.13	10.40 1	1.27	11.53	
Barnstaple Town	8c20	9a17	10c19	10a44	11a31	11.57	
Pottington SB	8.21	9.18	10.20	10.45	11.32	11.58	
Wrafton	8c29	9a25	10a27	10a52	11a39		
Braunton	8j36	9g31	10c31	10c56	11c43	12n21	
Mortehoe	8.38	8c55	9c50	10c50	11a14	12a1	12m50
Ilfracombe a.	8.46	9.4	9.58	10.58	11.22	12.9	1.0
Formation	WC 2	43xx 4	43xx 6 M7 Note 3	WC 6	M7 N 4 Note 4	WC 4	M7

	7.38 Wloo	11.39 Ex.C	8.22 Wloo	8.35 Wloo	8.57 Wloo	10.15 Wloo	12.50 Tn
Barnstaple Jn a.	12.36	1.14	1.30	1.43	2.36	2.51	3.0
d.	12.41	1.20	1.34	1.52	2.39	2.56	3.9
Barnstaple Town	12c46	1c25	1c39	1e58	2a43	3c1	3c14
Pottington SB	12.47	1.26	1.40	1.59	2.44	3.2	
3.15Wrafton	12a54	1a33	1c48	2c7	2a51	3c23	
Braunton	1g0	1e38	1g54	2j14	2e56	3g13	3g29
Mortehoe	1c19	1c57	2c13	2c33	3a14	3c32	3c48
Ilfracombe a.	1.27	2.5	2.21	2.41	3.22	3.40	3.56
Formation	WC 5	N 6 (M7)	WC 4 (M7)	WC 7 (M7)	WC 5 (M7)	WC 6 (M7)	N 4

	11.0 Wloo	11.30 Padd	12.5 Wloo	12.15 Ports	3.36 Tn	1.0 Wloo	
Barnstaple Jn a.	3.45		4.25	4.41	5.25	5.34	6.30
d.	3.51		4.28	4.46	5.31	5.50	6.35
Barnstaple Town	3a55		4a32	4a50	5a35	5c55	6a39
Pottington SB	3.56		4.33	4.51	5.36	5.56	6.40
Wrafton	4a3				5a43	6a3	6a47
Braunton	4j10		4g44	5j3	5e48	6g9	6c51
Mortehoe	4e30		5a2	5e23	6c7	6a27	7a9
Ilfracombe a.	4.38		5.10	5.31	6.15	6.35	7.17
Formation	WC 7 (N)		43xx 6 (M7)	WC 9 (N)	WC 5 (M7)	43xx 6 (M7)	N 3

	4.35 Tn	3.0 Wloo
Barnstaple Jn a.	6.42	8.15
d.	6.55	8.24
Barnstaple Town	6a59	8a28
Pottington SB	7.0	8.29
Wrafton	7a7	8a36
Braunton	7c11	8c40
Mortehoe	7a29	8a58
Ilfracombe a.	7.37	9.6
Formation	N 4	WC 3 (M7)

All Pottington SB times are passing times.
General Note. Unless otherwise stated all down trains with assisting locomotive were banked from Braunton to Mortehoe only.
All Pottington SB times are passing times.
Note 1. The M7 worked from Barnstaple Junction to Braunton.
Note 2. The N and 43xx worked from Barnstaple Junction to Ilfracombe
Note 3. The M7 worked from Braunton to Ilfracombe
Note 4. The M7 and N worked from Barnstaple Junction to Ilfracombe.

UP TRAINS

	K Nymp	Wloo	Manch	Wloo	Card	Wloo	Wolver
Ilfracombe d.	6.50	8.10	8.25	8.50	9.25	9.40	10.12
Mortehoe	7.2 1/2	8c24	8c39	9c4	9c39	10q0	10c26
Braunton	7.13 1/2	8a35	8c51	9c16	9c51	10g14	10e39
Wrafton	7.16	8a38	8a54	9a19	9c55		10c43
Pottington SB	7.22	8.44	9.0	9.25	10.1	10.21	10.49
Barnstaple Town	7a24	8c47	9c3	9a27	10c4	10c24	10c52
Barnstaple Jn a.	7.27	8.50	9.6	9.30	10.7	10.27	10.55
d.	7.29	8.55	9.12	9.48	10.14	10.31	11.5
Formation	WC 2	WC 3	N 7 (WC)	WC 7 (N)	43xx 6 (WC)	WC 8 (N)	43xx 4

	Wloo	Wolver	Wloo	Wloo	Padd	Wloo	Wloo
Ilfracombe d.	10.30	10.55	11.30	12.0	12.25	1.45	2.10
Mortehoe	10c44	11e10	11e45	12a13	12c39	1c59	2a23
Braunton	10e57	11g24	11e58	12a24	12c51	2c11	2e36
Wrafton	11c1	11c28	12a1	12a27	12a54	2a14	2a39
Pottington SB	11.7	11.34	12.7	12.33	1.0	2.20	2.45
Barnstaple Town	11e11	11c37	12c10	12a35	1a3	2a22	2a47
Barnstaple Jn a.		11.40	12.13	12.38	1.6	2.25	2.50
d.	11.14	11.44	12.20	12.40	1.12	2.30	2.55
Formation	WC 11 (N)	M7 43xx 6 Note 5	WC 9 (N)	WC 11 (N)	N n.a. (M7)	WC 6 (M7)	N 3

	Wloo	L.E. Ex Jn	Fgt	Ex.C	Tn		Tn
Ilfracombe d.	2.55	3.25	3.40	4.48	5.10	5.50	6.30
Mortehoe	3a8	3.37	4k0	5a1	5a23	6a3	6a43
Braunton	3c20	3e50	4p38	5c13	5a34	6a14	6c55
Wrafton	3a23		4l51	5a16	5a37	6a17	6a58
Pottington SB	3.29	4.0	5.0	5.22	5.43	6.23	7.4
Barnstaple Town	3a31	4.1	5.1	5c25	5a45	6a25	7a6
Barnstaple Jn a.	3.34	4.5	5.5	5.28	5.48	6.28	7.9
d.	3.41	5.24		5.35	5.55		7.17
Formation	N WC 5 Note 6	WC	M7	WC WC 4 Note 7	WC N Note 8	WC 6	43xx N 6 Note9

	ECS Ex.C	Ex.C	Tn				
Ilfracombe d.	7.0	7.42	8.0	8.30			
Mortehoe	7e15	7a55	8a13	8a43			
Braunton	7.26	8a6	8a24	8a54			
Wrafton		8a9	8a27	8a57			
Pottington SB	7.34	8.15	8.33	9.3			
Barnstaple Town	7.35	8c18	8c36	9c6			
Barnstaple Jn a.	7.38	8.21	8.39	9.9			
d.	7.53	8.30	8.45				
Formation	n.a.	WC WC 6 Note 7	M7 43xx 6 Note 5	N 2			

KEY

a	arrives 1 minute earlier	Card	Cardiff General
b	arrives 1 1/2 minutes earlier	Ex.C	Exeter Central
c	arrives 2 minutes earlier	Ex.Jn	Exmouth Junction
d	arrives 2 1/2 minutes earlier	K.Nym	Kings Nympton
e	arrives 3 minutes earlier	Manch	Manchester Exchange
f	arrives 3 1/2 minutes earlier	Padd	Paddington
g	arrives 4 minutes earlier	Ports	Portsmouth and Southsea
h	arrives 4 1/2 minutes earlier	Tn	Taunton
j	arrives 5 minutes earlier	Wloo	Waterloo
k	arrives 6 minutes earlier	Wolver	Wolverhampton Low Level
l	arrives 10 minutes earlier	Yeov	Yeovil Town
m	arrives 11 minutes earlier		
n	arrives 15 minutes earlier	LE	Light Engine
p	arrives 19 minutes earlier	ECS	Empty Coaching Stock
q	arrives 8 minutes earlier	Pcl	Parcels
		Fgt	Freight

All Pottington SB times are passing times, as is the Barnstaple Junct time for the 10.30am Ilfracombe.
General. Unless otherwise stated all up trains with a second locomotive were assisted from Ilfracombe to Mortehoe only.
All Pottington SB times are passing times, as is the Barnstaple Junction time for the 10.30 Ilfracombe.
Note 5. M7 and 43xx work from Ilfracombe to Barnstaple Junction.
Note 6. The N assists from Ilfracombe to Braunton
Note 7. The two WCs work from Ilfracombe to Exeter Central.
Note 8. The WC and N work from Ilfracombe to Barnstaple Junction.
Note 9. The 43xx and N work from Ilfracombe to Barnstaple Junction

The interior of Ilfracombe station and its steel platform gates. Returning holidaymakers were marshalled in an orderly queue in the station approach, and admitted through the gates when their train was ready. The Southern had considerable experience of coping with large numbers of passengers at many of its stations. *Reg Spurway courtesy David Watts*

ing vehicles arrived, usually unadvertised to the public, together with a extra coaches on some arrivals from Waterloo. Taking summer 1955 as an example, on a typical weekday there might be about 12 coaches berthed at Ilfracombe overnight, in position for the next day's services, whereas on Friday nights there were some *fifty* coaches in the sidings ready for Saturday morning departures. On Saturday nights there were another fifty, which had arrived

that afternoon and evening. These extra coaches were either worked away as extra vehicles on Sunday and Monday departures, or remained in Ilfracombe carriage sidings until the next weekend.

Shunting carriages into and out of the sidings was only part of the story. All carriages had to be thoroughly cleaned and the water tanks filled. These jobs were done in the platform on arrival the day before if at all possible, but for trains

which arrived during Saturday and then formed departing services, the work had to be done quickly, as soon as the passengers had cleared the train. A time-consuming job was the labelling of seat reservations for the principal expresses to Waterloo; although the reservation tickets could be prepared in advance in the booking office station staff had to allocate them to the right seats. This was a long job on the 11 coaches of the Atlantic

The Southern necessarily had wide experience of dealing with large quantities of passenger luggage in advance, and the Ilfracombe store could deal with two delivery lorries at once. Passenger barriers can be seen to the right. *Reg Spurway courtesy David Watts*

TABLE 2 LOCOMOTIVE DUTIES
Summer 1957 Saturdays Only

Nine Elms Duty No.15 — 7P5F (WC class)

Arrive	Location	Depart	Notes
	Nine Elms	10.9am	
10.22	Waterloo	10.45	P
12.16pm	Salisbury		
	Salisbury Loco	1.35pm	
	Salisbury	1.55	P (12.15 Ports)
5.56	Ilfracombe		
	Ilfracombe Loco	7.25	
7.30	Ilfracombe	7.42	P
10.7	Exeter	115	P
11.32	Honiton	11.47	
11.54	Sidmouth Junction	12.5	
12.25	Exmouth Junction		

Taunton Duty No.70 — (43xx class)

Arrive	Location	Depart	Notes
	Taunton	4.5am	F
6.43	Barnstaple Vic Rd	7.18	F
7.23	Barnstaple Jn (turn)	7.45	(ANR)
7.50	Barnstaple Vic Rd	8.5	P (6.20 Tton)
9.4	Ilfracombe		
	Ilfracombe Loco		
	Ilfracombe Loco	10.12	P
11.10	Barnstaple Vic Rd	11.35	
11.40	Barnstaple Loco	12.20pm	
	Barnstaple Junct	12.43	P (11.50 Tor'tn)
2.29	Taunton		
	Taunton Loco		
	Taunton	4.35	P
6.42	Barnstaple Jn (turn)	7.17	P (6.30 Ilfrme)
9.18	Taunton		

Taunton Duty No. 71 — (43xx class)

Arrive	Location	Depart	Notes
	Taunton	4.45am	F
8.20	Barnstaple Vic Rd	8.35	
8.40	Barnstaple Loco	9.0	
9.5	Barnstaple Jn	9.12	P (8.25 Ilfrme)
9.17	Barnstaple Vic Rd	9.25	P
11.0	Taunton		
	Taunton Loco	2.10	
	Taunton	2.26	P
4.9	Barnstaple Vic Rd	4.26	
4.31	Barnstaple Loco	5.5	
5.10	Barnstaple Vic Rd	5.29	P (3.36 Tnton)
6.35	Ilfracombe		
	Ilfracombe Loco		
	Ilfracombe	8.0	P
8.39	Barnstaple Junction	9.0	
9.5	Barnstaple Vic Rd	9.15	
9.20	Barnstaple Junction		

Taunton Duty No.72 — (43xx class)

Arrive	Location	Depart	Notes
	Taunton	5.20am	P
7.16	Barnstaple Jn (turn)	7.45	
9.31	Taunton		
	Taunton Loco		
	Taunton	12.50pm	P
2.38	Barnstaple Vic Rd	3.10	
3.15	Barnstaple Jn (turn)	3.55	P ANR
4.0	Barnstaple Vic Rd	4.20	P (2.26 Tnton)
5.10	Ilfracombe (turn)		
	Ilfracombe	6.30	P
7.9	Barnstaple Jn (turn)	7.30	
7.35	Barnstaple Vic Rd	8.0	F
10.22	Taunton		

Taunton Duty No.73 — (43xx class)

Arrive	Location	Depart	Notes
	Taunton	6.20am	P
7.55	Barnstaple Vic Rd	8.20	
8.25	Barnstaple Jn (turn)	8.45	
8.50	Barnstaple Vic Rd	9.5	P (7.15 Tnton)
9.58	Ilfracombe		
	Ilfracombe Loco		
	Ilfracombe	10.55	P
11.49	Barnstaple Vic Rd	11.55	
12 noon	Barnstaple Loco	2.39pm	
2.44	Barnstaple Vic Rd	3.5	F
7.34	Taunton		
	Taunton Loco		

Taunton Duty No.77 — (43xx class)

Arrive	Location	Depart	Notes
	Barnstaple Loco	7.10am	
	Barnstaple Junction	7.29	P (5.20 Tnton)
8.14	Ilfracombe		
	Ilfracombe Loco		
	Ilfracombe	9.25	P
10.23	Barnstaple Vic. Rd	10.50	
10.55	Barnstaple Jn (turn)	11.30	F
11.35	Barnstaple Vic. Rd	11.56	P (10.55 Ilfrme)
1.30pm	Taunton		
	Taunton Loco		
	Taunton	3.36	P
5.11	Barnstaple Vic. Rd	5.25	
5.30	Barnstaple Jn (turn)	5.55	P (5.10 Ilfrme)
7.51	Taunton		

Salisbury Duty No.461 — 7P5F (BB class)

Arrive	Location	Depart	Notes
	Salisbury Loco	11.34am	
	Salisbury	11.54	P(10.15 Waterloo)
3.40	Ilfracombe		
	Ilfracombe Loco		
	Ilfracombe	5.10	P (ANR)
5.49	Barnstaple Junction	6.12	F (4.5 Torrington)
9.33	Exmouth Junction		
	Exmouth Jn Loco		

Salisbury Duty No. 464 — 7P5F (BB class)

Arrive	Location	Depart	Notes
	Salisbury Loco	10.22am	
10.27	Salisbury	10.32	P (8.35 Waterloo)
2.41pm	Ilfracombe		
	Ilfracombe Loco	4.25	
4.30	Ilfracombe	4.48	P
7.3	Exeter	7.12	
7.17	Exmouth Jn Loco		

Exmouth Junction Duty No. 515 — 7P5F (WC class)

Arrive	Location	Depart	Notes
Off No. 609 Friday			
	Barnstaple Loco	7.45am	
7.50	Barnstaple Junction	8.0	P
8.46	Ilfracombe	9.25	P (Bank)
9.37	Mortehoe		
	Ilfracombe Loco	11.15	
11.20	Ilfracombe	11.30	P
3.20pm	Salisbury	3.24pm	
3.29	Salisbury Loco	5.0	
	Salisbury	6.10	P (4.48 Bas'toke)
7.25	Yeovil Junction	7.45	
7.50	Yeovil Loco		

Exmouth Junction Duty No. 516 — 7P5F (WC class)

Arrive	Location	Depart	Notes
	Exmouth Junction	11.48am	
11.52	Exeter	12.10pm	P (8.22 Waterloo)
2.21	Ilfracombe (turn)	3.25	
6.44	Exmouth Junction		

Exmouth Junction Duty No. 520 — 7P5F (WC class)

Arrive	Location	Depart	Notes
	Exmouth Junction	4.35am	
4.39	Exeter	5.17	P (ANR)
6.2	Okehampton	7.0	P
8.46	Plymouth Friary		via Cattewater Jn
	Plymouth Loco	10.45	
10.52	Plymouth Friary	11.0	P
12.52pm	Exeter	1.11	
1.14	Exmouth Junction	3.14	
3.18	Exeter	3.38	P
5.28	Ilfracombe		
	Ilfracombe Loco		
	Ilfracombe	7.42	P (ANR)
8.24	Barnstaple Junction	8.25	
8.30	Barnstaple Loco		

Exmouth Junction Duty No. 523 — 7P 5F (WC class)

Arrive	Location	Depart	Notes
	Exmouth Jn Loco	1.1am	
1.4	Exmouth Junction	1.20	F (4.30 Wdebr'ge)
3.8	Yeovil Jct (turn)	3.57	P
4.1	Yeovil Town	4.15	
4.20	Yeovil Loco	6.0	
6.5	Yeovil Town	6.25	P
10.58	Ilfracombe		
	Ilfracombe Loco	11.45	
11.50	Ilfracombe	12 noon	P
1.51pm	Exeter	1.53	
1.57	Exmouth Jn Loco	4.15	
4.19	Exeter	4.35	P
7.54	Salisbury		
	C. shunting	8.0 - 8.30	
	Salisbury	8.30	
8.35	Salisbury Loco		

Exmouth Junction Duty No.524 — 7P 5F (WC class)

Arrive	Location	Depart	Notes
	Yeovil Loco	5.15am	
5.20	Yeovil Town		
	C. shunting	5.20 - 7.20	
	Yeovil Town	7.45	P
12.9pm	Ilfracombe	12.20pm	
12.25	Ilfracombe Loco	1.30	
1.35	Ilfracombe	1.45	P
3.58	Exeter	4.9	
4.12	Exmouth Junction	6.6	
6.10	Exeter	6.52	P
9.6	Ilfracombe		
	C. shunting	9.10 - 9.25	
	Ilfracombe	9.25	
9.30	Ilfracombe Loco		

Exmouth Junction Duty No.525 — 7P5F (WC class)

Arrive	Location	Depart	Notes
	Exmouth Junction	10.49am	
10.53	Exeter	11.26	P (7.38 Waterloo)
1.27	Ilfracombe		
	Ilfracombe Loco	2.40	
	Ilfracombe	2.55	P
5.26	Exeter	5.28	
5.31	Exmouth Junction		

Exmouth Junction Duty No. 526 — 7P5F (WC class)

Arrive	Location	Depart	Notes
	Exmouth Junction	4.35am	
4.39	Exeter	5.6	P (1.15 Waterloo)
6.53	Ilfracombe	7.0	
7.5	Ilfracombe Loco	9.20	
9.25	Ilfracombe	9.40	P
11.33	Exeter	11.35	
11.38	Exmouth Junction		

Exmouth Junction Duty No. 527 — 7P 5F (WC class)

Arrive	Location	Depart	Notes
	Exmouth Junction	1.52am	
1.56	Exeter	2.6	F
4.55	Barnstaple	5.30	F
6.14	Ilfracombe		
	F. shunting	6.25 -6.40	
	Ilfracombe	6.40	
	Ilfracombe Loco	7.55	
8.0	Ilfracombe	8.10	P
10.11	Exeter	10.13	
10.16	Exmouth Junction	12.52pm	
12.56	Exeter	1.12	P (8.57 Waterloo)
3.22	Ilfracombe		
	Ilfracombe Loco	4.25	
4.30	Ilfracombe	4.48	P (AR)
7.3	Exeter	7.12	
7.15	Exmouth Jn Loco		

Exmouth Junction Duty No. 528 — 7P 5F (WC class)

Arrive	Location	Depart	Notes
	Exmouth Junction	4.35am	
4.39	Exeter	5.26	P
7.42	Ilfracombe	8.25	P (Bank)
8.39	Mortehoe		
	Ilfracombe Loco	10.0	
	Ilfracombe	10.30	P
12.21pm	Exeter	12.23	
12.26	Exmouth Junction	1.44	
1.48	Exeter	2.1	P (10.35 Waterloo)
5.0	Padstow	5.20	
5.30	Wadebridge Loco		

Exmouth Junction Duty No. 529 — 7P5F (WC class)

Arrive	Location	Depart	Notes
	Barnstaple Loco	7.15am	
7.52	Ilfracombe	8.50	P
9.30	Barnstaple Junction	9.48	P (9.10 Torrington)
10.50	Exeter	10.52	
10.55	Exmouth Junction	12.52pm	
12.56	Exeter	1.26	P (8.57 Waterloo)
3.43	Plymouth Friary		via Mount Gould Jn
	Plymouth Loco		

Exmouth Junction Duty No. 530 — 4P 5F (N class)

Arrive	Location	Depart	Notes
	Exmouth Junction	4.25am	
4.29	Exeter	4.30	P (12.35 Waterloo)
6.34	Ilfracombe		
	C. shunting	7.0 - 7.30	
	Ilfracombe Loco		
	Ilfracombe	8.25	P
9.6	Barnstaple Junction	10.37	P
11.46	Yeoford	1.49pm	P (ANR)
2.18	Exeter	2.23	
2.27	Exmouth Jc Loco		

Exmouth Junction Duty No. 531 — 4P 5F (N class)

Arrive	Location	Depart	Notes
	Exmouth Jn Loco	3.15am	
3.18	Exmouth Junction	3.30	F
4.37	Yeoford		
	F. shunting	4.45 - 6.55	
	Yeoford	7.9	F(6.0 Exmouth Jn)
8.35	Barnstaple Junction	10.2	
10.7	Barnstaple Vic. Rd	10.30	P (8.30 Taunton)
11.22	Ilfracombe	12 noon	(Bank)
12.11	Mortehoe	12.20	
12.28	Ilfracombe		
	Ilfracombe Loco	1.50	
1.55	Ilfracombe	2.10	P
4.11	Exeter	4.13	
4.16	Exmouth Junction	5.25	
5.29	Exeter	5.52	P
6.56	Okehampton	7.45	P
8.55	Bude	9.20	
9.23	Bude Loco		

Cont. from overleaf

Barnstaple   **Duty No. 572**   7P5F (WC class)

Arrive		Depart	
	Ilfracombe Loco	6.35am	
	Ilfracombe	6.50	P
7.52	Kings Nympton	8.30	P
8.52	Barnstaple Junction		
	Bnstple Loco (coal)	11.15	
11.20	Barnstaple Junt	11.28	P (10.48 Tor'gton)
12.39pm	Exeter Central	1.0pm	P (11.0 Plymouth)
2.49	Salisbury	3.0	
3.3	Salisbury Loco	7.35	
7.38	Salisbury	7.56	P
9.21	Yeovil Junction		
	F. shunting	9.55 - 10.20	
	Yeovil Junction	2.0am	
2.5	Yeovil Loco		

Barnstaple   **Duty No. 573**   4P 5F (N class)

Arrive		Depart	
	Barnstaple Loco	6.35am	
7.14	Ilfracombe		
	C. shunting	7.30 - 6.30pm (less 30 min. meals and E.R.)	
	Ilfracombe	6.30	P (Assist at rear)
7.9	Barnstaple Junction		
	Barnstaple Loco		

Barnstaple   **Duty No. 574**   4P 5F (N class)

Arrive		Depart	
	Barnstaple Loco	2.45pm	
2.50	Barnstaple Vic. Rd	2.55	P (12.50 Taunton)
3.56	Ilfracombe		
	Ilfracombe Loco		
	Ilfracombe	5.10	P
5.49	Barnstaple Junction		
	Barnstaple Loco		

Barnstaple   **Duty No. 575**   4P 5F (N class)

Arrive		Depart	
	Barnstaple Loco	7.20am	
	Barnstaple Junction	7.39	P (7.0 Torrington)
8.56	Exeter Central	8.58	
9.2	Exmouth Junction	10.58	
11.2	Exeter Central	11.39	P
2.5pm	Ilfracombe	2.55	P (AR)
3.18	Braunton	4.9	P(B'k 11.0 Wat'loo)
4.26	Mortehoe	4.40	
4.50	Braunton	5.3	P(B'k 12.0 Watloo)
5.18	Mortehoe	5.40	
6.5	Barnstaple Junction	6.55	P (4.35 Taunton)
7.37	Ilfracombe		
	Ilfracombe Loco	8.45	
9.19	Barnstaple Loco		

Barnstaple   **Duty No. 577**   2PT (M7 class)

Arrive		Depart	
	Barnstaple Loco	4.45am	
4.50	Barnstaple Junction	5.15	F
6.8	Torrington		
	F. shunting	6.15 - 6.30	
	C. shunting	6.30 - 6.45	
	Torrington	7.5	P
7.33	Barnstaple Junction	8.14	P
8.45	Torrington		
	C. shunting	9.0 - 9.20	
	F. shunting	9.20 - 10.0	
	Torrington	10.48	P
11.21	Barnstaple Junction	11.25	
11.30	Barnstaple Loco	12.20pm	
12.40	Braunton	1.38	P(B'k 11.39 Exeter)
1.55	Mortehoe		
	Braunton	2.14	P(B'k 8.35 Watloo)
2.31	Mortehoe	2.35	
2.45	Braunton	2.56	P(B'k 8.54 Watloo)
3.13	Mortehoe	3.18	
3.28	Braunton	4.44	P(B'k 2.26 Tauntn)
5.1	Mortehoe	5.10	
5.20	Braunton	5.48	P(B'k 12.15 Portsm)
6.5	Mortehoe	6.10	
	Ilfracombe		
	C. shunting	6.45 - 7.50	
	Ilfracombe	8.0	P (AR)
8.49	Barnstaple Junction		
	Barnstaple Loco		

Barnstaple   **Duty No. 581**   2PT (M7 class)

Arrive		Depart	
	Barnstaple Loco	10.25am	
	Barnstaple Junction	10.40	P (AR 8.30 Tntn)

11.22	Ilfracombe	12.25pm	P (Bank)
12.37	Mortehoe	12.40	
12.55	Braunton	1.54	P(B'k 8.22 Watloo)
2.11	Mortehoe	2.35	
2.45	Braunton	3.13	P(B'k 10.15 Watloo)
3.30	Mortehoe	5.36	
5.46	Braunton	6.9	P(B'k 3.36 Tnton)
6.26	Mortehoe	6.30	
6.40	Braunton	8.40	P(B'k 6.52 Exeter)
8.57	Mortehoe	9.5	
9.30	Barnstaple Loco		

Barnstaple   **Duty No. 583**   2PT (M7 class)

Arrive		Depart	
	Barnstaple Loco	5.40am	
	Barnstaple Junction	5.49	P (ANR)
6.3	Braunton	6.27	P(B'k 1.15 Watloo)
6.44	Mortehoe	6.55	
7.5	Braunton	7.14	P(B'k 5.26 Exeter)
7.31	Mortehoe	8.45	
8.55	Braunton	9.31	P(AR 7.15 Taunton)
9.58	Ilfracombe		
	Ilfracombe Loco	10.40	
	Ilfracombe	10.55	P(AR)
11.40	Barnstaple Junction	11.53	F
1.0pm	Ilfracombe	1.45	P (Bank)
1.57	Mortehoe		
	Ilfracombe	3.40	F
5.5	Barnstaple Junction	5.32	F
5.37	Barnstaple Vic. Rd	5.48	F
5.53	Barnstaple Junction	6.0	
6.5	Barnstaple Loco		

Barnstaple   **Duty No. 584**   4P 5F (N class)

Arrive		Depart	
	Barnstaple Loco	6.46am	
	Barnstaple Junction		
	C.shunting	6.50 - 7.15	
	Barnstaple Junction	7.27	P (AR 5.20 Tnton)
8.14	Ilfracombe	8.50	P (Bank)
9.2	Mortehoe	9.15	
9.23	Ilfracombe	9.40	P (Bank)
9.53	Mortehoe	10.0	
10.8	Ilfracombe	10.30	P (Bank)
10.42	Mortehoe	10.50	P (ANR)
10.58	Ilfracombe	11.30	P (Bank)
11.42	Mortehoe		
	Ilfracombe	12.25pm	P
1.6	Barnstaple Junction	1.24	P (12.45 T'gton)
2.50	Exeter	2.54	
2.58	Exmouth Junction	4.28	
4.32	Exeter	5.5	P
7.17	Ilfracombe	7.37	
7.42	Ilfracombe Loco	8.10	
8.15	Ilfracombe	8.30	P
9.9	Barnstaple Junction	9.30	
9.35	Barnstaple Loco		

Wadebridge   **Duty No. 603**   7P 5F (WC class)

Arrive		Depart	
	Wadebridge Loco	7.0am	
7.4	Wadebridge	7.5	F
7.19	Padstow		
	F.shunting	7.35 - 7.50	
	Padstow	8.30	P
11.50	Exeter	11.52	
11.55	Exmouth Junction	2.20pm	
2.24	Exeter	2.36	P (11.0 Waterloo)
4.38	Ilfracombe	5.0	
5.5	Ilfracombe Loco	5.20	
5.35	Ilfracombe	5.50	Mixed
6.28	Barnstaple Junction		
	Barnstaple Loco		

Wadebridge   **Duty No. 609**   7P 5F (WC class)

Arrive		Depart	
	Wadebridge Loco	10.2am	
10.7	Wadebridge	10.15	P
10.24	Padstow	11.0	P
2.4	Exeter	2.6	
2.10	Exmouth Junction	6.6	
6.10	Exeter	6.52	P
9.6	Ilfracombe		
	C. shunting	9.10 - 9.25	
	Ilfracombe	9.25	
9.30	Ilfracombe Loco		

ANR	Assistance not required
AR	Assistance required
P	Passenger
F	Freight
ECS	Empty Coaching Stock

All other movements are light engine.

---

drivers also had a hectic day shuttling to and fro between the stations and the resorts. It was not the easiest of jobs ensuring that holidaymakers and all their luggage arrived at the stations in good time for their departures, as road traffic hold-ups could be disruptive. This was particularly true in and around Braunton, which was literally cut into two when a train passed through and every level crossing was shut to road traffic. Caen Street, which formed part of the main B3231 road to Saunton and Croyde, was particularly vulnerable to traffic jams when down trains had to halt on the level crossing to allow the attachment of assisting engines. And the only entrance to Braunton station was from Caen Street.

A TYPICAL YEAR - 1958

The train service details in the next few paragraphs are taken from the 1958 summer working timetable. They are 'typical' but varied in detail from year to year. There were a limited number of early morning and later evening services catering for local traffic only. The first long distance trains were overnight services, the 12.25am and 1.15am from Waterloo, and the 5.20am, 6.20am and 7.0am from Taunton, which arrived at 6.14am, 6.53am, 8.14am, 9.4am and 9.58am respectively. The Taunton services were provided for travellers from the Midlands and the North who arrived there on overnight trains destined for Paignton and the Cornish resorts, changing for Ilfracombe. Surprisingly, there were fewer through trains from the North and Midlands to Ilfracombe than in the reverse direction. Once the passengers and all their luggage had cleared these trains station staff could prepare them for departing services.

The morning's long distance departures commenced with the 8.10am Waterloo, 8.25am Manchester Exchange, 8.50am Waterloo, 9.25am Cardiff, 9.40am empty coaching stock which became the 10am Mortehoe to Waterloo, 10.12am Wolverhampton, 10.30am Waterloo Atlantic Coast Express, 10.55am Wolverhampton, 11.30am Waterloo, 12noon Waterloo formerly the Devon Belle, 12.25pm Paddington, 1.45pm, 2.10pm and 2.55pm to Waterloo. Station staff at Ilfracombe became very adept at managing passengers waiting for their trains. As many as 600 or 800 would line up patiently on the station approach road, and when their train was ready for boarding the steel lattice gates were opened up and station staff called them in. Porters could supplement their wages with tips for looking after passengers and their luggage.

The daytime long-distance trains arrived in the afternoon and early evening with the 1.27pm, 2.21pm, 2.41pm, 3.22pm, 3.40pm arrivals of the 7.38am, 8.22am, 8.35am 8.57am, 10.15am from Waterloo, then the 3.56pm arrival from Taunton, 4.38pm Atlantic Coast Express from Waterloo, 5.10pm arrival from Taunton including through coaches from the 11.30am Paddington, 5.31pm arrival of the 12.05pm Waterloo (formerly the

---

Coast Express. Incidentally, Ilfracombe staff had to deal with the reservations for all stations for which the facility was advertised. For example, the 1964 Atlantic Coast Express offered reservations to Waterloo for all stations to Barnstaple Junction as well as Exeter Central. Restaurant cars received their provisions of fresh food and drinking water on the day.

It was not just the railwaymen who had a very busy summer Saturday. Very many holidaymakers were destined for accommodation further than walking distance from the stations so taxi and bus

TABLE 3 CARRIAGE WORKING NOTICES ILFRACOMBE SATURDAYS ONLY 16th July - 13th August 1955

Train	Destination	Formation	Previous Service Time	From	Due
6.42am	Barnstaple Jn	2-set(63-75)		Berth	
8.10	Waterloo	3-set(770)		Berth	
8.25	Manchester	7 LM corrs		Berth	
9.0	Waterloo	2-set(63-75)	5.26am	Exeter C.	7.42am
		5-set		Berth	
9.25	Cardiff	6 WR corrs	5.20	Taunton	8.12
9.40	Waterloo	5-set		Berth	
		3-set(770)		Berth	
10.12	Taunton	4 WR corrs	6.20	Taunton	9.1
10.30	Waterloo	3-set(770)		Berth	
		1 third		Berth	
		1 refreshment car		Berth	
		1 kitchen buffet		Berth	
		5-set		Berth	
10.55	Wolverhampton	6 WR corrs	7.15	Taunton	9.58
11.30	Waterloo	1 third	1.15	Waterloo	6.53
		5-set	"	"	"
		1 Bk Cpo	12.35	Waterloo	6.34
		2 Thirds	"	"	"
12noon	Waterloo	2 Thirds		Berth	
		2-set(63-75)	8.0	Bple Jn	8.46
		1 Open Third		Berth	
		1 restaraunt car		Berth	
		5-set		Berth	
1.45pm	Waterloo	3-set	6.25	Yeovil Tn	10.58
		3-set(770)	"	"	"
2.10	Waterloo	3-set(770)	7.45	Yeovil Tn	12.9
2.55	Waterloo	1 News Van	5.26	Exeter C.	7.42
		1 News Van	1.15	Waterloo	6.53
		3-set(770)	7.38	Waterloo	1.27
4.48	Waterloo	1 PMV		Berth	
	Exeter Central	3-set	11.39	Exeter C.	2.5
5.10	Taunton	4 WR corrs	12.50	Taunton	3.56
5.45	Barnstaple Jn	2 Thirds	8.35	Waterloo	2.41
		4 WR corrs	8.30	Taunton	11.18
6.30	Taunton	6 WR corrs	2.26	Taunton	5.10
7.45	Exeter Central	3-set	11.39	Exeter Central	2.5
		1 refreshment saloon	11.0	Waterloo	4.36
		1 kitchen buffet	"	"	"
		1 van	5.26am	Exeter Central	7.44
8.0	Taunton	6 WR corrs	3.36	Taunton	6.16
8.30 ECS	Barnstaple Jn	2-lav set	5.55	Barnstaple Jn	6.37
8.45	Barnstaple Jn	4 WR corrs	4.35	Taunton	7.37
	Berth	1 third	7.45am	Yeovil Town	12.9
	Berth	2 thirds	7.38	Waterloo	1.27
	Berth	1 third	8.22	Waterloo	2.21
		5-set	"	"	"
	Berth	5-set	8.35	Waterloo	2.41
	Berth	5-set	8.57	Waterloo	3.22
	Berth	1 third	10.15	Waterloo	3.40
		5-set	"	"	"
	Berth	2 thirds	11.0	Waterloo	4.36
		3-set	"	"	"
	Berth	5-set	12.0	Waterloo	5.28
		1 open third	"	"	"
		1 kitchen car	"	"	"
		1 open first	"	"	"
		1 Bk Compo	"	"	"
	Berth	2 thirds	12.15	Portsmouth	5.56
		3-set	"	"	"
	Berth	2-set(63-75)	5.55	Barnstaple Jn	6.37
	Berth	3-set	1.0	Waterloo	7.17
	Berth	3-set(770)	3.0	Waterloo	9.4

down and one up service missed out the Wrafton stop. Further afield four up expresses ran non-stop between Barnstaple Junction and Exeter St David's. The Atlantic Coast Express was non-stop between Barnstaple Town and Yeoford, and four trains also ran non-stop from Exeter Central to Salisbury. In the down direction three were non-stop between Salisbury and Exeter Central, and three non-stop between Exeter St David's and Barnstaple Junction. The 1.15am from Waterloo had no stop from Exeter Central to Barnstaple Junction. Other Waterloo expresses had a limited number of stops. On the Taunton line, the long distance trains missed out several stops and normally called only at South Molton, Dulverton and Wiveliscombe, although one down train passed Wiveliscombe and a couple also called at Bishops Nympton. On summer Saturdays the sheer volume of traffic precluded really fast running; the 11.0am Atlantic Coast Express on weekdays arrived at Ilfracombe at 4.2pm, but at 4.38pm on Saturdays. Delays could always be expected at Exeter St David's where the Western Region had great difficulty in coping with its huge volume of traffic. More time was needed, for passengers with luggage had to change trains at Salisbury and both the Exeter stations, and bankers had to be attached for the Mortehoe and Exeter banks. The weekday Atlantic Coast Express was allowed five minutes for loading and unloading at the four intermediate stations, but on

Saturdays ten minutes. As one Southern railwayman put it drivers were expected to 'Keep up with the one in front, stay ahead of the one behind'. Table 1 is extracted from the peak Summer 1958 Passenger and Freight timetables, and includes all movements shown for the period 14th June to 13th September, although some trains ran for a shorter period than this. It would have been preferable to use the locomotive duties and carriage workings for the same period, but these have yet to come to light, so the available 1957 locomotive duties and 1955 carriage workings have been used to complete the picture. Unfortunately, there were some changes which lead to some inconsistencies between the years, but these were limited. Missing from these timetables are the details of the return of light engines from Mortehoe to Ilfracombe or Braunton, so these sections were considerably busier than the timetable indicates. Barnstaple Victoria Road timings have been omitted for reasons of brevity, but it usually took 30-40 minutes from arrival at Victoria Road to departure from Barnstaple Town, a journey which could be walked in ten minutes. The train formations illustrate a marked frequency of double-heading, sometimes when the train did not justify it. This was to get locomotives in place without occupying paths, the trains being light enough for one engine only. Table 2 is extracted from the Summer 1957 Locomotive Duties and shows that no less than 30 different engines worked on the line on a summer Saturday. The five Western Region duties for 43XX 2-6-0s were for Taunton engines, but none worked its train right through to (or from) Ilfracombe, since this required turning on the only available turntable at Barnstaple, at the Junction, and running round at Victoria Road. In earlier years some of these duties were covered by 55XX 2-6-2Ts. On the Southern there were some long through workings of West Country Pacifics, with three of them working trains right through from Salisbury and two through from Yeovil to Ilfracombe. In the up direction a Pacific worked through from Ilfracombe to Salisbury.

Nine Elms Duty No.15 took a West Country to Salisbury on one train, and after a visit to the shed there on to Ilfracombe with another. The provision of banking engines illustrates the difficulty of the ascent from Ilfracombe station with an N or West Country, rather than the M7 often rostered up from Braunton. In earlier years an E1R might have appeared, and later the Ivatt 2-6-2Ts took over the M7 duties. Table 3 provides details of the carriage workings for Summer 1955. On the principal trains most Southern stock at this time was Bulleid, but some Maunsell coaches and even the odd South Western vehicles also appeared. Some BR Mark 1 stock appeared, including the triple restaurant car set on the 12 noon from Waterloo.

When Dr Beeching made his report in 1963 he found that such peak summer traffic, requiring extra rolling stock which lay idle for much of the year, and overtime payments to the men, was uneconomic.

Devon Belle), 6.15pm arrival of 12.15pm from Portsmouth and Southsea, 6.35pm arrival from Taunton including through coaches from Wolverhampton, and 7.17pm, 7.37pm and 9.6pm arrivals of the 1.0pm Waterloo, 4.35pm Taunton and 3.0pm Waterloo.

Normally all passenger trains called at all stations between Ilfracombe and Barnstaple Junction, although three

Saturday 29th August 1964, a week before an end was put to through expresses from Waterloo. The 5.57pm from Ilfracombe to Taunton consists of six Western Region coaches, hauled out of the terminus by 43XX 2-6-0 No.7303, piloted by N 2-6-0 No.31834. *S.C.Nash*

He felt much of the traffic was being taken over by the family car, and that what remained on the railway could be made profitable by controlling it with compulsory seat reservations, like the airlines. Subsequently, vast sums of money have been spent in building west country roads and motorways which are only fully used on those same summer Saturdays; what verdict would Dr Beeching hand down on that? The family travelling in a car along the M5 or A303 to a holiday in Ilfracombe, stuck in traffic jams or queuing to get into a motorway service area, do they have a better journey than a previous generation, enjoying a relaxed journey in reserved seats on the Devon Belle or Atlantic Coast Express, punctuated by the glorious views, a read of a paperback or a stroll along the corridor to the refreshment car?

Centre. The 4.50pm from Ilfracombe to Exeter Central consists of two luggage vans and a rake of Bulleid coaches hauled past the Slade reservoir by Hymek No.D7098 piloted by Battle of Britain class 4-6-2 No.34079 141 SQUADRON. Saturday 29th August 1964. *S.C.Nash*

Right. Saturday 29th August 1964, the last summer Saturday but one before the demise of through expresses from Waterloo. The full length Atlantic Coast Express, the 10.30am from Ilfracombe to Waterloo, consisted of nine Bulleid coaches hauled by Hymek No.D7100, banked by D7097, is passing Mortehoe up distant signal. The leading three coach set was built by the Birmingham RCW Co. *S.C.Nash*

APPENDIX
TIMETABLES

BARNSTAPLE AND ILFRACOMBE LINE.

THE SPEED MUST NEVER EXCEED 25 MILES AN HOUR.

No Engines except those specially constructed to work Light Railways can be admitted on to the Ilfracombe Line.

VERY GREAT CARE AND CAUTION MUST BE USED IN WORKING OVER THE INCLINES.

BARNSTAPLE JUNCTION TO ILFRACOMBE.

DOWN TRAINS.—WEEK DAYS.

Miles.	STATIONS.	1	2	3	4	5											
		a.m.	p.m.	p.m.	p.m.	p.m.											
	Barnstaple Junction ...dep.	8 57	12 8	3 34	3 50	8 35	...	...	...	...	...	...	...	...			
¾	Barnstaple Quay........... ,,	9 4	12 15	3 41	5 57	8 42										No Sunday Trains.	
5	Wrafton.................... ,,	9 17	12 28	3 54	...	...											
5½	Braunton .... ,,	9 22	12 33	3 59	6 12	8 57											
11¾	Morthoe.................... ,,	9 42	12 53	4 19	6 33	9 18											
14½	**Ilfracombe** .... arr.	9 52	1 3	4 29	6 43	9 28											

ILFRACOMBE TO BARNSTAPLE JUNCTION.

UP TRAINS.—WEEK DAYS.

Miles.	STATIONS.	1	2	3	4	5											
		a.m.	a.m.	p.m.	p.m.	p.m.											
	Ilfracombe..............dep.	6 35	10 10	2 0	4 45	7 20											
3	Morthoe.................... ,,	6 47	10 21	2 12	4 57	7 32										No Sunday Trains.	
9	Braunton .... ,,	7 5	10 38	2 30	5 15	7 50											
9¼	Wrafton .... ,,	7 9	...	2 35	...	7 54											
14¼	Barnstaple Quay........... ,,	7 23	10 54	2 49	5 32	8 8											
14½	**Barnstaple Junction** ... arr.	7 30	11 0	2 54	5 39	8 15											

N.B.—These Trains between Barnstaple Junction and Braunton and Ilfracombe will be worked under the Staff and Ticket system, as well as under the absolute Single Line Block Regulations—See separate Instructions.

BARNSTAPLE AND ILFRACOMBE LINE.

This Line is now Double throughout, except between Barnstaple Junction and Pottington Level Crossing (about ¾ mile west of Barnstaple) and between Morthoe and Ilfracombe. It has been converted from a Light Railway into the Company's standard type for every class of Traffic.

Very great care and caution must be used in working over the inclines, and especially on approaching Ilfracombe Station.

N.B.—The Trains between Barnstaple Junction and Pottington Level Crossing and between Morthoe and Ilfracombe is worked under the Staff and Ticket system, as well as under the absolute Single Line Block Regulations— See separate Instructions. The Line is double between Pottington Level Crossing and Morthoe, and is worked under the absolute Double Line Block Regulations between these Stations.

Boards bearing the words "Speed not to exceed 4 miles an hour" have been erected one on the right hand side of the Line approaching Ilfracombe Station, 150 yards east of the Facing points, and another at the Up Loop points approaching Barnstaple Junction Station from the Ilfracombe Branch. Drivers must be careful to observe the instructions given on these Boards and to regulate the speed of their Trains accordingly.

DOWN TRAINS.—WEEK DAYS.

A No. 3 Down does not convey Horses or Carriages. B Slacken for Train Staff or Ticket.

C No. 1 will convey Goods Wagons and Traffic to Ilfracombe, but only Road Box Traffic to Wrafton, Braunton and Morthoe. The Train must stop short of Shapland and Petters Crossing to enable the porter, who will ride on the Engine from Barnstaple Junction, to alight and to take charge of the Gates while the Train passes.

UP TRAINS.—WEEK DAYS.

A No. 3 Up does not convey Horses or Carriages.   B Slacken for Train Staff or Ticket.   C No. 3 Stops at Braunton by Signal to take up Passengers for Stations East of Salisbury only, or for Bristol and Stations beyond.

STONEHOUSE POOL BRANCH.

Miles from Devonport.	DOWN TRAINS.	1 Goods.		2 Goods.		3 Goods.		Miles from Stonehouse Pool.	UP TRAINS.	1 Goods.		2 Goods.		3 Goods.	
	WEEK DAYS.	arr.	dep.	arr.	dep.	arr.	dep.		WEEK DAYS.	arr.	dep.	arr.	dep.	arr.	dep.
		a.m.	a.m.	p.m.	noon	p.m.	p.m.			a.m.	a.m.	p.m.	p.m.	p.m.	p.m.
...	Devonport............		8 0		12 0		5 0		Stonehouse Pool......		8 20		12 20		5 20
¼	Stonehouse Pool......	8 5		12 5		5 5		¼	Devonport............	8 25		12 25		5 25	

The above Trains will run when required and as ordered by Mr. Samson, Devonport.

Table 83

TIVERTON JUNCTION and HEMYOCK   SUMMER 1957
WEEK DAYS ONLY—(Second class only)

	Miles		am	am	pm	pm	pm	pm	pm	pm	pm
						E	E	E	S		S
Tiverton Junction ... dep	—		8 45	11 25	12 51	4 04	3 05	0 7	5	5 57	52
Coldharbour Halt ...	2		8 55	11 35	1 35	50 4	4 05	87	15	56	07 57
Uffculme ...	5		9 59	11 38	1 38	5 34	4 35	1 27	18	5 24	136
Culmstock ...	5		9 22	12 02	12 43	4 45	4 45	307	37	38	05
Whitehall Halt ...	6½		9 38			2 135	35	307	37	42	
Hemyock ... arr	7½		9 42			2 205	75	357	42	52	

Miles		am	am	pm	pm	pm	pm
							S
—	Hemyock ... dep	7	15	10 39			
1	Whitehall Halt ...	7	20	10 34			
3	Culmstock ...	7	38	10 43			
3½	Uffculme ...	7	42	10 54			
5	Coldharbour Halt ...	7	52	11 10			
7½	Tiverton Junction ... arr	7	56	11 28			

E Except Saturdays   S Saturdays only

Table 84

TAUNTON, DULVERTON, BARNSTAPLE and ILFRACOMBE
WEEK DAYS ONLY

MONDAYS TO FRIDAYS / SATURDAYS

[Detailed departure/arrival timetable for stations: Taunton, Norton Fitzwarren, Milverton, Wiveliscombe, Venn Cross, Morebath, Morebath Junction Halt, Dulverton, East Anstey, Yeo Mill Halt, Bishop's Nympton and Molland, South Molton, Filleigh, Swimbridge, Barnstaple, Victoria Road, Barnstaple Junction, Ilfracombe]

Notes:
- V Refreshment Car Train. From 29th June to 31st August passengers can arr 1 20 pm without Refreshment Car
- W Will not run after 7th September
- X Through Carriages Wolverhampton (L.L.) to Ilfracombe (Tables 61 and 169). Will not run after 7th September
- Z Through Train. Torrington dep 11 50 am and Bideford dep 12 0 noon to Taunton
- § Second class only
- M Through Train Ilfracombe to Bristol. Commencing 29th June extended to Manchester (Exch.) arr 6 57 pm (Table 168)
- N Through Train Ilfracombe to Cardiff (Tables 61 and 104)
- P Through Carriages Ilfracombe to Wolverhampton (L.L.) (Tables 61 and 169)
- R Refreshment Car between Paddington and Taunton
- T Through Train between Taunton and Ilfracombe
- A Road Motor Service is operated by the Southern National Omnibus Company between Barnstaple Junction and Cheltham Cross, Bratton Fleming, Blackmoor Gate, Parracombe, Woody Bay Cross and Lynton
- K Through Carriages between Paddington and Dulverton
- For OTHER TRAINS between Taunton and Norton Fitzwarren, see Tables 81 and 82—Morebath Junction Halt and Dulverton, Table 87

NORTH DEVON LINE.   SUMMER 1924

This is a Single Line from Coplestone to Umberleigh, from Barnstaple Junction to Torrington, and from Barnstaple Junction to Pottington Signal Box, between which points it is worked under the Regulations for working Single Lines by the Electric Train Tablet Block System.

For Special Instructions as to the working and load of Trains and List of Catch Points between Braunton and Ilfracombe, see pages 101 and 102 of the Appendix to the Book of Rules and Regulations and Working Time Tables dated 26th July, 1921.

DOWN TRAINS. WEEK-DAYS

[Stations include: Exeter (Queen Street), Yeoford, Coplestone, Morchard Road, Lapford, North Molton Road, Eggesford, Portsmouth Arms, Umberleigh, Barnstaple June., Barnstaple Town, Pottington Box, Wrafton, Braunton, Heanton, Morthoe, Ilfracombe, Fremington, Instow, Bideford (Town), Bideford (New), Torrington]

Notes:
- A—Stops at Morchard Road for crossing purposes only.
- B—Barnstaple (Town) times not to be advertised.
- C—Stops at Portsmouth Arms for crossing purposes only.
- D—Stops at Lapford and Eggesford for crossing purposes only. Through carriage Portsmouth to Torrington attached to this train.
- E—G.W. Co.'s engine and guard will work through to Ilfracombe.